PERSONAL FINANCE

PERSONAL FINANCE

Margaret Magnarelli

AMSCO

Amsco School Publications, Inc.,
a division of Perfection Learning®

About the Author

Margaret Magnarelli is a senior editor at *Money* magazine, where she writes and edits articles on a wide variety of personal finance topics; she also blogs at Cnnmoney.com. Magnarelli has previously worked at *Good Housekeeping*, *Budget Living*, and *Seventeen* magazines, and has written for numerous other publications. She received bachelor's and master's degrees from the Medill School of Journalism at Northwestern University.

Reviewers

Diane Charnov
Social Studies Department Chair
The Langley School
McLean, VA

Louis M. DiCesare
Business Teacher
Irondequoit High School
Rochester, NY

Kelley Gallagher-Vlosich
Instructor
Economics America Center
 Ashland University
Cleveland, OH

Douglas Kramer
Teacher
Herricks High School
New Hyde Park, NY

Donna Shepardson
Business Teacher
Columbia High School
East Greenbush, NY

Lois A. Stoll
Family and Consumer Sciences Teacher,
 Nationally Board Certified
Benjamin Logan High School
Bellefontaine, OH

Jamie Walker
Business Teacher, Chair
Oakwood Senior High School
Dayton, OH

Cover Design: Meghan Shupe
Cover Image: © Artifacts Images/Cultura/Corbis
Text Design: A Good Thing, Inc.
Composition: Sierra Graphics, Inc.
Line Art: Hadel Studio
Illustrations: Angela Martini

Please visit our Web sites at: *www.amscopub.com* and *www.perfectionlearning.com*

When ordering this book, please specify:
either **13492** or **PERSONAL FINANCE**.

ISBN: 978-1-56765-694-7 / NYC Item 56765-694-6

This book is dedicated to those who will use it—and to my husband, mother, in-laws, and friends, who supported me while I was writing it.

PREFACE

Until now, you probably haven't had to take full responsibility for yourself financially. Most likely, it's your parents who have worked hard in order to pay for most of what you own, where you live, and other expenses. If you're lucky, you haven't had to contribute much to the household. Any money you have made has been yours to keep—no bills to pay, no obligations. A pretty sweet deal.

Unfortunately, that deal is about to expire.

In the next few years, you will take on more and more financial responsibility. Maybe you will head to college, or perhaps into the workforce. Either way, you will have to make more financial decisions on your own, and you will be in charge of your financial life. You may have to pay for rent, utilities (such as electric, phone service, and Internet), food, entertainment, transportation, clothes, or anything else you may want or need. At college, you may pay for textbooks and supplies, your parents may expect you to help with paying tuition, and you may even have some loans in your name. No matter what your situation, you will likely have to manage a checking account and a savings account, and maybe one or more credit cards. You may find yourself purchasing some expensive items on your own, like a new TV, a better car, furniture for your apartment; and you will have to figure out how you'll pay for them.

Financially speaking, you are becoming an adult. You're embarking on a major transition—one that comes with significant responsibility, but also some liberating rewards.

This book is designed to prepare—and empower—you to deal with what's to come. These early years on your own will make a big difference in your financial future. Pay attention now, and you will be ready for any money challenges that will come your way later. You'll have a better chance at ending up financially secure, and who wouldn't want that?

Consider yourself lucky: You're going to graduate prepared to set off on the road to financial security and wealth. Personal Finance isn't just a class—it is a roadmap for your life.

The Author

CONTENTS

Chapter Six: Managing Risk — 201

CHAPTER 1

Financial Planning Basics

Chapter Objectives

Students will:

- ✔ Analyze interest rates, learn how they affect the time value of money
- ✔ Calculate net worth to assess one's current financial situation
- ✔ Understand the difference between assets and liabilities
- ✔ Be able to make smart financial decisions and set achievable goals

> **Personalize It!** *Close your eyes and think about your financial circumstances. How would you describe your situation? Now imagine yourself five years down the road. What might your finances be like? Where will you be living? What will you be driving? How will you be spending your time? Now think of yourself ten years down the line. How has the picture changed? This chapter is about planning for your life in the long term, so that your goals and dreams can become reality.*

Introduction

Let's start by defining **personal finance**, since that's what this book is all about. *Finance* refers to the allocation or distribution of money or things of monetary value; *personal* means it's about individuals, as opposed to societies, corporations, or governments. So, personal finance relates specifically to how you—as an individual or part of a household—manage your money.

It makes sense, then, that we are going to get personal.

Over the course of the book, you are going to learn the basics of **financial planning**. This is the term for the process by which you apply personal finance principles to manage your money in ways that will help you achieve financial security and other money-related goals.

There are several components to financial planning. At the least, a comprehensive financial plan should include:

- Statements of where you are and where you want to be financially (Chapter One)
- A plan for working, income and understanding taxes (Chapter Two)
- Strategies to manage cash for current expenses and to save for short-term goals (Chapter Three)
- Investment planning for long-term goals (Chapter Four)
- Tactics for using credit and managing debt (Chapter Five)
- A plan for managing financial risk associated with health, safety, and the chance of death (Chapter Six)

In this chapter, we'll get an overview of why you must take responsibility for your finances. We'll also look at the first stage of financial planning: taking stock of your financial situation right now, and setting some goals for the future.

By the time you finish this book, you will learn to organize resources in such a way that you will be able to live securely and comfortably, for the present, future, and very distant future (like retirement). You will learn how to balance your income against your expenses. You will learn how to invest and grow your money, and learn how to protect your money against various risks. In other words, you'll have your own financial plan.

The Time Value of Money and Its Advantages

TERMS TO KNOW

time value of money	principal	Rule of 72
interest	interest rate	mortgage
simple interest	compound interest	financial planner/advisor

Getting Started

Perhaps you're wondering why you should care about financial planning at your age. You have plenty of time to make sense of your finances, right? But *time* is exactly the reason why you should care.

Time is money, as the adage goes; and it's true in several different ways.

It's more than a pithy saying. Just consider what's known as the **time value of money**, which boils down to this: a certain amount of money saved today is worth more than the same amount saved in the future. The reason is that money saved now has time to grow.

The Power of Compound Interest

Imagine you win a sweepstakes and have the option of taking $1,000 today, or taking it in one year. Which would you choose? If you wait a year, you may think you are saving it, keeping it safe instead of spending it on things you don't need, right? If you take the money now, however, you could invest it in an account that pays interest. **Interest** is money paid to you by banks and other institutions, in exchange for borrowing your money. Let's assume you find a bank account paying 3% interest annually. The formula for **simple interest** is:

Interest earned = principal × interest rate × years

The **principal** is the amount you are investing, or in this case $1,000. The **interest rate** is the percentage of the principal that the investment will return, which in this case is 3% per year. We're looking at investing for one year to see the difference between taking the money now and taking it a year from now.

As the equation above shows, you would multiply $1,000 × 0.03 × 1 to calculate interest. That equals $30 by the end of the year. Add that to the principal, and the future value of your money, at the end of the year, would be $1,030. There's a $30 advantage to taking the money now.

To figure out what you'd have at the end of ten years, multiply $1,000 × 0.03 × 10 to get $300. That means your balance at the end of the ten-year period would be $1,300.

"That piggy bank is for my college fund."

 Look at this cartoon. How old do you think the children are? Why is the piggy bank so big? What is the cartoonist saying about college costs and money?

Impressive to be sure, but it gets even better. *Simple interest* means that the interest is only applied to the principal every year. But many accounts pay **compound interest**. Compound means that interest earnings from previous periods become part of the principal for the following period, and then the interest rate is applied to this larger principal. Compounding happens on annually or monthly periods, and when you sign up for an account you'll be told which.

It's easier to understand this idea when you see it in numbers, so let's go back to that $1,000 example. In this case you have the same $1,030 at the end of year one. But in year two, the 3% applies not just to the $1,000, but to the whole $1,030. So, you multiply $1,030 (new principal) × .03 × 1 and find out that your interest in year two is $30.90, and your balance is $1,060.90. With simple interest, you'd have only $1,060, so you're already 90 cents wealthier, thanks to compounding!

Every year, the principal gets bigger, and therefore the interest payment gets bigger, too. To calculate compounding—which is a bit more mathematically sophisticated than simple interest—use this formula:

Future value = principal (1 + interest rate) $^{\text{number of compounding periods}}$

So, for ten years of annual compounding at 3% interest; enter $1,000(1 + 0.03)^{10}$ on a calculator with an exponents function. (Note that the interest rate of 3%, which means *three out of a hundred*, is expressed as 0.03, or *three hundredths*.)

 Alternatively, you could use the search term "interest rate calculator" to find an online calculator that can calculate compounding interest. Or try *www.mindyourfinances.com/calculators*.

Timeline	Simple Interest	Interest Compounded Annually	Interest Compounded Monthly
Initial Deposit	$1,000	$1,000	$1,000
End of Year 1	$1,030	$1,030	$1,030.42
End of Year 2	$1,060	$1,060.90	$1,061.76
End of Year 3	$1,090	$1,092.73	$1,094.05
End of Year 4	$1,120	$1,125.51	$1,127.33
End of Year 5	$1,150	$1,159.28	$1,161.62
End of Year 6	$1,180	$1,194.06	$1,196.95
End of Year 7	$1,210	$1,229.88	$1,233.35
End of Year 8	$1,240	$1,266.78	$1,270.87
End of Year 9	$1,270	$1,304.78	$1,309.52
End of Year 10	$1,300	$1,343.92	$1,349.35

Compounding annually, the total is $1,343.92, which represents a *34% growth of your money*. As you can see from the preceeding table, that's $43.92 more than you would have with simple interest. The more frequently the interest is compounded, the bigger the difference. So, time is a major factor in compounding, meaning that if you start saving early, your money will earn more on itself.

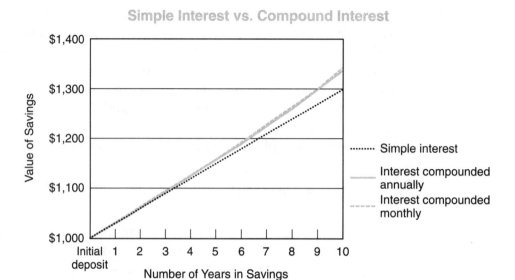

Simple Interest vs. Compound Interest

Based on the graph above, which is the least effective savings plan? What is the difference between simple and annual compound interest after ten years?

Pretty cool, isn't it? Recognize that the greater the starting principal, the greater your earnings will be, because you're applying the same interest rate to a higher number (for example, 3% of $2,000 is $60, 3% of $10,000 is $300). Of course, you may not be able to save a huge sum of money all at once. But you can reap some of this benefit by continually adding to the principal yourself—in other words, regularly adding money to the account. If you add only $100 a year to the original $1,000, a total addition of $1,000 over the decade, you'd have about $2,525 by the end of year ten. The $1,000 in deposits—of $100 a year—adds $1,180 onto the total. In this example, the interest is compounded annually. If it were compounded monthly, you would see even more growth.

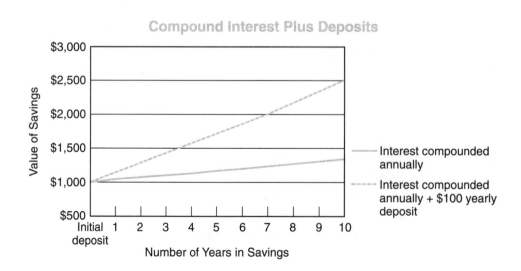

Compound Interest Plus Deposits

Q: Based on the previous graph, how apparent is the difference between the two savings plans? How can you tell? What happens to the difference over time?

These examples all use a 3% interest rate, but a higher rate would pay even more. At 4% with similar yearly deposits, the total would come to about $2,729 by the end of ten years.

A small difference in interest rates can make a big difference over time. Imagine you started saving $50 each month. The graph below depicts the growth of savings given four different interest rates, with interest compounded monthly.

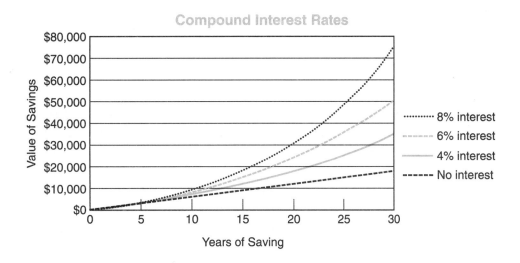

 Q: Based on this graph, after 30 years of saving $50 a month, what is the difference between the no interest account and the account with 4% interest? What is the difference between the 6% account and the 8% account? List the four accounts and the final value of savings for each.

To sum up, how quickly your money will grow depends on these factors: the interest rate, the frequency of compounding, the amount you are saving, and the time you have.

Time being such a key factor in saving means that if you start early, you could end up with more in the bank than a peer who didn't save so early. To see how this works in the long term, let's imagine that at age 20 you start saving $125 a month—or $1,500 a year—in an account with a 3% interest rate that compounds monthly. Your best friend, on the other hand, saves the same amount at that rate, but doesn't start until she's 30.

At 60, you will have $116,461. At the same age, your friend will only have $73,331. Your savings will be $43,130 more, even though you saved only $15,000 more than your friend.

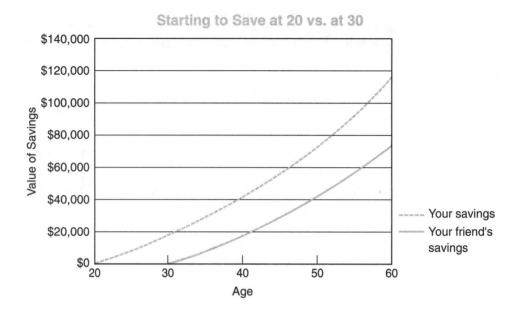

Starting to Save at 20 vs. at 30

 Which features of this graph would you point out if you wanted to convince your friend to begin saving earlier? What numbers and figures would you highlight?

What all these graphs are telling you is that the more time you have, the more money you can have, and the easier it will be to get things when you need them. Now do you understand why we all should care about personal finance?

Developing Good Habits Early

Getting on a path to wealth and financial security requires more than just compound interest; you also have to practice good financial habits, like saving money and avoiding debt. Developing these habits now is easier than overcoming damage from bad money habits later. The way interest on savings compounds to your benefit, bad financial moves can compound to your detriment. It may seem like no big problem if you wait to pay a bill for a few months, but such missteps can affect your opportunities later in life. Actions like these go on record, accessible by financial professionals, rental agencies, car salesmen; and could lead to trouble getting a loan to buy a home or a car later on (most people need loans for these big purchases). Even if you are approved for a loan, you might have to pay more to borrow money than if you had paid your bills on time. Your financial mistakes can have negative effects on others, too—a roommate, a spouse, your kids.

Of course, you can overcome a few missteps. All of us make mistakes with money over a lifetime. But the fact is, you'll have a better financial future—with more and better options—if you start establishing good money behavior as soon as possible. Time is money, and the time to start thinking about your money is today.

Fast Facts *Double Your Money!*

To find out how long it will take to double your money at a certain interest rate, you can use an economic principal called the **Rule of 72**. The rule states that if you divide 72 by the interest rate, you will get an estimate of the years required to double your money.

$$\frac{72}{\text{annual rate}} = \text{years to double your money}$$

For example, at a 3% annual interest rate, it will take 24 years to double your money since $72 \div 3 = 24$. How long would it take at a 4% rate? How long at a 6% rate? What pattern do you notice? (Notice here, 3% is translated as 3, not as 0.03 like in other percentage equations.)

MAKING CENT$ OF IT

Determine the time value of money in each of the following scenarios.

1. What would you have after ten years if you put $12,500 in an account earning 3% yearly interest, compounding annually?

2. What would you get if it compounded monthly? (Note: 3% yearly interest needs to be converted to a monthly rate, then compounded monthly.)

3. You put away $600 in an account earning 2.5% per year, compounding annually. You decide soon after to save $5 per month and add what you saved to the account at the start of each year. How much would you have after five years?

4. a. You put $120 each year in a savings account earning 3.5% per year, but compounding monthly. How much will you have in six years?

   b. How much would you have if you had hidden the same amount every month in your mattress for six years?

The Other Side of Compounding

Compound interest benefits you when you're a saver, but it can hurt when you're a borrower. Whenever you take out a loan or "borrow" money with a credit card, you're *charged* interest (on top of having to pay back the principal). That's how the bank makes money with loans. On many credit cards, and on **mortgages** (the loans people use to buy homes), interest is compounded, meaning you pay interest not just on the principal borrowed, but on interest as it compounds, too. Say you borrow $1,000 on a five-year loan with a 7% interest rate. The first year, you would owe $70 in interest; the second year you would owe 7% of $1,070, which is $74.90; and so on. In the end, you pay $188 in interest!

The longer it takes you to pay off a loan, the more the loan will cost you in interest due to compounding. If you are borrowing, time is money for the bank rather than you.

Getting Help With Financial Planning

In this book, you'll create your own financial plan. At the early stages of financial independence, your finances are pretty straightforward. But as your life situation grows more intricate—once you have a house, a spouse, a car, a few kids, or a good salary, for example—you may want to get help making important money decisions. You may decide to hire a **financial planner** or **financial advisor**. This professional can suggest a comprehensive, individualized action plan to help you reach goals.

Some planners and advisors get paid on commission by investment companies, meaning that they get money for selling you on certain products. Other "fee-only" planners are paid solely by their clients, either by a flat rate (hourly, or negotiated in advance) or by a percentage of "assets under management" (usually 1% or so a year of what they manage for you). The risk of working with a commission-based planner is that you might be sold investments that make less sense for you, but provide better money (in commissions) for the planner. Going to a fee-only planner eliminates some of the potential conflict of interest. On the other hand, it costs money, so it's a tradeoff.

The best way to find a good planner is to get a referral from family or friends. Alternatively, you could get references from the Financial Planning Association (*www.fpanet.org*). For fee-only planners specifically, go through the National Association of Personal Financial Planning (*www.napfa.org*).

Right now, however, you can be your own financial planner. The skills you will develop while reading this book will be useful to you, even if you do decide to hire someone else to manage your money later on.

1.2 Assessing Your Current Financial Situation

TERMS TO KNOW

net worth statement	assets	appreciation/appreciate
liabilities	equity	depreciation/depreciate

Getting Started

As you just read, the financial planning process can help you achieve financial security and afford the life you'd like to have. Before we discuss more future plans, however, we must start with a point of reference. So, its time to ask yourself, what is your financial situation right now?

One way to answer this question is through a **net worth statement**. This financial planning tool classifies the two categories of what you owe and what you own—or your **liabilities** against your **assets**. Liabilities are any debts you have outstanding, such as a credit card balance, student loans or the money mom and dad lent you that they expect to get back. Assets are all the property you own of value, plus any cash or investments you have.

The formula that we use to calculate net worth is:

Assets – liabilities = net worth

It's good to do a net worth statement at the beginning of your financial planning, because then you have a benchmark that you can compare to later on. Each one you do gives you a sense of how far you are from your goals, and a way to get the big picture of your financial progress.

What Is Included in Net Worth?

The best way to figure out net worth is to make a comprehensive list of assets and liabilities.

Assets include:

- value of real estate owned (this maybe more than your **equity**, or the amount you have paid on your property so far)
- value of personal property worth $500 or more (such as jewelry or a car)
- bank accounts
- savings bonds
- investment/retirement accounts

Liabilities include:

- a mortgage
- auto loan balances
- student loan balances
- credit card debt
- any other money owed

One thing you'll notice that's omitted from the above is income. Though a big income is very helpful in purchasing power, it doesn't figure into your wealth because it isn't something that you have at your disposal, to use at any one time. That means that you can have a high income without having a high net worth. People who make a lot of money—such as your favorite actors or musicians who are often photographed on shopping sprees around Hollywood—may seem rich, but unless they have been saving, they may not actually have financial security. The more you save, the more net worth, or wealth, you will have. Also, current bills like your cell phone bill are not considered a liability so long as you plan to pay them off when they're due.

You may also notice that you can count certain non-money items as assets. This applies only to goods that are expected to **appreciate**, or gain value as they age. Most items don't do this—instead they lose value quickly, and are worth less than what you paid for them (they **depreciate**). Among things that might appreciate: jewelry, art, collectibles or real estate.

 Let's say you save $1,500 and borrow $2,000 from your parents to buy your first car. You now own the car at the price you paid for it ($3,500), but you owe your parents their money back. What are your assets and liabilities in this scenario?

MAKING CENT$ OF IT

Differentiating between assets and liabilities is essential to creating an accurate net worth statement. Determine which items below are assets and which are liabilities by marking A for asset and L for liability.

1. _____ a diamond ring

2. _____ a house you own

3. _____ an outstanding student loan

4. _____ $100,000 in retirement savings

5. _____ $1,250 in an auto loan

6. _____ a painting by Picasso

7. _____ $4,000 in credit card debt

8. _____ $1,000 owed to your parent

How Much Are You Worth?

Once you have comprehensive lists of assets and liabilities, find the sum of each column, then subtract the liabilities from the assets to get the net worth. A finished net worth statement may look like this:

Net Worth Statement for Mrs. Cindy Yee

Asset	Value	Liability	Value
Home	$250,000	Mortgage	$150,000
Checking account	$5,000	Student loans	$10,000
Savings accounts	$30,000	Credit card debt	$2,000
Retirement accounts (401k/IRA)	$170,000		
Brokerage account	$2,000		
Total assets =	$457,000	Total liabilities =	$162,000
Total net worth = $295,000			

You probably have very little, if any, debt, so you'll probably find your net worth is positive—albeit low. This may change in the next few years. If you take on college debt, or further down the road as you buy a house, you may end up with negative net worth. It's not necessarily a bad thing to have a negative net worth, if your liabilities are ones that are meant to create more wealth (a house might appreciate, a college education promises a better paying job). Someone on the negative side ought to have a plan for moving toward a positive net worth. There are two ways to do this: decreasing liabilities (paying down debt), or increasing assets (saving more money).

Measuring Progress Through Net Worth

You probably go to the doctor every year or so for your annual checkup. The point is to make sure you continue to be healthy. Your finances need the same checkup. That's why you should assess your net worth regularly.

It's a way to measure progress, and to help you foresee trouble before you get buried too deep. (For example, the net worth statement may help you realize if you're increasingly relying on credit cards, in which case you might reduce spending.) Also, seeing the cold, hard numbers can be very motivating. It puts the goal in perspective, and makes it a reality—much as a dieter might weigh him or herself on a weekly basis. Just as one pound lost encourages this person to steer clear of ice cream for another week, so too can getting closer to your financial goals inspire you work harder toward them.

Regular net worth checkups are essential for building wealth. It might be interesting to know that according to one study compiled by the authors of the book *The Millionaire Next Door*, 80 percent of American millionaires were not born rich. That means they made their money. And to bank $1 million, they likely saved diligently and planned often over their lifetime. For most people, wealth doesn't happen overnight. It's accumulated over time.

MAKING CENT$ OF IT

1. Calculate your own net worth by completing a table like the one below. Add as many rows for assets and liabilities as you need.

My Net Worth Statement

Asset	Value	Liability	Value
Total assets =		Total liabilities =	
Total net worth =			

2. Use the same kind of table to calculate Ming's net worth based on the financial information she has listed here.

   - $1,100 monthly income from grocery clerk job
   - $525 in a checking account
   - $680 in a savings account
   - $75 signed I.O.U. to her older brother
   - $400 antique necklace from her grandmother
   - $169 owed to her mother for new cell phone

1.3 How to Make Decisions and Set Financial Goals

TERMS TO KNOW

scarcity   opportunity cost   needs   wants

Getting Started

Now that you've established where you are in your financial life, you can move on to planning for the future. Let's start with a simple, fun exercise: Take ten minutes to write out a list of all the things you wish you could buy, as well as things you have been needing to purchase recently. Your list might look like something like this:

- a better bike
- a new MP3 player
- new sneakers for track practice
- tickets to see a favorite band in concert
- a car
- more up-to-date cell phone
- a new bag/backpack for school
- a new set of tires for the bike

Now think back to your financial situation, established by making your net worth statement. Do you have the money to get *everything* on your list right now?

Unlikely. Aside from maybe Microsoft founder Bill Gates (net worth: $50 billion), few people are able to indulge their every whim. What you're experiencing is a key concept that applies to both economics and personal finance: scarcity. **Scarcity** refers to the conundrum of having insufficient resources (in this case, money) to cover all that you might like. It's simply the normal condition of life. Scarcity requires us to make choices, which are not always easy.

The Cost of Scarcity

Whenever you make decisions, you are choosing between multiple options. In the end, you must give up something in exchange for what you are getting. You make tradeoffs. The next best option that you pass up—that is to say, the most valuable thing you sacrifice in making one choice over another—is referred to as the opportunity cost. To understand **opportunity cost**, you might ask yourself these questions: What am I losing by taking advantage of this opportunity? What else could I be doing with that money?

Say you get your allowance for the week—$15—and the same day your friends call to see if you want to go to a movie. You'd been planning to save the money toward a new computer. Now you have a decision to make: the computer or the movie? If you choose the movie, the opportunity cost is that you lose $15 saved for the computer, so it may take you longer than you'd planned to save. If you choose to save for the computer, the opportunity cost is losing that time spent with friends.

There is no right choice; it's up to you. One thing you can do to help make the decision easier is to assess the benefit against the cost. Are you prepared to delay the computer purchase by a week in order to enjoy that time spent with friends? If you are, then you can enjoy the movie knowing you thought it through. If you know the options and make your choice, you'll be satisfied knowing you made an informed financial decision, either way you choose.

Be sure you are considering not only the short-term consequences of little actions, but also the long-term ones. For example, if you decide to go to college, the opportunity cost of doing so might be the earnings sacrificed by not working full time for those years. On the other hand, research shows that college graduates earn significantly more money than high school graduates do. So in that case, the opportunity cost of working right away is the future income benefits of having a college degree.

Another way to think about financial decisions is in terms of risk versus reward. Much of personal finance comes down to these terms, which you will see again and again in this course, in regards to everything from investments you make to how much you use your credit cards. The question is how much you might lose compared to how much you might gain. Usually, the greater the risk, the greater the potential reward. That means, though, that you have the potential to lose a lot as well. So you might ask yourself: What are the risks? Is it worth the reward?

LIVING TODAY, PLANNING TOMORROW

In today's recession (or post-recession) economy, a financial plan is crucial. Things happen, jobs are harder to come by, and expenses will keep accruing whether you can pay them or not. Read about how the 20-somethings of today are coping with financial security, and future plans.

"Life on Hold"
By Jessica Bliss
The Tennessean

Four hours before he boarded a plane for a vacation to Ireland, Brett Kling was laid off. "I was cut the same day as the Christmas party and the company picnic," he said.

With a mortgage, student loans and a '99 Saturn with 196,000 miles on it, the then-29-year-old technical trainer was "completely freaking out." Four months later and still unemployed, his anxiety hasn't subsided.

"I am terrified," he said. "I am skittish."

He is not alone. The recession, now pronounced near an end by financial gurus, has affected many. But for the young adults of Generation Y, it has completely altered a once-inviting future.

Raised in better times, 20-somethings were brought up to believe they could do anything and become anyone. They assumed they would have a job, plenty of credit, a place of their own—and that it would be at their text-happy fingertips as soon as they were ready.

When the economy sank, those assumptions died. Unemployment escalated, mortgage restrictions tightened, and all those lofty expectations unraveled.

Now many 20-somethings must learn skills they may have thought unnecessary growing up in more financially stable times. Often unversed on budgeting, living frugally, saving or avoiding debt, they now have to learn to sacrifice luxuries, pool resources and alter expectations.

"Being a 20-something, you wish you could have a little more freedom and have more fun and just be able to spend the money," said Mark Peters, 27. "But it's a different day and age."

It is an age in which unemployment is the undercurrent of many troubles.

Labor statistics for August show that 15.1 percent of Americans age 20 to 24 are without a job, up 4.4 percentage points from this time last year. Among 25- to 29-year-olds, that number is slightly lower, at 11 percent, but it is no less disconcerting. Overall, the U.S. jobless rate was 9.7 percent in August.

"I would expect that this generation would have a pretty good reason to not be very happy," said Ted Klontz, a financial behavioral consultant and president of Nashville-based Klontz Consulting Group.

"Which is hopeful. That's when change occurs. The previous generation didn't have it right, so let's make it right."

But change isn't easy—especially for a generation spoiled by the convenience of the Internet, cell phones, quick-to-please parents and a marketplace keen on meeting its mercurial tastes.

The situation can be as difficult on parents as it is on sons and daughters.

To some degree, parents feel a need to prove they can provide for their struggling children, Klontz said, so they support them longer than appropriate to avoid feeling inadequate.

"I don't think it is bad to shield your kids," Klontz said. "But there is a difference between keeping them from hitting the ground really hard and enabling them to live a lifestyle they can't support."

When Brittany Byrd, 22, lost her apartment complex job in June, her mother, Love Wilson, immediately stepped in to cover her daughter's expenses. Byrd already lived at home, but to that point she had paid her mom for rent and cable. Wilson didn't want to see her daughter struggle, but she also made it clear this wasn't an extended free ride.

"I told her, 'I will help you out in every way I can,'" Wilson said. " 'I will help cover your part of the rent and some of your bills, but I can't do it all, because I live on a paycheck, too.' "

Byrd never finished college. After one year at Volunteer State Community College, she took time off to "discover" herself, so finding a job was even more of a challenge. Even with her mother's support, she faced $450 in car loan and insurance payments each month, forcing her to cut out morning trips to the coffee shop and long-distance drives to see out-of-town friends.

Wilson believes her daughter learned from being forced to make financial sacrifices. After two months of unemployment, another apartment complex hired Byrd.

"I think everybody should go through this," Wilson said. "As hard as that may sound—or as mean as that may sound—it makes you appreciate what you have, when you have it, even more."

1. What is this piece saying about 20-somethings in our culture today, as compared to generations past?
2. What percentage of 20-24 year olds are unemployed according to this article?
3. Imagine your life in the next five years. Your expenses, what will they be? What are your plans for securing a way to pay them? Would you consider a back-up plan after reading this article? What would it be?

Prioritizing Your Resources

What scarcity means is that you can't have everything on your wish list. There just isn't enough money to go around. But it doesn't mean you can't have *anything* you'd like. One of the ways to deal with scarcity is by prioritizing your wishes, or deciding what the most important use is for your money.

To some extent, you may already do this. For example, if you got to the counter of your favorite fast-food restaurant for lunch and discovered you had only $3 in your pocket, you would reassess your menu choices. Maybe you would decide to give up the fries and the soda to have something more filling, like a burger. That's called prioritizing—deciding what comes first on your list of food choices, what you want or need the most.

Penny and Nick

Penny and Nick, pictured above, are two best friends who have grown up together. They live on the same block and have been in the same class since elementary school. This semester, they are taking a senior-year elective course on personal finance. They both are good students, but have always loved spending their extra money on movies, shopping, video games, or going out to eat; so this class has been a challenge to their money habits. For each scenario throughout the book, help Penny and Nick give each other smart personal finance advice as you watch them face difficult choices.

   Penny has been desperate for some new clothes. "I have nothing to wear!" she complained to her best buddy, Nick. At the Denim Hub, she tried on two pairs of jeans.
   "This pair is on the sale rack, marked down to $25, and looks good," she said to him outside the fitting room. "But the other is a premium designer brand. They cost $100, and they look *great*."
   "Get the ones you like more, Pen," said Nick, whose mind had admittedly drifted to the Xbox game he'd been wanting to buy.
   "But, I kind of wanted to save that money and put it towards a car for next year," she thought out loud. "But it's not *that* much more . . ."

   Pretend you're Nick, and explain to Penny what the opportunity costs (tradeoffs) might be for each pair of jeans.

In prioritizing what to spend money on, it also helps to think about whether the items are needs or wants. **Needs** are those things that you can't do without, such as food, water, and shelter. A notebook for your personal finance class is a need if your teacher says it's required. New sneakers would be a need if your old pair has a few holes in the soles and you have phys. ed. tomorrow. **Wants**, on the other hand, are the video games, the fashionable sunglasses, the football game tickets, a new pair of skis, or that new lacrosse stick when your old one is still in good condition—anything that you desire, but can do without. If you can put off buying it, it's probably in the category of want.

Your needs should come first. For example, you'd want to prioritize paying rent over buying a new wardrobe—because if you don't pay the rent, your new wardrobe won't be all that impressive when you're without a place to live.

The good news: for now, your parents may help take care of some of your needs. That means you get to focus the majority of your resources toward wants. But that won't last forever.

MAKING CENT$ OF IT

Part 1: To prioritize your resources, you'll need to be able to tell wants from needs. Mark wants with a W below and needs with an N. Some of these things could fit in both categories, so categorize them as you see fit.

1. _____ a video game
2. _____ concert tickets
3. _____ a new bicycle
4. _____ extra cash to buy lunch at school
5. _____ pencils for school
6. _____ a guitar
7. _____ a soccer ball
8. _____ a new coat for winter

Part 2: Take the wish list you created at the beginning of this section, and list the items in order of importance, being sure to place needs at the top. Explain your choices. If you need help figuring out which goals are more important to you, try the "Set Your Financial Priorities" tool at *cnnmoney.com/tools.*

How to Make Smart Decisions

As you're attempting to prioritize your resources, or when making purchasing decisions, you may have to make some tough choices. Some financial decisions are more difficult to make than others are. Like the example, choosing whether to apply the $15 to the movie or the computer fund may take just a few minutes of weighing in your head. But when there are larger decisions involved, like deciding on college, or picking an apartment to rent—you may want to spend more time assessing your choices. It may be wise to apply a systematic decision-making process, which can help you fully consider your options and their consequences.

Such a process can reduce outside influences, also including those from family, friends, and the media, that may push you in one direction. While you can't eliminate such influences, it is often best to put them in perspective. As you are choosing a college, for example, your best friend may want you to go with to the one she plans to attend. But with something as crucial as your education, you'll want to consider more than just your friend's predisposition. Majors offered and tuition costs are just two of the factors you should probably weigh over other people's opinions. Not to say that your friend's point of view shouldn't count, but you just want to make sure it doesn't overwhelm other considerations.

The decision-making process uses facts and figures rather than feelings and emotions to help you make choices. The following process will work with any difficult money decisions—whether it's determining which laptop to buy, choosing a savings account, or figuring out which colleges to apply to.

Step One: Define the problem. As you begin this process, make sure to have a clear idea of what issue needs to be solved. Maybe phrase it as a question to help define it. Write it down somewhere you can refer to it as you are thinking it over.

Example: Raquel has been thinking about buying a new netbook for a while. She has wanted her own computer to be able to write her blog and do her homework; without her pesky brother bothering her to get off the home computer. She decided during the summer to save up for one, so that by fall she could afford her own. She managd to save $500 from her summer job for the netbook. The question is: which netbook should she buy?

Step Two: Identify your choices. The next step is to figure out what all the possible responses to the problem are. This may require some research; you may not yet be aware of all your options. Perhaps you will ask your parents, look online, or consult with a professional to determine your choices. In some situations, you may have too many choices, in which case you'll want to narrow down your problem, or rule out undesirable options right away so that you have a finite, manageable number of possibilities.

Example: A quick Web search reveals that there are more than 50 netbooks available. Raquel has a few requirements for the netbook that limit the number suitable to her desires. She's looking only at models under $500. She also wants a model with at least one gigabyte of RAM. With these features in mind, she goes to the electronics review site *Cnet.com*. There she enters those features into their search engine, to eliminate some netbook choices from consideration.

Step Three: Evaluate the choices. Once you know what your options are, you must differentiate them. In some cases, you may have to elaborate on specific features of the options; in others, you may need to lay out the pros and cons for each decision. Define the opportunity costs of choosing one over the other. Once you have this figured out, create a chart (like the following) so that you can see the choices side by side.

Example: Raquel looks at the specs on each of the three computers that meet the needs she outlined above. Here is a table with her choices:

Comparing Netbook Specs

Spec	Netbook A	Netbook B	Netbook C
Processor speed	1.6 GHz	1.8 GHz	1.8 GHz
RAM memory	2 GB	1 GB	2 GB
Battery life	4 hours	7 hours	6 hours
Webcam	Yes	No	Yes

Step Four: Make the choice and act on it. Seeing a few possibilities up against one another, you should have an easier time making a decision. Once you've decided, you can go ahead and act on it.

Example: Based on the chart above, Netbook C seems to be the best option. It has the most memory, the longest battery life, and a camera. The next step would be for Raquel to go buy Netbook C.

Step Five: Evaluate the decision. Even once you've made a final decision, you may want to reassess periodically to make sure it's still the best option. Certain economic or personal conditions, or your experience with what you choose, can help form your future decisions.

Example: In six months' time, Raquel wonders whether she made the right decision with the netbook. "If I had this to do over again, would I buy the same computer? Why or why not?" She asks herself. (She decides she would have made the same decision.)

Decision-Making Tools

The decision-making process described may require you to find more information to make an informed decision. There are countless sources of financial information available to you, including:

Government agencies. Several branches of government—federal, state, and local—focus on consumer money issues. These agencies may serve to raise awareness or enforce laws that protect consumers.

Examples: The Securities and Exchange Commission (SEC), the Federal Trade Commission (FTC), the Arizona Department of Insurance.

Trade organizations. These are groups of businesses or people in the same industry that get together as a unit to increase consumer awareness, provide training or other resources for members, or lobby the government as a unified force. They can be very useful for gaining a general understanding of their field.

Examples: The American Bankers Association (ABA) for information on banking; the Insurance Information Institute to find out about insurance needs.

The media. Numerous newspapers, magazines, and newsletters' sole aims are to cover the topic of personal finance. There are also Web sites and blogs devoted to the subject, as well as entire TV stations, TV shows, or just segments of shows.

Examples: Magazines like *Kiplinger's Personal Finance*, *SmartMoney* and *Money*; news/information sites like *marketwatch.com* and *bankrate.com*; newspapers like The *Wall Street Journal* and The *New York Times*; TV options such as CNBC, CBS evening news, *House Hunters* on HGTV.

Companies. The companies that work to provide financial services to consumers—which include banks, brokerages, credit card issuers or investment companies—may have Web sites or offices where they offer information.

Examples: Bank of America, E*TRADE brokerage, the mutual fund company Vanguard.

People. Right now, your parents may offer you financial advice. Certainly your personal finance teacher does. Later on, you may consult with any number of professionals whom you would pay for advice.

Examples: Stock brokers, financial planners, accountants and tax preparers, insurance agents, attorneys.

Not every source of information is credible. You undoubtedly know by now that there are many Web sites—Wikipedia among them—that shouldn't be your only resource for facts and information. The problem with sites like Wikipedia is one of authorship; since so many people are contributing, it's difficult to know whether the last person to update it was someone who is truly knowledgeable. You can use sites like this as a starting point, not as a final word.

With financial information, use a three-part lens to determine if a source is trustworthy:

Objective. The best financial information comes from sources that attempt to be unbiased, meaning they have no affiliation with any one commercial service or product. Many sources of personal finance information do, unfortunately, have an agenda. They are trying to sell you something. (For example, a bank Web site provides guidance about savings, while it is in that bank's interest that you save with them). It's important that you ask what their motivation is. How do they earn their money? Are they speaking with your interests in mind? All that said, just because a source has a bias doesn't make it worthless, it just means you have to consider their opinion as you weigh the advice. And you will surely have to consult other sources along with it.

Accurate. Of course, it's crucial for any source you use, in this class or any other, to contain correct information. After all, basing decisions on a source riddled with errors can change the results. It can be tough, as a consumer, to evaluate the validity of information. With financial information, reputation is key—the *Wall Street Journal*, for example, is a well-regarded publication read by Wall Street executives, who wouldn't stand for errors. A relatively unknown blog with few readers, however, means less certainty about accuracy.

Current. Financial information is changing constantly. If you're consulting a source that's out-dated, it can mean a big difference in knowledge. For example, the Federal Reserve may change interest rates (how much borrowing money will cost you or how much saving money will earn you) several times a year. These rates may affect what you do with your money, so you want to make sure the source you are consulting to find them is as current as possible.

Just knowing these three factors doesn't always make it easy to evaluate a source. Plenty of experienced adults have trouble judging whether a site or periodical or person is giving them objective, accurate, and current information. That's why, throughout the book, we'll suggest sources that are trustworthy in these three areas. These will provide a good groundwork.

MAKING CENT$ OF IT

1. Imagine you have saved $3,000 to buy a car, and your parents have agreed to match that, giving you $6,000 to spend. Using Web sites like *Edmunds.com* or Kelley Blue Book (*KBB.com*), research three used cars that fall within your budget. Organize the information you find in a comparison table like the one shown here.

Car Choices

	Car A	Car B	Car C
Make/model			
Year			
Price			
Miles driven			
Body style			
Color			
Transmission			
Gas mileage (city/highway)			
Rating			

2. State which of the three cars you would choose. Explain how you used the information in your comparison table to make your decision.

How to Set Achievable Financial Goals

It is possible—even with limited resources—to achieve what you want from your money. But to do so, you'll need to set goals. Financial goals need not be only things you want to buy. They can be anything from wanting to set up a bank account, to paying off debt, to saving for a time to travel after you finish school, or just a long spring-break trip. You have to think about savings for getting married, renting or owning where you live throughout your life, or having children.

Achieving something, as you know, requires commitment. Goal setting is the first step of that commitment. Writing out your objectives turns them into a kind of contract that you're entering with yourself; you begin to feel accountable for them. Crafted correctly, a goal statement also helps turn an idea that's floating in your head into a practical, actionable reality.

Chess, like decision-making and planning, involves strategy. It always helps to think a few steps ahead.

As you saw from the examples on compounding, time is a big factor in your ability to accumulate wealth. So too does time affect how you need to plan in order to achieve your goals. Generally, goals fall into three categories:

Short-term goals: things you would like to accomplish between now and one year from now.

Examples: Buying a 10-speed to compete in bike racing competitions, buying March Madness basketball tickets for you and a friend.

Medium-term goals: things you would like to accomplish one to three years from now.

Examples: Getting a car, paying for moving to a college out of state, going on a road trip to visit Graceland in homage to your favorite singer Elvis.

Long-term goals: things you would like to accomplish in five years or more.

Examples: Renting an apartment, buying a house, getting married, raising children, moving to Thailand to start your own tea exporting company.

At this point in your life, with a more limited income, you may want to stick to one short-term, one medium-term, and one long-term goal at a time. Later, when you have more financial resources, you may be able to expand to more than that. In general, it's best to concentrate on a handful of goals.

The best goals are SMART. That means:

Specific

Measurable

Action-oriented

Realistic

Time-framed

Specific

Be as clear and detailed as you can. So, instead of "taking a summer trip with friends," you might want to say, "spending three nights in New York City." This helps narrow the parameters—the prices of hotels, for example, are going to be much higher in New York City than, say, Manchester, New Hampshire.

Ask: *What exactly do I want to accomplish?*

Measurable

Quantify your goal as much as possible. Don't just generally assume you'll need "a few hundred dollars" for that trip to New York. Pin down your costs. In this case, expenses would include hotel, meals, gas if you're driving, or train tickets/airfare if you're not. You might want to set aside a certain amount money to see some Broadway shows, go to museums, or buy souvenirs.

Ask: *How much do I need to save to make this happen?*

Action-oriented

Your goal should be something that you can take action to achieve. So, say you determined that that the trip will cost $400. The action you'll need to take is to save $400.

Ask: *What do I need to do to make this happen?*

Realistic

 If the goal isn't realistic, it will be frustrating trying to keep up with it. A four-star hotel in New York, for example, might make the cost of the trip out of reach. That said, it's okay if it's a little ambitious, or a little bit of a stretch. Just know your limits. If you aren't sure whether one of your goals is realistic, go to the calculator at *mindyourfinances.com/calculators/savings-goals* to see how long it would take you to reach your goal. You may find, for example, that saving for a three-day trip to New York is much more realistic than saving for a six-day trip.

Ask: *Can I achieve this goal given my time and resources?*

Time-framed

It's best to have a deadline on your goal so that it feels more urgent. This also helps you to complete it in small time frames split up over the longer period. For example, with a savings-oriented goal, you may be able to save $10 a week to get to your goal of saving $100 by ten weeks from now. Some goals have a pre-set timeframe. That summer trip with your friends, for example, has to happen in the summer—so you know how long you have to save for it. Other goals may be more flexible. If you want to buy a new car in the next few years, you may not have a specific date in mind. In such cases, you may want to start with how much money you will need to make the goal happen, and then plan from there in establishing a time frame. You can use the calculator noted earlier to help you come up with a time frame that is realistic for you.

Ask: *When would I like to accomplish this by?*

Your Personal Action Plan

As you run each goal through the SMART rubric, you determine what you need to do to accomplish the goal. But a general statement of your plans may not be enough, especially when it comes to a savings-oriented goal. The "action-able" part of your goal may be "to save $3,500 to buy a used car." However, that doesn't exactly tell you *how* you're going to save $3,500.

That's why you need an action plan, or a method of achieving your goal.

For savings goals, it's most effective to save a set amount on a recurring basis, and have this amount automatically transferred from your paycheck or your checking account to your savings account. (You'll learn to do this in Chapter Three.) That way you won't spend it or forget to put it aside. Financial experts call that "paying yourself first," because you're prioritizing your goals above all other spending.

Let's say you have a part-time job working at a grocery store, earning $100 a week after taxes, and you start setting aside half of your weekly pay in a savings account.

You could use this formula to find out how long it would take you to save up:

$$\frac{\text{Cost of item}}{\text{weekly or monthly savings}} = \text{weeks or months needed to save}$$

For the car:

$$\frac{\text{(cost of car)}}{\text{(monthly savings)}} = \text{(months to save)}$$

$$\frac{\$3,500}{\$200 \text{ per month}} = 17.5 \text{ months}$$

That's just about a year and a half. Plus, if you put it into a savings account, your money will grow, and you'll hit your goal even faster. At a 2% interest rate, you drop a month off your plan. It's not instant gratification, but it helps prove you can achieve your goal of your own car, and you can do it on your own.

One thing to keep in mind is that the more time you have before you need the item, the less you'll have to save each week or month, meaning the less you'll have to sacrifice. In order to save $50 a week you may have to give up a number of other expenses; but if you need to save just $20, you have less to give up. You might decide that $20 is a more realistic savings goal. As it goes, however, the less you save the longer it will take you to reach your goal. At $20 per week, it would take almost three years to get the car. A third solution might be to aim for a less expensive car, which would allow you to get to your goal more quickly while saving just $20 a week.

There's no right answer here. You get to determine what's most realistic for you: what you can save, sacrifice, or the total money you need to save. The most important thing is that you choose a plan you think you'll stick with.

Once you have a plan to achieve your goal, write it down, and post it somewhere where you can see it. That way, you will hold yourself more accountable for achieving it. You may also want to tell your parents or friends, so they will keep you accountable to it as well.

SMART Personal Action Plan	
Goal	Spend a weekend in New York City with friends from July 10–12
Money needed	$300 (includes two nights at a hotel, split four ways; gas; five meals)
How to achieve it	Save $13 a week from my paycheck, and put it into my savings account each payday
To be completed by	July 1

Specific
Measurable
Actionable
Realistic
Time-framed

This action plan is SMART, isn't it?

It's best if you can come up with a way to track your progress. You may want to keep a running tally on your computer of how much you have saved toward the goal. If it's a long-term goal, you might even want to open a separate bank account to keep that money in. (More information on bank accounts is in Chapter Three.)

Setting financial goals will help you not just as you're beginning your financial journey, but for the rest of your life. It's rather certain that in the coming years, you'll hit some serious financial milestones where you'll need to lay out a lot of money all at once. For example, you may soon be responsible for your college tuition. You may start renting your first place. You might buy your own car. Eventually you will want to buy a house—which on average costs $313,000, according to the Census Bureau.

All of these steps will require some forward thinking. If you don't end up planning for some of them, you'll end up behind, either having to rely heavily on debt or having to put off something you want to do. But if you set these as goals, and set out on a path before you need to achieve them, you'll be ready when the time comes. It'll be a lot easier to rent an apartment in a few years, for example, if you've thought ahead about saving up for the security deposit and few months' rent you'll have to put down to guarantee it. Otherwise, you might have to wait a few months longer than you'd like so that you can save enough rent.

MAKING CENT$ OF IT

1. Identify three of your personal financial goals; one short-term, one medium-term, and one long-term goal.

2. Create a SMART Personal Action Plan for each of the goals you identified. This may require some research. If your medium-term goal is to backpack around Europe, you would need to research the cost of airfare, hostels, and food. Use the Internet to estimate the amount of money you'd need for your goals.

SMART Personal Action Plan

Goal	
Money needed	
How to achieve it	
To be completed by	

CHAPTER REVIEW

Master the Vocabulary

Use the personal finance terms from the start of each section to complete the following sentences.

1. _____ is the process of setting financial priorities and goals, then developing a plan and method to achieve them.

2. The _____ is how to describe why having $1 today is worth more than $1 tomorrow.

3. _____ is money paid to you by banks and other institutions in exchange for borrowing your money.

4. _____ is the amount you have deposited in an account or have borrowed, to which interest is applied.

5. If an account pays _____ interest, the interest never becomes part of the principal.

6. _____ is the name for the interest earned in the current period on both principal and on interest accrued from previous periods.

7. To figure out how long it would take to double your money at a certain interest rate, you could use the _____ .

8. A(n) _____ is a professional whose job it is to help individuals and households manage their money to reach their goals.

9. The difference between what you owe and what you own is your _____ . The things you own are called your _____ ; _____ are what you owe.

10. _____ is the basic economic term explaining that we have limited resources but unlimited wants.

11. When you make a decision, the _____ is the price you paid by giving up one option when you chose another.

Apply What You've Learned

1. Show your understanding of the time value of money by solving these problems.

   a. You deposit $200 in an account earning 2.6% a year and compounding annually. How much will be in the account after 20 years?

   b. You deposit the same amount in an account earning 2.6% annually that does not compound. How much is the account worth after 20 years?

2. Identify four factors that affect how fast your money grows in an account that compounds. Explain the effect of each factor.

3. When might you expect your money to double at a 6% annual interest rate? At a 3.2% rate? At a 10% rate?

4. Give examples of three assets and three liabilities.

5. Create a net worth statement for the following scenario; include a total net worth.

   Becky and Jon Hickoh are a married couple living near San Francisco, California. They live in a two-bedroom house that cost them $280,000. They have paid $100,000 of that. They also have set aside $400,000 in a retirement account; they have $12,000 in a checking account, and $9,000 in savings bonds. Right now, they have $5,000 charged on a credit card. They also have a $6,000 auto loan.

6. List five wants and five needs that you have now.

Wants	Needs
1.	1.
2.	2.
3.	3.
4.	4.
5.	5.

7. Imagine that you've just won $300 in a school raffle. There are two things you could buy with the money, but you couldn't afford both. Explain the opportunity costs of choosing and buying one.

8. Use the five decision-making steps to come to a conclusion on the following scenario: Imagine you are looking to buy a new cell phone, and you get a $50 loyal-customer credit on whatever you buy. Identify what your five top choices would be (assuming you stay with your current carrier). Then identify the costs of each (using the list price), as well as any opportunity costs, and make a decision. Assume you would stick with a two-year contract. Show your work for each step.

9. What are the three most important factors in evaluating sources of financial information?

10. Indicate S, M, or L next to each of these to indicate short-, medium- or long-term goals. (For those that require spending, assume you have a $10 per hour job and work 10 hours per week, and that you could put half of that money towards the goal in question.)

a. _____ Being able to afford a used car ($5,000)

b. _____ Saving $75 by bringing lunch to school this month

c. _____ Buying a starter house ($250,000)

d. _____ Opening a savings account

e. _____ Getting yourself a good quality digital camera ($300)

f. _____ Planning a six-week backpacking trip to Europe for your 21st birthday ($4,000)

g. _____ Buying a sweater ($50)

h. _____ Getting a complete new wardrobe for back-to-school ($350)

i. _____ Buying your mother a gold bracelet as a gift ($100)

11. You have set a short-term goal of buying a TV for your bedroom. The TV costs $300. You earn $7 an hour, and work 10 hours a week. Come up with an action plan to save for the TV. How much will you save per week, and how long will it take you?

CHAPTER 2

Working and Earning

Chapter Objectives

Students will:

✔ Analyze factors that affect earned income
✔ Understand how to investigate careers and apply for work
✔ Learn the types of benefits offered in a full-time job
✔ Calculate taxes on income, and consider tax forms and procedures

> **Personalize It!** *Take a moment to think about where your money comes from. Do you make money through a job? An allowance? Occasional handouts from your parents? Gifts from relatives for your birthday? What factors influence how much income you have?*

Introduction

If you have an after-school job, you probably celebrate payday.

Right now, making money may allow you certain freedoms, such as being able to go out to eat with friends or being able to buy clothes for yourself. Soon enough, making money will be a necessity. You'll need income to support yourself.

As an adult, the amount of money you earn is directly related to the standard of living you can sustain: it dictates what you can afford in terms of where you live, what you wear, how you get around, even what you eat. Imagine how your life might be different if you had $100,000 in income versus $20,000.

Your income also figures into how financially secure (or insecure) you might feel. Knowing you are able to pay bills, pay off debt, or put aside some savings for unknown emergencies are types of securities that your income may allow. Your earnings also determine how quickly you can reach financial goals.

In this chapter, you will learn about the factors that influence income. Since career planning is a key component of financial planning, you will also find out how to explore career paths and how to find work. Finally, you will learn about taxes, which reduce your earnings in a significant way, whether you like it or not.

2.1 Factors That Affect Income

TERMS TO KNOW

earned income	formal education	recession
commission	informal education	lay off
tips	apprenticeship	unemployment rate
unearned income	internship	inflation
wage	tuition	deflation
minimum wage	financial aid	Social Security
salary	circular flow	pension
cost of living		

Getting Started

Earlier, you began thinking about where your own income comes from. There are actually are several different types of income. **Earned income** is money received as compensation for labor. Money a teen makes from a job at the grocery store, or an adult makes as a lawyer are both examples of earned income. **Commission** (money earned as a percentage of a sale of an item) and **tips** (money from a customer for good and friendly service) are also earned income.

Another kind of income is **unearned income**. This type of income is passive—you don't have to work to gain it. Types of unearned income include:

- Growth of invested money, including interest (interest income)
- Profits shared by companies you own a part of (dividends)
- Profits on assets you sell for more than you paid for them (capital gains)
- Rent payments you receive on property you own
- Gifts (including allowance)
- Inheritance
- Prize or award money
- Certain payments from the government

In Chapter Four, you will learn more about unearned investment income. This chapter will focus on earned income, which represents the majority of income for most working adults. Your ability to earn income is about your human capital—that is, what you bring to the workforce in terms of skills and education that make you an economic asset.

Your Earned Income

Why do some workers make $20,000 a year, while others make $200,000? There are many factors that can affect your potential earned income, such as:

- The type of occupation you choose
- The state and city where you live
- The education and skills you acquire
- Race, gender, and other social and cultural factors
- The health and needs of the economy

While the last two of these are outside your control, the first three are affected by the choices you make and the type of life you choose to pursue.

Type of job and industry. Obviously, not all fields of work offer the same range of pay. Thus, your income potential will depend in part on which type of occupation you choose.

Many people who work in retail and service industries—store salespeople, waiters, and hairstylists—are paid a **wage**, or hourly rate, such as $8 per hour. The same goes for many of those who do some kind of manual labor, such as carpenters, machine operators, and plumbers. These jobs typically do not require a college education, but some may require specific vocational or technical training.

The **minimum wage** is the lowest amount that a company can legally pay its hourly workers. The federal minimum wage in 2010 was at $7.25 per hour, but your state may have a law that guarantees workers a higher minimum. (You can find out your state's minimum wage at *www.dol.gov/whd/minwage/america.htm*, or by searching by state name and the key words "minimum wage.") As you can see in the following table, many wage jobs pay more than the minimum. The *annual* pay for wage work depends on the number of hours worked—not all positions are full time.

Sample Wages	
Job	Median Hourly Wage
Waiter/Waitress	$8.01
Janitor	$10.31
Hairdresser	$11.13
Auto parts manufacturer	$13.76
Auto mechanic	$17.81
Carpenter	$18.72

Source: Bureau of Labor Statistics, 2008.

In contrast, many professional and administrative positions pay workers a set **salary** for the full year—for example, $40,000 a year—with an expectation of 40 hours or so of work per week. People who work in salaried jobs often have higher annual earnings than wage workers. The table that follows shows average incomes for a variety of salaried jobs.

Sample Salaries	
Job	Median Salary
Fitness trainer/Aerobic instructor	$29,210
Executive secretary	$40,030
Medical/public health social worker	$46,650
Funeral director	$52,210
Aerospace engineer	$95,520
High school principal	$97,486
Anesthesiologist	$197,570

Source: Bureau of Labor Statistics. *Note:* Anesthesiologist assumes more than one year in specialty.

Whether you are paid by wage or salary, your income will also depend on your experience level. In most industries, there are positions that are ranked, that are attained through experience in either work or education. For example, in public relations you may start as an assistant, and then get promoted up to account executive, account supervisor, vice president, and senior vice president. The entry-level person would make less than the senior V.P., as expected, given years of work and educational attainments. Just as the starting income is often higher for a salaried position than for a wage position, often there tends to be more room for career and salary growth in a company or industry that offers salaried positions.

Wage jobs don't always equal dead-end jobs. For many positions, learning on the job and passion for the work are what it takes to get ahead. A few years of experience and this prep cook could become a manager, run his own kitchen, or own his own restaurant!

So, the question is, why do certain fields pay better than others? This, like many questions in economics, boils down to supply and demand. Consumer demand for a certain product or service leads to industry demand for workers that can provide those things. The supply of qualified workers then directly influences the potential level of income. The best-paying industries are those involved with producing something for which there is significant consumer demand, *and* for which there are fewer qualified laborers than jobs. In such fields, companies are desperate to attract talent, and that pushes up the pay scale. For example, there are few anesthesiologists due to the educational requirements (becoming a doctor), so anesthesiologists are always in demand. Furthermore, people will always need surgery.

The lowest paying jobs, typically, are those for which there are many qualified applicants. This is why wage jobs requiring less than a high school diploma and no special skills—grocery store clerk or retail store salesperson—tend to pay the least. Almost anyone can do the tasks required. This is an example of a high supply of available workers. Applicants competing with each other drive salaries down. The more specific the skills needed in a wage job, the higher the pay, as the skill requirements reduce the number of potential applicants. (So, a carpenter could expect better pay than a fast-food worker.)

Wage and employment possibilities are affected by the changing demands of consumers over time. Changing technologies and needs play a role, too. Innovation also causes significant shifts. For example, as personal computers started becoming more available and affordable in the 1980s, fewer people bought typewriters. Companies that made typewriters saw revenue fall, and many of those workers who had designed, manufactured, or marketed these products lost their jobs. Meanwhile, the computer revolution led to the creation of many new jobs.

The Bureau of Labor Statistics, an arm of the U.S. Department of Labor, tries to predict the needs of the job market with its Occupational Outlook Handbook (*www.bls.gov/oco/home.htm*, or search for it by name). The handbook, updated yearly, reports facts on hundreds of different positions in different industries, including the nature of the job, the training necessary, market outlook for job demand, and earnings.

Location. The same job can pay differently in different areas. For example, curators—those who organize art or historical exhibits—could expect median earnings of:

$77,530 in Washington, D.C.
$65,890 in Illinois
$59,020 in California
$52,490 in Vermont
$40,510 in Wyoming
$35,970 in Montana

Why such a wide range? In part, it's due to demand. Washington, D.C. has a variety of museums and libraries, and many of them—like the Smithsonian Institution—are world-renowned. These top organizations might demand the most talented and experienced staff, which requires paying higher salaries.

More significantly, the income differential is also a factor of **cost of living**, or how much it costs for food, housing, transportation, and other necessities to live in that city or area. This too, can vary by a lot. Using the cost of living comparison tool at sites like *www.salary.com* or similar sites, you can find out that to maintain the same lifestyle as you could afford on

$35,970 in Helena, Montana, you would need to earn $62,222 in Washington, D.C. So, employers in D.C. know they need to pay more to attract high-caliber employees who also must be able to afford to live there.

Skills and education. As mentioned before, different jobs require different skills and knowledge. For example, a public relations professional would need to be good at making contacts and communicating persuasively in writing and over the phone. The anesthesiologist needs an understanding of the human body, of certain drugs and their impacts, and of the methods in which those drugs are best applied.

Some skills you develop on your own, while others require education. A **formal education** happens in a classroom; as you finish high school, you complete one level of formal education. College and graduate school are also formal education. So is trade school, a place at which you can get training for a specific technical field like cosmetology, hospital or health care work, plumbing, automotive repair, or cooking.

Informal education is training that happens outside of a traditional school. It may happen on the job; for example, a plumber may complete an **apprenticeship**, in which he or she works alongside someone more senior to learn the ropes. High school or college students often take on **internships**, in which they work in a low-level position in their field of interest in order to try it out and gain experience.

Formal post-secondary (post-high school) education can be expensive, as you can see it the following table. In this country, you must pay **tuition**, a set educational fee, to attend college. The benefit of a college education can mean a wider range of career choice, as many careers require a college degree. The trade-off is that you are spending money to attend school when you could be working—and earning.

Costs of College

Type of School	Degree Earned	Yearly Tuition and Fees	Total Cost
Public two-year college, community college	associate's	$10,000	$20,000
Public four-year college, in-state resident	bachelor's	$15,000	$60,000
Public four-year college, out-of-state resident	bachelor's	$27,000	$108,000
Private four-year college	bachelor's	$36,000	$144,000

Source: College Board "Trends in College Pricing," 2009. *Note:* Four-year college costs include room and board.

Even though most students get **financial aid**—tuition help from outside sources in the form of grants or loans—college can be a huge investment. It is an investment that typically pays off in higher earnings. As you can see in the following graph, average salaries tend to increase the more formal education you have. So, you can understand why the anesthesiologist—who must complete ten years of education at minimum, in a very challenging field of study—makes more on average than the aerobics instructor.

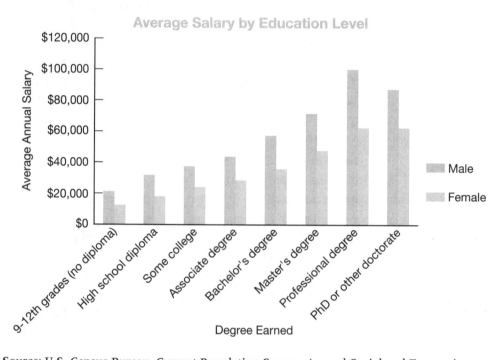

Source: U.S. Census Bureau, Current Population Survey, Annual Social and Economic Supplements; 2007.

 Take a look at the graph; roughly how much more per year would the average male make if he finished his associate's degree versus just finishing high school?

These are average annual salaries. Looking at it over a longer term, Americans with a college degree *earn twice as much over the course of their lives* as people with a high school diploma only, as estimated by the U.S. Census Bureau. This is one major reason why your teachers and guidance counselors encourage you to consider going to college rather than entering the workforce right after high school. After college, your starting salary could be tens of thousands of dollars higher than it would be if you started work right after graduation. And since future raises are based on that starting salary, you have the potential for significantly higher lifetime earnings by attending college.

Another reason education is important: as the graph that follows shows, the more schooling you have, the less likely you are to be unemployed.

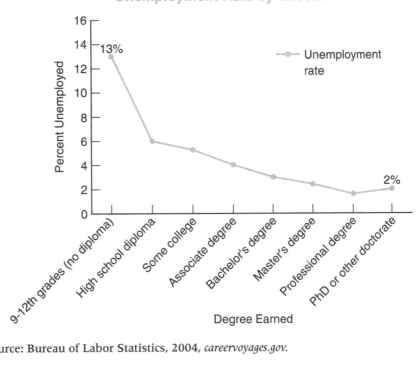

Unemployment Rate by Education Level

Source: Bureau of Labor Statistics, 2004, *careervoyages.gov.*

 What is the unemployment rate of those who are just high school graduates? What is the unemployment rate of bachelor's degree holders?

Social and cultural factors. There have been many attempts over the last century to level the playing field in the United States in job and income opportunities for every citizen. The Civil Rights Act of 1964 prohibits employment discrimination based on race, color, religion, sex, and national origin. Later laws have included age, disability, and sexual orientation as factors that cannot be used to discriminate. While these laws—and the Equal Pay Act of 1963, which dictated that men and women doing equal work should receive equal pay—have lessened the wage gap between majority and minority groups in the workplace, there still remains wage inequality. The phrase *wage gap* is used to describe the fact that there remains an invisible but very real divide between the salaries of women or minorities and the salaries of their workplace counterparts.

In 2007, working males earned on average $37,828 per year, while working females made only $23,052. (You can also see the differences by gender on the earnings by education graph on page 42.) In the table here, you can see how average income also varies by race:

Average Income

Race	Average Income
Asian	$30,875
White	$27,238
Black	$21,888
Hispanic	$21,151

Source: U.S. Census, 2007.

These differences may be attributed in part to an inequality of educational opportunities; but the truth is that discrimination still exists in some workplaces. It isn't easy to prove, but those who see it or have experienced it can file a charge with the nearest office of the Equal Employment Opportunity Commission, the agency that oversees the execution of the law. What you can do to lessen the wage gap is to know what the average salary for your desired field is, so that you can know when you're not being paid enough, and have leverage to ask for more money.

Economic forces. Your individual potential for income is also directly related to the needs and health of the economy as a whole. To understand this, consider the model of **circular flow**, which economists often use to show how money cycles through the economy.

The circular flow model demonstrates, in a simplistic fashion, the reciprocal relationship among businesses, households, and government. Money, goods and services, taxes, and incomes exchange among these institutions and keeps the economy flowing. Ideally, the economy is in a state of equilibrium, meaning consumers are buying what producers are making, money continues to flow, and employment levels are high. Supply and demand are fairly equal.

Sometimes, however, the circular flow falls out of equilibrium. In a **recession**—a period of economic decline—producers are making products that people are not buying; supply outpaces demand. As production slows down, producers stop hiring, and they may even have to **lay off** workers, or let them go. (This is different from being fired, which is a dismissal for cause.) The **unemployment rate**—or the percentage of the workforce not employed but looking for work—rises. Those workers fortunate enough to keep their jobs may have to take a pay cut. In these ways, a recession can be detrimental to income. This cycle continues through the circular flow as consumers continue to buy less, nervous about their own income and job security. As an example, the economic downturn of 2008–2009 led to a reduced demand for new cars, which caused a decline in demand for autoworkers. When these people lost their jobs others became uncertain of their own economic security, which led to even less demand for cars, and so on.

Comparatively, in a period of economic expansion there is high demand for certain goods or services. Therefore, producers need to start producing more, which means they need more workers. Unemployment tends to be low. Workers are paid better because they are in demand. This can be good for you.

While it might be nice to have economic growth all the time, it doesn't work that way. The economy goes through cycles, and you will likely experience both boom and bust in your career.

Circular Flow of the U.S. Economy

Resources, Payments

Goods and Services, Income

Businesses

Households

Goods and Services, Taxes

Taxes, Resources

Services, Payments

Services, Income

Governments

Where do you fit in this model? Once you start working and living on your own, where would your money come from? Where would the taxes you pay the government be spent?

Penny and Nick

"Want to grab some lunch?" Nick asked Penny as they packed up their books after personal finance class.

"Maybe tomorrow," she answered. "I have a meeting with my guidance counselor about college and careers. I think, after doing mock trial last semester, that I could be a pretty tough lawyer. Hey, what's *your* plan for after high school?"

"I plead the fifth."

"Oh, come on!"

"I don't really know what I want to do. I guess I might go to community college; on the other hand, if I just go straight to work I can make money right away," Nick said.

"That's true, but . . ."

Help Penny explain to Nick why he might want to go for the degree, and how he might start investigating career possibilities now, during high school.

How Inflation Reduces Income

There is another economic factor that influences income, but this one doesn't directly affect your wage or salary; instead, it changes what that money is worth. **Inflation** refers to price increases on goods and services over time. In the United States, inflation of the dollar can be measured through fluctuations in the Consumer Price Index (CPI), which follows the prices of some 400 common consumer items (such as milk, bus fare, electricity). It is expressed as a rate, which refers to the amount of change over a certain period, often a year. Prices historically rise over time (only rarely does the CPI drop, indicating **deflation**, or prices falling); but generally inflation is thought to be a problem for the economy only when it's over 3% per year.

The problem with inflation as it relates to income is that it shrinks your purchasing power—it causes your dollar to be worth less later because you cannot buy as much with it as you could today. Let's say item X costs $100 this year. If inflation is 3%, you could expect it to cost $103 next year. Inflation is compounded in the same way that savings are—but in this case, it's to the detriment of your money. So, if the next year prices on the item go up another 3%, it means that item would then cost $106.09.

In an inflationary economic environment, cost of living rises. Your income may not keep pace. So, as your needs—food, shelter, clothing—go up in price, you have less money to put toward goals, savings, or daily fun activities. If inflation is particularly high—in the 1970s prices were rising by between four and 13% a year—it means you may have to cut back significantly on nonessential spending.

Inflation is of particular concern to people who live on a fixed income, such as retirees, who typically get a set amount of money each month from the government (in the form of **Social Security**), or their former employer (like a **pension**). This income does not rise annually. So, if prices rise, they must reduce their spending.

MAKING CENT$ OF IT

Understanding the impact of inflation is easier once you see it in real numbers. Find an online inflation calculator by searching for key terms, or head to *www.bls.gov/data/inflation_calculator.htm* to find out:

1. What is $50,000 of income in 1980 equivalent to in today's dollars?

2. What income would you have needed in 1980 to have the same purchasing power as $100,000 today?

3. Something that cost:
   a. $1 in 1960 costs what today?
   b. $1 in 1970 costs what today?
   c. $1 in 1980, 1990, and 2000 costs what today?

2.2 Researching and Planning for a Career

TERMS TO KNOW

job	benefits	union
career	health insurance	entrepreneur
résumé	disability insurance	profit
cover letter	life insurance	business plan
job interview	401(k)/403(b) plan	

Getting Started

Right now, if you work after school or on the weekends, you probably have a **job**. Most likely, it's not a **career**. What's the difference? While the words are often used interchangeably (even in this book), a *job* is meant to refer to work done in the short term for the goal of making money. It doesn't necessarily have to be something you see yourself doing for the long term. A *career* is more of a journey: something you are aiming to do for some time, something for which you may have a passion. It is a professional course in which there is room for growth. Staying on one path for several years allows you to advance within that field, and promotions may come with significant raises.

Thus, to maximize income potential, it is best to have a career path in mind. In this section, you'll learn how to find your dream career, as well as how to apply for work within that field.

Investigating Career Paths

How do you find the right path for you? While it may seem wise to opt for the highest paying field—say, anesthesiology—it's actually better to choose a career that you have an interest in, and the appropriate talents for. If you care about your work, you're more likely to be successful at it. The goal is to balance personal satisfaction with special talent and an income that will afford the lifestyle you would like to have.

One way to narrow your options is by first looking at different industry sectors, or wide-spanning categories under which there are hundreds of professions. The Bureau of Labor Statistics' Career Guide to Industries has labeled these ten industry groupings:

- Natural resources, construction, and utilities
- Manufacturing
- Trade
- Transportation
- Information
- Financial activities
- Professional and business services
- Education, healthcare, and social services
- Leisure and hospitality
- Government and advocacy, grant making, and civic organization

 Investigate this list in the Occupational Outlook Handbook at *www.bls.gov/oco/cg*. Take some time to navigate career pathways, learn about job opportunities, and read more about what having a certain occupation may entail. For example, under "transportation" you might choose "air transportation." From there you can search employment, occupation types, and different job responsibilities.

Spend some free time playing out different scenarios, following different career pathways that may interest you. Finding out about various careers, what you need to study to get there, how much you might get paid, and what the job prospects are can help you when it comes time to plan your future, and to help you consider what you can do to get started today.

Explore what careers you might like. Think about your favorite class. Ask the teacher of that class what careers you might pursue given your interest in this area. Think about your strengths, and then talk to your guidance counselor about how you might apply those in the workforce. For example, if you are great at problem solving and math, you might make a good engineer (or bookkeeper, or accountant, or theoretical physicist, or business manager, etc.). Your guidance counselor can be an excellent resource, as it is his or her job to help you find direction in terms of college and jobs. Get to know this person. You may also find out more about careers by talking to people whom you admire. Ask them about their current job, but also work backward. Ask what their previous job was, and the job before that, so that eventually you can envision the path they took to get to where they are now.

As you narrow down your career options, you can return to the Occupational Outlook Handbook or your guidance counselor to talk about what preparations you will need to make. Will you need a college degree or vocational training? Should you be better equipped at math or pump up your writing skills? How should you prepare for taking the next step?

Fast Facts — *Taking It Step by Step*

Not sure what you want to pursue as your career path? Take time to recognize the things you enjoy doing. Solving difficult puzzles, peer reading your friend's papers, taking on responsibilities for your sports team, keeping your locker organized, or decorating your room are all valuable traits that show insight into your possible career strengths. Take the first steps by joining a club or getting an after school job that coincides with these, *just to try it out*. Maybe you don't know where your path will lead, but giving yourself the opportunity to explore will put you in a better position to achieve your future goals. In many ways, your future depends on what you do today.

MAKING CENT$ OF IT

It's a good idea to start investigating career possibilities early, as it can help you get onto the right track to pursue your dreams.

Part 1: Make a table like the one here. Use the Occupational Outlook Handbook at *www.bls.gov/oco/* to find the duties involved, training necessary, median earnings, and number of jobs available on the following types of work, plus two of your choosing. Fill out the table with your findings.

	Basic Duties	Training Necessary	Median Earnings	Jobs Available
Nurse				
Architect				
Judge				

Part 2: Interview someone in your community whose career you admire, and come up with a list of jobs they have held. Write the list in reverse order, starting with the job they have now, and work your way back through the jobs that got them there. Ask the person which early jobs were most important in building their career and why.

Applying for Work

If you apply for jobs now, you will likely have to fill out an application similar to the one here:

Manny's Dog Grooming

Application For Employment

Manny's Dog Grooming is an equal opportunity employer committed to diversity in the workplace and dedicated to a policy of non-discrimination in employment on any basis including age, sex, race, color, ancestry, religion, creed, citizenship status, disability, national origin, marital status, military status, sexual orientation, genetic information, gender identity and expression, or any factors not related to the job and will comply with all applicable laws.

Personal Information (Please print)

Name	Last	First	Middle		Date

Present Address	(Street, City, State, Zip Code)

Home Phone	Business Phone	Cell Number	Email Address

Are you legally authorized or permitted to work in the United States? (All new hires will be required to provide proof of eligibility to work in the U.S.) Yes _____ No _____	Are you (Please check the box that applies): *16___ *17___ 18 or over ___? [*A work permit or age certificate may be required for employment.]	Prior to answering this question you must read the instructions to applicants about criminal convictions section (on the reverse side) of this form. Have you ever been convicted of a crime? (Answering yes to this question will not be an absolute bar to an offer of employment.) Yes _____ No _____ If yes, explain _____

Employment Desired (If you are applying for a retail hourly position, please keep in mind that the availability of hours may vary.)

Position

	Sunday	Monday	Tuesday	Wednesday	Thursday	Friday	Saturday
Specify hours available for each day of the week _____ Full Time _____ Part Time _____ Seasonal/Temp							

Have you ever worked for Manny's Dog Grooming? If yes, when?_____

How did you hear about us? _____

Education

	Name and Address of School	Circle Last Years Completed	Did You Graduate?	Subjects Studied and Degrees Received
High School		1 2 3 4	Y N	
College		1 2 3 4	Y N	
Post College		1 2 3 4	Y N	
Trade, Business, or Correspondence School		1 2 3 4	Y N	

List skills relevant to the position applied for _____

SKILLS Computer Proficiency: Word ☐ Excel ☐ Others: _____

References

Give below the names of three professional references, which you have known at least one year.

Name	Company/Job Title	Address & Phone Number	Years Acquainted How do you know this person?
1			
2			
3			

Signature	Date

Q: Notice how even a basic job application has room for you to fill in your educational background. Why do you think that might be important to the company?

It may also help to start creating your own **résumé**, which is a sort of application for professional jobs that highlights experiences and education. This document is a starting point, growing as you grow in your career. It showcases your experience along your career path. Eventually, you will target your résumé to the job you're applying for, highlighting certain aspects of your experience that are relevant to the position. The basic format of the document, however, tends to remain the same. A good résumé is a one-page document that includes:

Contact information. At the top of the résumé, include name, address, phone number, and an e-mail address. Because this is a formal document, it is best to avoid abbreviations—such as St., or Ave.

Education. State the name of your school(s), the dates you attended, and the degree or diploma achieved (or expected date of achievement).

Work experience. This is the most important part of the résumé! It can include jobs, and, at this point, school leadership positions, internships, and volunteer positions you may have had. The listings, which should start with most recently held, should each include job title, company or organization, dates you worked there, and the duties you had. Duties should be written in an action-oriented fashion. For example, "Tutored children in mathematics and reading"; or "Photographed sporting events for the school newspaper"; or "Provided lawn care to clients." You need not include every task, just the more important or relevant ones.

Achievements/activities. You may want to list groups you participate in at school or outside of school, particularly if they show leadership or other important skills or traits. It can also be helpful to show any awards you've won or other special achievements that don't show up elsewhere in the résumé.

References. The company or organization may want to talk to people who know you professionally—not family or friends—to verify what you say about yourself. Supervisors from past jobs who liked your work are the best choice, but ask their permission before listing them. (If you are asking a boss from a current job, make sure they know you are looking for other work.) For each reference, list the person's name, title, connection to you (for example, "parent of family I babysat for"), and contact number or e-mail address.

Madison Stevens
125 Davis Street
Evanston, Illinois 60201
(847) 224-XXXX home
(847) 967-XXXX cell
mstevens@XXXX.com

EDUCATION
- **Northwestern University**, will begin pursuing a B.S. in child psychology in September 2012
- **Evanston Township High School**, diploma expected in June 2012

WORK EXPERIENCE
Retail clerk, Shale's Department Store   fall 2011–present
- Assist customers in coat department
- Run the cash register
- Oversee stock inventory

Lifeguard, City of Evanston Pool   summer 2011
- Monitored pool area for unsafe conditions and people in distress
- Rescued swimmers in need of assistance
- Performed first aid and resuscitation as needed

Babysitter, various clients   fall 2010–present
- Have watched children ages 9 months to 8 years

ACHIEVEMENTS
National Honor Society, 2010, 2011, 2012
All-state Softball Team, 2011

ACTIVITIES
Vice President, Key Club   fall 2011–present
- Organized clothing drive for homeless shelter
- Sold candy to raise money for elementary school playground

SKILLS
- Good with children
- Fluent in Spanish
- Red-Cross certified in lifeguarding and CPR

REFERENCES
Mrs. Gretchen Smith
Manager, Schale's Department Store
(847) 974-XXXX

Mr. George Yoa
Director, City of Evanston Parks and Recreation
(847) 837-XXXX

Ms. Melissa Ingerman
English teacher, Evanston Township High School
(847) 273-XXXX

Q: Note how Ms. Stevens's work experience is detailed. Action verbs like "operate," "monitored," and "organized" convey a sense of responsibility and active engagement. What action verbs would you use to describe some of your responsibilities?

Once you have created a résumé—and highlighted your key achievements and experiences, you will probably also need to have a **cover letter**. This is a letter in which you introduce yourself to the hiring manager, and make a case for why you are the best candidate for the position being offered. It should not repeat the résumé, but can elaborate on the parts of your experience that are most relevant to the position. Read the job description for clues about what the company is looking for. As you write the letter, keep in mind the key words used in the description.

The letter will be different each time, but most letters follow the same sort of outline: First, it should be under one page. The first paragraph should state the position you are applying for. The body paragraphs should explain why you are qualified, given the experience, education, and knowledge you have that would make you an asset to the company. The last paragraph should provide contact information, ask for an interview, and express your thanks.

Even though cover letters can be e-mailed, they should be written as formal business letters. Include your address at top (often this matches your résumé style, since the two will be sent together), and address the hiring manager as "Dear Mr. Smith:" or "Dear Ms. Jane Smith:"

Madison Stevens
125 Davis Street
Evanston, Illinois 60201
(847) 224-XXXX home
(847) 967-XXXX cell
mstevens@XXXX.com

March 15, 2012

Ms. Sheryl Grantham
Director, Sycamore Summer Camp
Post Office Box 535
Wisconsin Dells, WI 53965

Dear Ms. Grantham:

I am writing to apply for the position of junior counselor at Sycamore Summer Camp for this coming June.

I am a recent high school graduate with a great deal of experience working with children. I have been babysitting in my spare time since 2010. One of my regular clients has four kids—ages 6, 8, 9 and 11—and caring for them has helped prepare me for this job. I am able to keep children of different ages engaged by creating fun games and activities to keep them entertained (I often bring an arts and crafts kit with me on babysitting gigs now!). I have also worked as a lifeguard at the town pool, a skill I imagine would be useful as your campers do quite a bit of swimming. I have truly enjoyed working with children, both as a babysitter and a lifeguard; and my experiences have led me to an interest in child psychology, a degree I will be pursuing at Northwestern University starting in the fall.

Sycamore Summer Camp seems to be an engaging place, where children create summer memories. I would be delighted if I could take part in making them happen. I welcome the opportunity to meet with you to discuss my experiences further; I can be reached at (847) 224-XXXX. In the meantime, I have attached my résumé. Thank you for your time and consideration.

Sincerely,

Madison Stevens

At the Job Interview

Once you have applied for a position, a representative from the company may call you in for a **job interview**, during which you'll have to answer questions about why you want the position, and what makes you qualified. Before you go in, you'll want to do some research on the company or organization.

Look at the company's Web site; maybe enter the company's name into the "news" feature of a search engine to see what types of articles have been written on it. Of course, jobs you look at now may or may not have Web sites. In that case, call the information line, or visit the location yourself if it is in the neighborhood. Some things to keep in mind:

- What is this company's primary business?
- What makes it different from its competition?
- What is its reputation?
- How is what they do in line with what I want to do?

Arrive at the interview on time and dress professionally—typically you want to wear something a notch up from what you might expect to wear to work. For many jobs, it's appropriate to wear a suit. Bring a few copies of your résumé with you, in case you meet someone who hasn't yet seen it.

When you arrive, you will be directed to the interviewer's office. Introduce yourself, offer the person a firm handshake, and be prepared to answer questions such as:

- Why are you interested in this position? In this company?
- What skills/attributes/experiences do you have that are relevant to the position?
- What is a strength of yours that you have exemplified in a work environment?
- What do you know about this company?
- Why should we hire you?

Answer honestly—never lie!—but succinctly. In responding, understand that your ultimate aim is to convince the person that you are a good fit for this job.

Have some questions of your own to ask; this will help you to be more involved in the interview, and it will help you determine whether you really are interested in this job. Some questions you may want to keep in mind:

- What are the basic position responsibilities/expectations?
- What would a typical day in this job be like?

- What is the office culture like?
- What are the opportunities for growth?

As the meeting draws to a close, thank the interviewer for taking the time to tell you about the position, reiterate your interest, and shake hands again. When you get home, write the person a thank-you note, either a letter or an e-mail, and send it later that week, as this shows you to be professional and gracious.

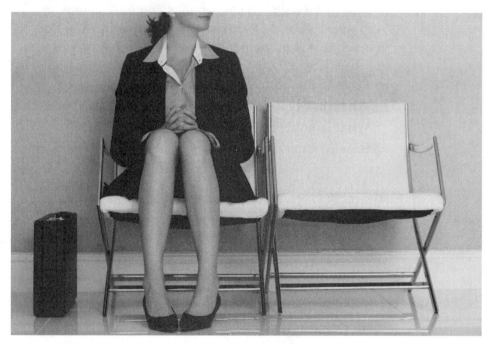

Interviews can make some people really anxious. Just remember to breathe, relax, and smile!

MAKING CENT$ OF IT

Part 1: Create your own résumé. Follow the outline on page 53, listing your contact information, education, work experience, achievements, activities, and references. If you don't have any work experience, describe a position you have held at school (for example, captain of the track team, math club treasurer). Include responsibilities you have at home such as housework, yard work, meal preparation, or childcare. Convey your experience vividly by using action words such as: aided, built, cared for, checked, coached, helped, prepared, provided, repaired, solved, taught, etc. Check your résumé carefully for spelling, punctuation, or grammar mistakes.

Part 2: Search the Help Wanted section of your local newspaper or an online job site like *Monster.com* for a job that you would want to have someday. (For this exercise, you can consider jobs for which you are not yet qualified.) Write a cover letter that you would submit to apply for the job. Follow the format suggested on page 54, but in the body paragraphs where you explain your qualifications, be creative. What experience, education, and knowledge would you need to be an asset to the company or organization?

Understanding Job Benefits: Beyond Salary Figures

When interviewing for a job, it will be worthwhile for you to know the typical salary for the position. You can find this information through the Occupational Outlook Handbook or sites like *www.salary.com.* Employers have a vested interest in keeping pay down, as they will reap greater profits with fewer expenses. It is typical to have to negotiate with the company to bring the salary up to a fair price. Knowing the market rate gives you leverage to do this. For jobs you may hold now, there is often very little room for negotiation; but soon enough when you start interviewing for positions that are salaried or require specific training, it will help to be aware of what your skills are worth.

In assessing a job offer, pay is not the only thing to consider. Once you get your first salaried job, you may be offered other **benefits**. These perks offered to workers are a form of compensation because they have monetary value (even though they're not paid in cash). Some begin once you start a job; others require that you stay on staff for a period of time. Among the more common benefits are:

Insurance. The majority of large and medium-sized employers offer **health insurance** plans to their workers; and most pick up part of the cost. Health insurance, which we will talk more about in Chapter Six, is a way of managing the financial risks of getting sick. In exchange for a monthly fee (called a premium), the insurance will cover the majority of your medical costs. It can be very costly to buy health insurance on your own, but if you get it through an employer it's significantly cheaper. The benefit of group health insurance, as it's called when offered by an employer, is so valuable in fact that many people narrow their job search only to positions that offer this benefit. Employers may also offer other types of medical coverage not typically included in a health plan; for example, they may offer dental coverage for your dentist visits and vision coverage for your eye doctor and eyeglasses needs.

Almost half of employers include long-term **disability insurance**, which will replace a portion of the employee's salary in the event that he or she becomes sick or disabled and cannot work.

Some employers also offer free **life insurance**, meaning that when the employee dies, a certain amount of money will be paid out to a person of his or her choice. Life insurance is particularly important for a person who supports a family. If that person dies, the insurance can help replace the lost salary.

Paid time off. Many salaried positions offer paid time off, meaning days you don't have to work but will still collect salary. Most employees get at least 10 federal holidays off (this includes New Year's Day, Memorial Day, and Christmas); but on top of that, paid time off can include vacation days, sick days, personal days (on which employees can make doctor's appointments or do other personal business), even paid lunches. Most Americans start with either 7 or 14 paid vacation days, though as you hit certain year milestones with a company, you may be given more time off. Before taking your days, you usually must approve them with a manager.

Retirement plans. Although becoming less and less popular, some of the nation's largest companies still offer a traditional pension plan, which (as noted earlier) guarantees workers a certain amount of income when they retire from the workforce. The amount of the payout depends on the person's age, number of years worked at the company, and salary. This is generally considered the most generous company benefit, as workers do not have to contribute any money toward a pension; the employer is contributing on the employees' behalf. A pension used to be the most common type of retirement benefit. Perhaps you have a grandparent or older relative who gets a pension from a past job.

Because pensions are so costly for companies to fund and maintain, many employers have moved—or are moving—to **401(k) plans** (or **403(b) plans** for public and nonprofit employees). In these retirement investing accounts, workers contribute their own money and pick their own investments from a selection the employer has chosen. Obviously, this is not as generous as a pension since it is your money instead of the company's. Some employers do, however, match dollar-for-dollar employee contributions up to a certain point. A special benefit of these plans is that money employees contribute is not subject to income taxes in the year it is saved—it will be later on, when it's withdrawn in retirement. That means that by saving in a 401(k), you're basically postponing that income and the taxes owed on it. You are reducing your taxable income for the present.

Flexible spending accounts (FSAs). These accounts offered by some employers allow workers to save money toward certain purposes. There are three common types. In a health care expense FSA, you can put aside money to pay for medical costs not covered by insurance—including over-the-counter medicines, eyeglasses, and the like. In a dependent care FSA, employees can save toward daycare, nanny service, even some nursing care for elderly parents. In a commuter expense FSA, employees can save toward bus or train fare or parking costs paid for a commute to work. You elect how much to save in such accounts, up to a set maximum. Then that money is contributed toward the accounts before taxes are taken from the paycheck, meaning that contributing to such accounts can lower taxable income, and therefore, taxes owed (we'll cover more about taxes on page 63).

Educational assistance. Some employers will offer to pay for all or part of additional education that will assist you in your job. This is a valuable benefit, especially given how expensive school can be. Taking advantage of this opportunity may make you a more valuable employee and put you in line for promotion. One important note: often the amount of reimbursement is tied to the student's grades; they may get 100% of tuition back only if they receive an A or B.

Overtime pay or bonus. Either of these can directly increase your salary. Overtime pay means you will get a certain extra sum for working beyond your set business hours. A bonus, or one-time lump sum of money, may be given as a reward for performance.

Suffice to say that when you consider any job opportunity, you must always consider not only the salary, but also the benefits. Consider being offered the following two jobs:

	Company A	Company B
Job title	Manager	Manager
Salary	$50,000	$44,000
Benefits	Two weeks vacation	Health insurance, a 401(k) plan with dollar matching up to 10%, two weeks vacation

Despite the difference in salaries, the job with Company B is worth more, because the total compensation package (job plus benefits) is worth well over $50,000.

In some occupations, employees have the choice or requirement to join a **union**, or collective of laborers in the field that bargains with the top managers of the relevant companies. Examples of unions include the Airline Pilots Association, the United Auto Workers (UAW), Major League Baseball Players Association, the American Federation of Teachers (AFT), and the Screen Actors Guild. The union represents workers, and argues for wage increases, pushes for certain working conditions, and negotiates policies on hiring, firing, and promotion. According to a recent study by the Center for Economic Policy Research, young workers in unions earn 12% more than peers who are not in unions, and are far more likely to be offered employee-sponsored health insurance and a pension.

Going a Different Route: Starting Your Own Business

Not everyone goes through the process of working for someone else. Some people start their own business, and work for themselves. Perhaps they have an idea for a product or service that doesn't yet exist; maybe they see a need that's not being met in a particular community; or possibly they think they can do something better or faster than other businesses.

These **entrepreneurs**, who start their own businesses, face considerable risks, but also considerable potential reward.

The greatest risk is of financial loss. Small business owners often must take on loans to start the business and to fund its operation before it generates revenue. These can be anywhere from a few thousand dollars to several hundred thousand. They are also not guaranteed a certain salary, or any salary at all. The hope is that within the first few years the business will start making enough money to cover its costs, and come out with a **profit**. But if it doesn't, the entrepreneur is left with lots of debt and a business that has gone bust.

On the other hand, if the business is successful, the owner gets to choose the direction of the company, be his or her own boss, and claim any revenue that exceeds business costs. This profit can be more significant than the income one might get working for someone else. For example, the entrepreneurs who founded Google, Amazon.com, and Nike are all on the *Forbes* magazine list of richest Americans.

To increase the potential for success and reduce the risk of failure, many would-be entrepreneurs painstakingly prepare a **business plan**: a proposal describing the idea for the business, analyzing the market and the competition, introducing the people involved, and stating financial needs and goals. This document is necessary to secure loans, but it's also a good idea because it helps assess whether the "brilliant idea" is really going to be profitable. Many successful entrepreneurs also work for someone else in the field they're interested in before striking out on their own. That gives them first-hand knowledge on what works and what doesn't.

THE IDEA THAT WAS WORTH MILLIONS

To be a successful entrepreneur, you have to create a product or service that people want to buy. The founder of Taco Bell did that, as you'll see in the obituary story below. Read this, and then consider the discussion questions that follow.

"Taco Bell entrepreneur started career in SB"
By Andrew Edwards
The San Bernardino County Sun

The first Taco Bell did not open in San Bernardino, but Bell's foray into the fast-food industry began in the same city where brothers Richard and Maurice McDonald opened their first restaurant.

Bell made his way in the restaurant business after serving with the Marines in World War II. He was a veteran of battles in Guadalcanal and Guam.

Bell, along with Baker's Drive-Thru founder and San Bernardino High School classmate Neal Baker, followed the example of the McDonald brothers by establishing their own fast-food enterprises.

"These were true entrepreneurs. These weren't people who did hostile takeovers," Stater Bros. Markets chairman Jack Brown said. "They took a risk, had a dream and went out and financed it. And nobody did it better than Glen Bell."

Bell was born Sept. 23, 1923, in Lynwood. He grew up in Muscoy, Brown said. "It was a very tough area in those days, and Glen was a tough guy."

Brown said he knew Bell for about 50 years. Around 1960, Bell, Baker and the McDonald brothers would eat breakfast at Sage's Complete Market in San Bernardino, where Brown was an assistant manager.

Bell opened his first restaurant, Bell's Drive In, in 1948. The restaurant initially served hamburgers and hot dogs, and Bell later developed a taco shell recipe in order to sell tacos to drive-through customers. The hard-shell taco became a fast-food legend overnight.

The emphasis with Mexican- influenced menu items continued. So in 1955, Bell and a business partner established a trio of Taco Tia restaurants.

Bell sold his stake in Taco Tia after his partner declined to expand into the Los Angeles market. He and another group of partners started a new fast-food chain called El Tacos around Long Beach, but again Bell sold his interests in the chain to try something new.

In 1961, Bell and employee John Galardi created Der Wienerschnitzel chain. The first restaurant to bear the name Taco Bell opened in 1962 in Downey.

Another influence on the fast-food industry was Bell employee Ed Hackbarth, who founded Del Taco. The first Del Taco opened in Barstow in 1964.

Bell may not have been as famous as the Carl's Jr. Founder Carl Karcher, or Ray Kroc, the businessman who developed McDonald's into an international powerhouse; but the founder of Juan Pollo, Albert Okura, said the Taco Bell founder did not get enough credit for his influence on the fast-food industry.

"Taco Bell is so far ahead of the nearest competitor, it's not even funny," Okura said.

Bell sold his 868 Taco Bell stores to PepsiCo in 1978. The chain is now owned by Yum Brands, which also owns Kentucky Fried Chicken, Pizza Hut, A&W Restaurants and Long John Silver's.

1. What was Bell's innovative idea that helped him differentiate himself from other fast-food entrepreneurs?
2. What kind of risks did Bell take in starting his own restaurant?
3. How can a would-be entrepreneur like Bell reduce these risks?
4. How might his story have been different if the tacos hadn't sold well?

MAKING CENT$ OF IT

Think you have what it takes to be an entrepreneur? Consider joining your school's Future Business Leaders of America club or your local Junior Achievement for hands-on experience. What kind of business do you think you could handle running? What might your business plan look like? With a partner, develop an idea for a business you would like to start. Together, draft a one-page business plan that includes:

a. a description of your idea for the business
b. an analysis of the market and the competition
c. a list people who would be involved in your business
d. the amount of money you would need to start the business

Understanding Taxes and Income

TERMS TO KNOW

taxes	progressive tax system
income tax	marginal tax rates
Form I-9	tax return
Form W-4	Form W-2
withholding	Form 1099
exemptions	Form 1040EZ
Internal Revenue Service (IRS)	adjusted gross income
disposable income	deduction
net pay	tax credit
FICA	tax liability
government transfer payments	audit

Getting Started

Flip back to the model of circular flow on page 45. In it, you'll see that households and businesses give a certain amount of their income to the government in the form of **taxes**. The government—whether federal, state, or local—then spends this tax revenue toward paying for items it deems necessary for society, putting money back into the economy.

Taxes pay for some of the services that the government provides—such as road upkeep, school funding, unemployment benefits, and military defenses. Taxes pay the president's salary, as well as those of other government officials. They help fund international policy, including aid to disaster-stricken countries. Taxes are also used to redistribute wealth; by taxing the rich at a higher rate than the poor, the government can reduce some of the gap between the highest and lowest earners. Finally, the government can also use taxes to influence the economy by means of what economists call *fiscal policy*. Reducing taxes leaves more money in the pockets of the people, which stimulates the consumer economy because consumers have more money to spend. Buying more means more production, more employment opportunities, etc. This is called *expansionary* fiscal policy; it expands the economy when it needs it. *Contractionary* fiscal policy, on the other hand, helps keep inflation in check, and keeps prices down. By raising taxes, the government curbs people's spending. Higher taxes leave people with less money to spend, so demand for things should go down, and prices usually follow.

There are several types of taxes collected in the United States. Among them:

- Sales tax, which is levied (or imposed) on purchases when you buy them
- Property tax, which is paid by landowners and homeowners
- Customs tax, which is paid on items imported from another country
- Estate tax, which is paid on large inheritances

The largest portion of revenue collected by the government comes from **income tax**, which is levied on income, both earned and unearned. Almost everyone who has income must pay income taxes.

Employment, Tax, and Income Forms

Your first day at a new job—or even before—you'll probably be handed an employee handbook and be asked to fill out some paperwork. This includes a **Form I-9**, which is a government form used to verify that you are a citizen or otherwise authorized to work in the United States.

The other piece of important paperwork you will fill out is a **Form W-4**, a tax document that signals to employers the estimated income tax you may owe over the year. In the United States, you don't pay your taxes all at once, but instead prepay a certain amount through every paycheck.

The amount you pay per paycheck, referred to as **withholding**, is determined by how many exemptions you elect on this form, as well as on your salary or wages. **Exemptions** are circumstances that reduce taxable income (basically, a certain portion of income is never taxed). For example, the bigger your household (the more people you support on your income), the more of your income is exempt.

The top part of the W-4 form is a personal allowances worksheet, which helps you determine your exemptions. The more you choose, the less tax will be withheld from your paychecks; in other words, your paychecks get bigger. Later in this section, we will talk about filing tax returns, which determine the exact amount of taxes you really owe. Even if you file for many exemptions to keep your pay during the year, you still will be held responsible for the allotted taxes you should owe given the number of people in your family, household income level, and other situations that may lessen or increase total taxes owed.

Your employer redirects your withholding to the **Internal Revenue Service**, or IRS, the agency that collects tax money. If your state has an income tax—a few states do not—you may have to fill out a withholding form for your state as well.

When it comes to receiving your paycheck, you may also have the option to fill out a direct deposit form. Direct deposit allows your paychecks to be deposited directly to your checking or savings account, so that you don't have to bother going to the bank to deposit a paper check. Also, with direct deposit, the money is often available immediately on payday, whereas the check may take a few days to clear. (This is mentioned in more detail in Chapter Three.)

Reading a Paycheck

When you get your first paycheck, you may be surprised at how small it is. That's taxes for you! As noted earlier, you prepay your taxes due through every paycheck. Thus, whether you're making $30,000 a year or $300,000, you'll never see the full amount. Taxes reduce **disposable income**, or the amount of income after taxes, for living expenses or savings.

A paycheck generally comes with a *pay stub*, as shown on the next page. The pay stub includes a section devoted to earnings, which should end with *gross pay*, or total earnings for the period before anything is subtracted. This section may also show how many of the days worked were regular days and how many were vacation or sick days. It may also list year-to-date totals of these categories.

The next section will be deductions from gross pay. The biggest of these are likely to be for income taxes, owed to federal, state, and local governments. The amount withheld will be based in part on what you have said on your W-4 and state withholding forms.

At the bottom of the pay stub, you will see **net pay**, or the amount remaining after all of the payroll deductions and income tax are taken out. That's the real number you will get to take home.

Employee benefits costs/contributions. If your employer offers health insurance, you may have to pay a share of the premiums. So, if you have elected this benefit, a regular amount of money will be deducted from every paycheck before taxes are calculated. If you decide to contribute to a 401(k) plan or FSA, that money will also be deducted pretax. The employer may list these as pretax deductions on the pay stub.

Payroll taxes. A small fraction of your income goes toward paying for specific federal programs, including Social Security (government-granted income for retirees and the disabled) and Medicare (government-sponsored health insurance for the same groups). Known as **FICA—** Federal Insurance and Contributions Act—these payroll taxes include 6.2% Social Security tax (on income up to a certain amount) and 1.45% Medicare tax. Your company pays the same amount on your behalf as you do, effectively splitting the bill with you. Depending on your state, you may also pay a small percentage to support unemployment insurance.

Union dues. If you are a member of a union, as mentioned in Section 1.2, you may be required to pay a certain small amount per paycheck (called your *union dues*) to support the actions of that union.

Model Pay Stub and Paycheck

	Co. FILE DEPT. CLOCK NUMBER						Earnings Statement			
	MCB 216543			02470383 0						

Manny's Dog Grooming
200 Main Street
Summerville, N.Y. 12345

Period ending: 6/30/20xx
Pay date: 7/13/20xx

Social Security Number: 999-99-9999
Taxable Marital Status: Single
Exemptions/Allowances:
  Federal: 3, $25 Additional Tax
  State: 2
  Local: 2

Janet Spelling
210 Oak Lane
Summerville, N.Y. 12345

Other Benefits and

Earnings	rate	hours	this period	year to date		Information	this period	total to date
Regular	9.50	25.00	237.50	4,628.75		Sick Hrs Left		16.00
Overtime	15.00	1.00	15.00	45.00				
Gross Pay			**$ 252.50**	$4,673.75		**Important Notes**		

Deductions Statutory

	this period	year to date
Federal Income Tax	− 23.75	462.88
Social Security Tax	− 2.38	46.29
Medicare Tax	− 1.81	32.01
State Income Tax	− 13.89	173.54
City Income Tax	− 4.06	96.17
SUI/SDI Tax	− 0.50	11.09
Other		
Union Dues	− 5.00	45.00
401(K)*	− 10.00	300.00

WE WILL BE STARTING OUR UNITED WAY FUND DRIVE SOON AND LOOK FORWARD TO YOUR PARTICIPATION.

Net Pay	**$ 191.11**

* Excluded from federal taxable wages

Manny's Dog Grooming
200 Main Street
Summerville, N.Y. 12345

60 102433

Payroll check number: 02470383
Pay date
Social Security No. 999-99-9999

Pay to the
order of: **Janet Spelling**

07/13/20xx

This amount: **One Hundred Ninety-One and 11/100**

$191.11

SAMPLE
NON-NEGOTIABLE
VOID VOID VOID

VOID AFTER 180 DAYS

John Brown
AUTHORIZED SIGNATURE

⑆02470383⑈ ⑆043301627⑈ 100844840 2⑈

Examine the pay stub and paycheck. What is the difference between the gross pay and the net pay? How can you account for that difference? What are the types of income tax deducted? What is the largest deduction?

Other People Your Taxes Help

Some of your tax money is used to redistribute wealth. **Government transfer payments** provide money, valuable services (such as health care), or vouchers for food to citizens with certain needs. Among the common beneficiaries of such programs are low-income individuals and families, retired persons, very ill or disabled people, and veterans. The following table describes some of the common programs. In theory, you will someday benefit from your own payroll tax payments. If you're ever laid off from a job, you'll qualify for unemployment compensation; and eventually, when you retire, you will be eligible for both Social Security benefits and Medicare. Social Security is meant to replace part of the monthly income you had as a worker. Your benefit depends upon your annual salary before retiring and the age at which you start taking benefits.

Government Transfer Payment Programs

Social Security, Survivors, and Disability Benefits	Guaranteed income to senior citizens, survivors of deceased workers, and people who are disabled or ill to the point of being unable to work
Medicare	Health insurance for those who are over age 65 or disabled
Medicaid	Health insurance and bill assistance for people with a lower income
Unemployment Benefits	Temporary income to people who have been let go from their jobs
State Children's Health Insurance Program	Health insurance for children
Temporary Assistance for Needy Families	Temporary income for families with children
U.S. Supplemental Nutrition Assistance Program	Vouchers or debit cards to be used on food for low-income families
Veterans' Benefits	Health insurance, educational assistance, income replacement and more for certain veterans and their families

How the IRS Determines Taxes

The United States has a **progressive tax system**, which means that the more income one makes, the greater percentage of it one pays in taxes. The idea is that those who earn higher incomes have more ability to sacrifice part of that income, whereas those at lower incomes need nearly every dollar. A progressive tax system is also intended in part to help equalize wealth. Those at the top pay for the services those at the bottom will need. This system also narrows some of the wage gap between income levels.

The alternatives to a progressive tax would be a *regressive tax*, which might tax everyone the same dollar amount—and would be hardest on those with the lowest income—or a *proportional tax* (also called a *flat tax*), which would tax everyone the same percentage of income.

In our progressive tax system, the amount owed by earners at each income level is determined by the federal government. It is explained in terms of **marginal tax rates**, or the rate that you would pay on the last dollar you earn. This also determines your "tax bracket," the highest bracket (rate of taxation) you fall into at your income. In the table, you can see the marginal tax rates for a single person in 2010 (the numbers are different for married couples and families).

Income Range	Marginal Tax Rate
$1–$8,375	10%
$8,375–$34,000	15%
$34,000–$82,400	25%
$82,400–$171,850	28%
$171,850–$373,650	33%
$373,650 and up	35%

This does not mean that a single person earning $50,000 would pay $12,500 (a flat 25%). Rather, income is taxed progressively more as it surpasses certain income limits. So, the first $8,375 of income would be taxed at the 10% rate; the next portion up to $34,000 taxed at 15%; and the last portion up to $50,000 at 25%. (Thus, the tax bracket—in this case 25%—represents the rate the last dollar of salary is taxed.) So, the math would be as follows:

$$(\$8,375) \times 0.10 = \$838$$

$$(\$34,000 - \$8,375) \times 0.15 = \$3,844$$

$$(\$50,000 - \$34,000) \times 0.25 = \$4,000$$

$$\text{Total tax owed} = \$8,682$$

In reality, $8,682 is not 25% of $50,000. To come up with an average tax rate, the actual percentage of income paid, you would divide the amount of taxes owed into total salary.

$$\frac{\$8,592}{\$50,000} = 0.173 \text{ or } 17\%$$

If you work for someone else, your company decides how much you will prepay based on the exemptions you selected on your form W-4 and the total amount the employer is expecting to pay you for the year. If you work for yourself, however, you must figure out your own withholding, for filing your personal taxes at the end of the year.

MAKING CENT$ OF IT

Using the marginal tax rates for a single person in 2010 (on page 68), calculate the total tax owed on the following incomes, and then calculate the average tax rate for each.

1. $34,522
2. $100,000
3. $181,087

Filing a Tax Return

Every American with a certain amount of gross income in a year—in 2010, this was $9,350 for single people—must file a **tax return** for that year on or before the following April 15. These standard forms are a way of reporting to the IRS all the income you've made (both earned and unearned) and the tax you have already paid. It's a way for the government to assess whether you have paid the appropriate amount of tax given your income. If you paid too little, you will owe the government—and will have to pay by the filing deadline, April 15. If you paid over what is owed, you will be given a refund from the government.

Up until age 19—or 24 if you are a qualified student—your parents may be able to include you on their tax return as a dependent, assuming you have under a certain amount of earned and unearned income. After that, you must file your own.

In order to help you file your tax return, your employer must send you a **Form W-2** by January 31 of the following year (so, you would get a W-2 for the year 2011 in January 2012). This form reports taxable income (salary before taxes) for the year. It also shows the federal and state income tax and payroll tax you have already paid.

Look at the sample Form W-2 and locate:

1. The person's name and Social Security Number (the 9-digit number used to identify you to the government)
2. The company that employed her
3. How much she earned
4. How much she paid in federal taxes
5. How much she paid in state taxes
6. How much she paid in local taxes

22222	a Employee's social security number 999-99-9999	OMB No. 1545-0008		
b Employer identification number (EIN) 000-00000			1 Wages, tips, other compensation 10,567.31	2 Federal income tax withheld 1,056.73
c Employer's name, address, and ZIP code Manny's Dog Grooming 200 Main Street Summerville , N.Y. 12345			3 Social security wages	4 Social security tax withheld 105.68
			5 Medicare wages and tips	6 Medicare tax withheld 69.72
			7 Social security tips	8 Allocated tips
d Control number			9 Advance EIC payment	10 Dependent care benefits
e Employee's first name and initial Last name Suff. Janet V. Spelling 210 Oak Lane Summerville , N.Y. 12345			11 Nonqualified plans	12a
			13 Statutory employee ☐ Retirement plan ☐ Third-party sick pay ☐	12b
			14 Other	12c
				12g
f Employee's address and ZIP code				
15 State Employer's state ID number NY 000-00000	16 State wages, tips, etc.	17 State income tax 610.27	18 Local wages, tips, etc.	19 Local income tax 242.06	20 Locality name

Form **W-2** Wage and Tax Statement   **2010**   Department of the Treasury–Internal Revenue Service

There is also a **Form 1099** for other types of income, such as interest or other investment income on which taxes are owed. A 1099 reports income on which tax was not withheld. In some jobs, usually project work or contract positions, tax is not taken out of your checks, and your income will be reported on a 1099. This doesn't mean you don't owe. It just means the employer isn't taking responsibility for sending the money to the IRS as withholdings.

Some time between receiving the W-2 or Form 1099 and April 15, you will have to fill out your tax return form. The main federal tax return is known as a Form 1040. Those who are single, or married filing together, and earning less than $100,000 a year can fill out a simpler, more abridged version called the **1040EZ**. There are many other forms, and the more complicated the finances, the more forms there are that might need to be filled out.

The beginning of the form asks for your **adjusted gross income**, your earned income (line 1 of the W-2) and your unearned income (from the 1099) added together.

You will then be asked to enter a standard deduction; this is the base amount of your income on which you do not owe taxes. For 2010 it is $9,350 for a single person. A **deduction** is something that directly reduces taxable income; the amount of the deduction is subtracted from the adjusted gross income, leaving a smaller amount that will be taxed. On the 1040EZ, there is space to take only the standard deduction; but those who file a standard 1040 have the option to itemize certain allowed expenses instead and deduct those from taxable income.

Q: What is this cartoon's commentary? What makes the tax code complicated? List three things from this section.

There may be other deductions you are entitled to take on top of the standard deduction on the regular 1040. For example, if you contributed to a retirement account, paid college tuition, or paid interest on student loans, you may be able to deduct even more. To figure out how much a deduction is worth in tax savings, take the value of the deduction and multiply it by your tax bracket. So, a $1,000 deduction in the 25% tax bracket is worth $250.

Next step on the 1040EZ: enter, from the W-2, the amount of federal tax paid during the year.

Then, the following few lines will ask about certain **tax credits** you may be eligible for. Tax credits reduce your taxes owed dollar-for-dollar. So, a $1,000 credit means you owe $1,000 less in taxes for the year. Recently, credits have been offered for buying a home, or buying a hybrid car. Again, not all credits will appear on a 1040EZ; you may need to use a regular 1040 form to claim them.

Next, you will be asked to look in the tax tables in the instruction book that comes with the form for the appropriate **tax liability**, or amount owed, on the newly calculated taxable income. You will compare this with the amount you actually paid, noted on your W-2. If the liability is greater than what you paid, you will owe the IRS that amount. If the liability is less than what you paid, you will be owed a refund.

Once you know how to fill out the federal 1040, filling out a state form will be easy, as they tend to follow the same basic structure.

MAKING CENT$ OF IT

Fill out a 1040EZ for the following person. Your teacher will hand out the instruction booklet, so that you can find the tax liability.

- Mr. Ira S. Taxman, 2432 K Street NW, Washington, DC 20037
- SSN: 123-45-6789
- single
- $33,000 in wages
- $1,023 in interest income
- $4,103 paid in federal income tax

 *Attempting to Cheat on Your Taxes*

Under-reporting income on your taxes (or claiming deductions or credits that you are not entitled to) is considered tax fraud, and is punishable by hefty fines or jail time. The IRS **audits** a certain number of returns each year, forcing those taxpayers to produce proof for what they have claimed on their returns.

CHAPTER REVIEW

Master the Vocabulary

Use the personal finance terms from the start of each section to complete the following sentences.

1. Wages, salaries and tips are examples of _____ , while prize money, gifts, and investment gains are considered _____ .

2. If you're paid by the hour, you earn a(n) _____ ; if you're guaranteed an annual income, that's called a(n) _____ .

3. _____ education happens in a classroom setting; _____ education happens on the job or through other activities.

4. The cost of college instruction is referred to as _____ . Some students qualify for _____ , which includes loans and grants to help pay for college.

5. _____ is a model showing how businesses, households and the government interact in the economy.

6. In a _____ , producers are making more than consumers are buying and the economy is slowing. So, companies may _____ workers, or let them go for financial reasons. This raises the _____ , or percentage of the workforce that is out of work or seeking work.

7. _____ refers to the general rise in prices over time. _____ occurs in the rare instances when prices are falling.

8. A _____ is work done in the short term for the goal of making money, while a _____ is something you plan to do for the long term that may allow you more room for growth.

9. When applying for a position, you may have to submit a(n) _____ , a one-page document that lays out your professional experience. You may also have to include a(n) _____ with your application, to explain why you are right for that specific position.

10. The hiring manager may ask you to come in for a(n) _____ , in which he or she will ask you questions about your experience and interest in the position.

11. When you are considering a job offer, you must consider the pay, but also the _____ —the other resources the employer will provide that have monetary value to you.

12. _____ helps pay medical bills; many employers subsidize costs for this.

13. When it comes to retirement plans, some companies may offer a(n) _____, which provides guaranteed retirement income paid by the company; whereas other companies offer a(n) _____, to which the employee contributes, investing in a fund set up by the company.

14. _____ start businesses of their own; they usually must write a(n) _____ in order to secure funding.

15. _____, which mainly come out of your paycheck, help to pay for the services the government provides. The _____ is the federal agency that collects these.

16. After taxes come out of your paycheck, the amount of money you are left with to spend on saving and living is your _____.

17. Before starting a job, you'll have to fill out a(n) _____ to verify employment eligibility and a(n) _____ to help your employer determine how much tax to withhold from your paycheck.

18. The more _____ you take on a W-4, the less money will be withheld from your paycheck.

19. A _____ represents people who work within an industry, and negotiates on their behalf. It is a collection of workers who come together to guarantee better benefits and job security for every worker in their group.

20. The name given to the payroll taxes used to pay for Social Security and Medicare is _____.

21. _____ is your compensation before taxes, employee benefit costs, and savings plan contributions. _____ is your pay after all these are taken out.

22. _____ is a federal welfare system that provides income to retirees and disabled people. It is an example of a(n) _____.

23. In a _____ tax system, the more you earn, the more you pay.

24. Your _____, or your "tax bracket," is the percentage tax rate you pay on the last dollar you earn.

25. A(n) _____ form shows your taxable income for the year; a(n) _____ shows income from investments.

26. The simplest tax return form, which can be filled out by single people who earn less than $100,000, is _____.

27. On a tax return form, claiming _____ reduces your taxable income; while claiming _____ reduces your tax owed, dollar for dollar.

28. Your _____ is the amount of tax you owe.

29. A(n) _____ occurs when the government asks for detailed proof of what you submitted in your tax return.

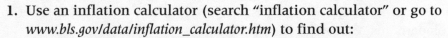

Apply What You've Learned

1. Use an inflation calculator (search "inflation calculator" or go to *www.bls.gov/data/inflation_calculator.htm*) to find out:

    a. What is $34,000 of income in 1969 worth in today's dollars?

    b. What is $34,000 in 1979 worth in today's dollars?

    c. What is $34,000 in 1989 worth in today's dollars?

    d. What is $34,000 in 1999 worth in today's dollars?

    e. What is $34,000 in 2009 worth in today's dollars?

2. Use the Occupational Outlook Handbook at *www.bls.gov/oco/*, to find the:

    a. Nature of the work

    b. Training necessary

    c. Median earnings

    d. Employment hiring trend over time (as a percentage)

    Of the following careers: atmospheric scientist, librarian, automotive mechanic, actor, funeral director, and fashion designer. (Hint: On the Occupational Outlook Handbook page, use the search box to find the occupation if you can't find which category it may fit into.)

    > **Example:** *Utilities Meter Reader*
    >
    > a. *Read meters on properties of electric, gas, or water consumption, and record volume used*
    >
    > b. *High school diploma, driver's license*
    >
    > c. *$32,950 a year*
    >
    > d. *Down 20% from last year*

3. Imagine you have a job interview next week with Wegmans supermarket chain. Before the interview, you decide to do some research. Go into the "about us" portion of the company's Web site (*www.wegmans.com*), and find the answers to the following:

    a. Where is the company headquartered?

    b. When was it founded?

    c. Who is the CEO?

    d. How many stores does the company have?

    e. What are some of the features it claims make it different from other supermarkets?

4. Steven Schwartzman wants to apply for the job described on the next page. He just graduated from the Culinary Institute of America with a bachelor's degree in culinary arts, and last summer interned at a wedding-planning venue in Poughkeepsie, New York, where he assisted

planners in setting up and running events. He served as a day-of coordinator for two of the weddings, and was told by one of the couples that he "helped make the day perfect." Help him write a cover letter to accompany his résumé for the position.

Job Description: Assistant event planner, The Catered Way

An event facility that handles weddings, birthdays, and corporate events is looking for an assistant event planner to work with clients to determine their needs.

Responsibilities:

- Developing event ideas
- Working with senior staff to take the event from idea to reality
- Negotiating with other vendors
- Handling day-of responsibilities

Requirements:

- One year experience in restaurant industry or event planning
- Bachelor's degree

Contact:

    Kim Clarke
    Director of Event Planning
    The Catered Way
    17 State Street
    Boise, ID 83701

5. Look at the sample pay stub and record the following.
    a. Gross pay for this paycheck
    b. Gross pay for the year
    c. Net pay for this paycheck
    d. State Unemployment Income tax for this paycheck
    e. Federal income tax paid for this paycheck
    f. State income tax paid for this paycheck
    g. Social Security tax for this paycheck
    h. 401(k) savings for this paycheck

Co. FILE DEPT. CLOCK NUMBER			Earnings Statement	

Co. FILE DEPT. CLOCK NUMBER
MCB 216543   02470383 0

Earnings Statement

Book E. Books
310 Court Way
Downtown, PL 11102

Period ending: 8/15
Pay date: 8/22

Social Security Number: 999-99-9999
Taxable Marital Status: Single
Exemptions/Allowances:
    Federal: 3, $25 Additional Tax
    State: 2
    Local: 2

Thomas Woods
7600 Asbury Place
Downtown, PL 11101

Earnings	rate	hours	this period	year to date
Regular	10.00	40.00	400.00	16,440.00
Overtime	15.00	0.00	0.00	380.00
Holiday	10.00	0.00	0.00	60.00
Gross Pay			**$ 400.00**	**$16,880.00**

Other Benefits and Information	this period	total to date
Vac Hrs Left		40.00
Sick Hrs Left		16.00

Deductions	Statutory			
	Federal Income Tax	– 31.00	2,351.44	
	Social Security Tax	– 15.75	1,551.67	
	Medicare Tax	– 3.25	362.89	
	State Income Tax	– 21.25	903.24	
	Income Tax	– 4.20	427.96	
	SUI/SDI Tax	– 0.50	31.20	
	Other			
	Union Dues	– 5.00	100.00	
	401(K)*	– 15.00	600.00	
	Stock Plan	– 15.00	150.00	
	Net Pay		**$ 289.05**	

Important Notes

EFFECTIVE THIS PAY PERIOD YOUR
REGULAR HOURLY RATE HAS BEEN
CHANGED FROM $9.00 TO $10.00 PER
HOUR.

* Excluded from federal taxable wages

6. Using the marginal tax rates for a single person in 2010 (on page 68), calculate the tax due on the following incomes, and then calculate the average tax rate.

a. $29,877

b. $55,000

c. $120,087

7. Fill out a 1040EZ for the following person. (Your teacher will hand out the 1040EZ form and instruction booklet, in which you can find the tax liability; or find the form and booklet at *www.irs.gov/pub/irs-pdf/f1040ez.pdf*.)

- Name: Sally McGinley
- SSN: 654-78-9878
- single
- $45,000 in wages
- $898 in interest income
- $11,250 paid in federal income tax

CHAPTER 3

Budgeting, Banking, and Money Management

Chapter Objectives

Students will:

✔ Manage a budget, and learn how to make smart spending decisions
✔ Find out what types of accounts banks offer
✔ Understand how to balance a checking account
✔ Learn about identity theft and protection

> **Personalize It!** *Take a second to look in your wallet: how much cash is in there right now? Think about what you're planning to do with it. If you'll spend it, what will you spend it on? How much of it will you allot for fun? And how much will you put toward responsibilities? How much of it will you save? Basically, what purpose will this money serve in your life?*

Introduction

If you have income right now, you know how easy it can be to spend these funds without even blinking. But it's important to blink—and think—about how you are allocating your resources.

You are the manager of your own money. As such, you are responsible for making sure you have enough cash to cover your expenses. Right now, these might be minimal. Your parents may require you to pay for only your cell phone bill, or your entertainment costs. In a few years, you will be responsible for a host of other expenses, including rent, groceries, utilities, and more. Both now and *especially* in the future, you will need to make sure you have the money to pay for your expenses at the time these expenditures are due—or else your cell phone might get cut off, you may get kicked out of your home, or you may have trouble providing basic needs for yourself and your family.

Smart money management also means making sure you have money left to put toward future goals; in other words, it requires trading away some instant gratification for even better delayed gratification. For example, a five-dollar cappuccino five days a week from your favorite coffee shop may make you happy in the short term. In total, that's $100 a month of money you might use toward something you've been really wanting. Buying something now can prevent you from reaching your goal later.

How do you ensure that your money achieves both current and future objectives? It's not as hard as it may sound. All you need is a plan that helps you balance expenses against income and a place to store your money so that it's available for expenses, emergencies and short-term goals. In this chapter, you'll learn everything you need to know about budgeting and banking—two essential tools for everyday money management.

 ## 3.1 Budgets and Spending Plans

TERMS TO KNOW

budget
discretionary income
philanthropy

recurring expenses
fixed expenses
variable expenses

budget surplus
budget deficit

Getting Started

Responsible money management comes down to living within your means. To live within your means is simply to keep the amount you spend below the amount you receive in income. You'll have the money to pay for the things you need, as well as some of the things you want. If you plan it right, you'll even have cash left over for saving toward future goals. You will also avoid unnecessary debt.

A spending plan, or **budget**, helps you figure out how much you can spend, save, and give to charity on a given income. Having such a plan can also help you make financial decisions, as you will have a better sense of your priorities.

You Can Get It if You Really Want

A budget requires reconciling (or balancing) your cash flow, which expresses the difference between the money that comes into and goes out of your hands in a given period. Cash inflow is income, while cash outflow is your expenses. A cash flow statement shows what's already happening. A budget, however, is what *should* be happening; it's a plan to balance the two cash flows so that you spend less money than you make.

When it comes to budgeting, almost any financial advisor will recommend that you "pay yourself first." This means that you should allot a portion of your income to savings before you spend any of it. By doing this, you prioritize your future goals ahead of the day-to-day. You're prevented from thoughtlessly using money on purchases that wouldn't matter as much to you as your goal. The spending plan makes you decide in advance how important your goals are to you, by asking you to consider how much you want to save before you consider how much you have to spend.

Next, the budgeting process will force you to consider your needs. Needs are those things that you can't do without, such as food, a roof over your head, a notebook for your personal finance class—while wants are things you desire but can do without (as described in Chapter One). Most people's wants far exceed their incomes. So, if you don't prioritize needs ahead of wants, you could easily spend all your income on things you want, and be left without money for rent or meals. If you allocate money to needs first, however, then the money left over—your **discretionary income**—can be used toward wants.

Where budgeting for needs gets complicated is that there is a huge continuum of what you could spend even on these "needs." For example, you need food, but do you need steak? Well, you can probably get by on hamburger. You need clothes, but do you need an $800 cashmere sweater fresh off the Paris runway? That nice sweater on sale at the mall will do just fine. You need a roof over your head, but do you need a million-dollar mansion? A budget helps you determine the most you can spend on your needs, based on your income. (Sorry, the mansion is unlikely to fit into your starting salary!) With this idea in mind, it's up to you to decide the appropriate amount to spend.

There are no right answers. No matter how much you choose to spend on your needs—and even your wants—there will be tradeoffs. This is a prime example of *opportunity costs*, from Chapter One. For example, imagine two people with the same income, just starting on their career paths: One might prefer to live in a roomy one-bedroom apartment that rents for $800 a month. The other might rather spend $300 on a small, compact studio apartment. In this example, the opportunity cost for the first person is that he or she has less money left for other things, because of the higher rent; for the second, the opportunity cost of saving that money is giving up living in a more comfortable apartment.

Create a Spending Plan

Now onto the practicalities: A budget can be done by day, week, month or year, but it is typically done by month because many expenses recur monthly.

Calculate monthly income. The first step in creating a budget is to know how much money you have coming in.

For most people, most income comes from one or more jobs. So, start by determining your income after taxes, your disposable income, from Chapter Two. (For comparison, *discretionary* income is after taxes *and* expenses). The easiest way to get this is to look at your pay stubs for your net pay. Multiply this figure by two if you're paid biweekly to get your monthly income. If your income is more variable (for example, you work from five to fifteen hours a week at your $10 an hour job), you may want to average out a few paychecks to estimate your average monthly income.

Teenagers might also have income from an allowance; make sure to add this. Adults may also have income from other sources, which could include unearned income from investments, child support, pensions, or government assistance, among other things.

Once you total your income, you know how much you have at your disposal every month to budget.

Example: Travis works after school and on weekends at the local pizza place, and his monthly net income averages $320.

Figure out saving and giving. To "pay yourself first," you must figure out how much you want to save before looking at your expenses. That way, you can see where you might need to trim your expenses to make your savings goal.

If you have something specific you're saving for, you'll need to determine how much you need to set aside on a monthly basis up until you have saved enough. For example, to save enough for a $280 gaming console within a year, you'd divide by 12.

$$\frac{\$280}{12} = \$23.33 \text{ per month}$$

If you wanted to get it within six months, you'd calculate:

$$\frac{\$280}{6} = \$46.66 \text{ per month}$$

Even if you don't have a specific goal in mind right now, it's always best to save some of your income, and many experts recommend setting aside at least 10%. That way you'll have money to use in the future, and you'll have more security. You should try to set some money aside for emergencies anyway, as we'll discuss more in Chapter Four.

A budget helps you save for your future goals. If there is a cause you believe in, a budget can also help you put aside money to support that cause. If you feel strongly about fighting homelessness, protecting the environment, or supporting a religious group, for example, you might consider making room in your budget for philanthropy. **Philanthropy** involves helping charities either with a donation of money or your time as a volunteer. If you decide to give money, there are two ways you might do it: give a one-time gift, or commit to give regularly. You should budget for these contributions, especially if you choose to give money regularly.

Example: Travis's biggest financial goal right now is to buy a new digital video camera so that he can create funny videos with his friends and post them on the Internet. After doing some research, he finds out the camera will cost $200. If he saves $25 a month, it will take him eight months to save. If he saves $50 a month, it will take four months. If he saves $100 a month, it will take two. He decides to save $50 a month, figuring that he can wait four months to have the camera.

 **Don't Trust Every Charity**

If you're considering donating some of your income to a charity, you should be aware that there are a lot of scammers out there posing as charities to get your money; and even legitimate ones may not spend donations in the way you'd like.

Ideally, 40% of a charity's donations should go to the costs of running the charity, and the rest to the actual charitable programs. You want to know where your money is really going; that means doing a bit of homework. All true service organizations, like charities, must be registered with the IRS. Check this by going to *www.IRS.gov*, typing "publication 78" in the search box, and then searching for the charity. You may also want to check out:

The U.S. Better Business Bureau (bbb.org/us)
The American Institute of Philanthropy (charitywatch.org) or
Charity Navigator (www.charitynavigator.org)

These groups describe charities with a number of factors, including how much money they raise is spent on programming compared to administrative costs.

Calculate expenses. The next step in creating a spending plan is to consider your necessary monthly *outflow* of cash: your expenses. Here are some common categories of expenses:

- housing (rent or mortgage)
- utilities (Internet, phones, heat, electricity, water, other such bills)
- food (groceries, buying lunch at school or work, and so on)
- gas, car insurance, bus pass, or other transportation costs
- healthcare costs (including prescriptions or doctor visits)
- debt payments (such as from a credit card or student loan)
- insurance premiums
- clothes
- home supplies
- personal care (like haircuts, dry cleaning, makeup, shampoo)
- entertainment

If you are a high school student, the majority of these likely do not apply to you, but some may. Not every adult will have all of the above expenses either; each person makes different choices and has differing costs as a result.

Make a list of the categories that affect you, and then try to figure out how much you have been spending on each. For most people, the easiest part is determining the **recurring expenses**, or those that you pay regularly. Some of these are **fixed**, meaning they are the same amount every month—like rent or a gym membership. Other expenses may be **variable**, meaning they change in amount. An electricity bill or a phone bill may be higher or lower every month depending on usage. If you have expenses that are variable, you'll have to estimate. You may want to average out a few months of bills, for example.

Average Household Income Expenses

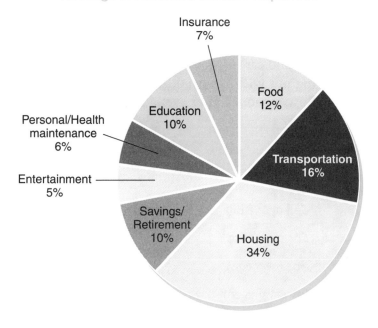

Insurance 7%

Food 12%

Education 10%

Personal/Health maintenance 6%

Transportation 16%

Entertainment 5%

Savings/ Retirement 10%

Housing 34%

 If you made $1,800 a month, how much on average might be spent on entertainment? How much on paying for rent or housing? How much might you try to save?

Many surveys on people's spending habits have shown that people cannot account for up to 20% of their spending. If, beyond your fixed expenses, you don't have an accurate sense of where your money is going, you may want to keep a *spending diary*, or a catalog of your expenses. To create such a diary, you'll need a notebook. Write the day of the week on top of each new page. Then every time you make a purchase that week, no matter how small, enter it.

Monday
$4 *US Weekly* magazine
$3.25 café latte
$30 gas
$4 piece of pizza and a peach iced tea
$10 dues for National Honors Society
Total: $51.25

Expect to be surprised. Many of us spend more than we actually think we do each day.

Example: Travis pays for his own cell phone, plus he has to pay for gas and car insurance. He also spends money going to movies and eating out with his friends. This is what he found was his monthly outflow of money after averaging his spending diary.

Travis's Average Expenses

Expense	Cost per Month
Cell phone bill	$50
Car insurance	$72
Gas (average)	$95
Entertainment	$53
Video games	$50
Total	$320

Balance the budget. The next step involves planning for your cash outflow to be less than your cash inflow. To do this, add how much you would like to save to how much you currently spend on expenses. Then, subtract this from your income to see if you would be spending less or more than you make.

Monthly disposable income – monthly money needed = $_____
(for expenses and savings)

If the end result is a positive number, you would be in excellent shape: a positive cash flow—or a **surplus**—means your expenses and savings are below your income. You could even be saving more, if you want. If you're at zero, you're also doing well; you already have a balanced budget, which means you are able to make your savings goals and live within your means.

For most people, however, expenses and savings will exceed the income number, which means they have a budget **deficit**. If you have a deficit, you must cut back on expenses by that amount to make the savings goal and balance the budget. (Or you'll have to earn more, though that's often not an easy solution.) There are usually items within the expenses that can be cut back. It's typically easier to trim the "wants" than the "needs." We've seen that a five-dollar latte five days a week comes to $100 a month. So you may want to make a vow to get them half as often and spend only $50. You don't have to give up your wants completely, but reducing your consumption now allows you to put more toward your personal goals for the future. If cutting back on your wants doesn't help, you may have to go back and amend your budget for other expenses, or adjust your savings goal, so that they are more realistic.

When you come up with enough expenses to cut back so that you can zero your budget, you'll want to make a revised statement that includes your income and your newly assigned expense and savings amounts all on one sheet. It may look like the worksheet that follows.

Example: Travis adds his current expenses to his savings and then subtracts that from his income:

$320 (income) – $370 (savings + expenses) = –$50

Realizing he has a budget deficit, Travis looks back at his expenses to see what he can cut in order to even it out. Since he can't give up the cell phone or the car, he focuses on entertainment and video games. Finally, he decides to postpone buying a new video game for four months—thus eliminating that spending, and balancing his budget.

Travis's Monthly Balanced Budget

A. Income	Budget
Pizza Heaven job	$320
A. Total	$320
B. Savings	
For digital camera	$50
B. Total	$50
C. Expenses	
Cell phone bill	$50
Car insurance	$72
Gas (average)	$95
Entertainment	$53
Video games	$0
C. Total	$270
A – (B + C) Total	$0

Track your budget. Once you've figured out how to balance the budget, you'll want to track your progress. When the next month is over, create another column in your budget in which you'll enter the actual amounts you spent in each category—as in the example below—to see how you did, or where you need to be more diligent. There will always be some variances: for example, a utility bill may go up in the summer with air-conditioning costs.

Overall, the goal is to get as close as you can to your budgeted amount. While you don't have to track your budget every month, you may want to revisit it periodically to make sure you are within range. If you make any big changes, like moving out of your parents' home, you will want to re-think your budget completely. You might look back to see how much surplus you have to put toward rent, and consider what expenses you'd be willing to trim in order to pay for your new place. The opportunity cost of moving out will be spending less on going out with friends, new clothes, or reaching your savings goals as quickly as you'd hoped.

Example: Travis fills in the following after his first month's budgeting. His income, which fluctuates, was above the average he assumed in his budget, and he spent less on gas. As a result, he ended up with a budget surplus of $30. He is considering putting that money toward his camera.

Travis's Monthly Budget

A. Income	Budget	Actual
Pizza Heaven job	$320	$340
A. Total	$320	$340
B. Savings		
For digital camera	$50	$50
B. Total	$50	$50
C. Expenses		
Cell phone bill	$50	$50
Car insurance	$72	$72
Gas (average)	$95	$85
Entertainment	$53	$53
Video games	$0	$0
C. Total	$270	$260
A − (B + C) Total	$0	$30

There's a new craze sweeping today's high schools: saving money. More teens are saving today than their parents were when they were young; and they have some good reasons why. Read the article and answer the following questions to find out more.

"Survey: College is top savings goal for teens"
By David Pitt
Associated Press

Stroll through the mall on a weekend and you get the impression teens save money to buy clothes or iPods and video game systems, but a new survey shows their priority is quite different—saving for college.

The survey by online brokerage TD Ameritrade Holding Corp. shows putting money away for higher education is the top savings goal for today's teens. The results showed 62 percent of teens aged 14 through 19 save their money for college, a much higher rate than the 40  percent of adults who said they saved when they were teens.

The results weren't expected by educators who are pushing for financial literacy education in schools.

"It's a pleasant surprise that we're seeing young people paying that much attention to the importance of this issue," said Joseph Peri, CEO of the nonprofit Council for Economic Education. "Part of teaching the importance of investing is showing that the best investment a young person can make is an investment in themselves."

The survey shows teens are not hesitant to sock more of their money away than their elders did when they were young. About 87 percent of teens say they save. That compares with 56 percent of adults who said they saved some portion of their income as teens.

The results also show 78 percent of teens said they want to establish a plan with their parents that involves splitting the cost of education.

That interest should prompt teens and their parents to discuss the options for saving. They can include a prepaid tuition plan that locks in costs of tuition and mandatory fees. There's also a 529 savings plan option that's an investment account offering tax-free earnings growth to cover tuition and other costs such as room and board and books. Other options include a Coverdell education savings account, which is similar to a Roth IRA in which taxes are paid up front but the savings grows tax-free and are taken out with no taxes due.

Custodial savings accounts, those set up by parents and turned over to students when they become adults, are also available. They typically help families set aside money for expenses not covered in the other plans such as sorority dues or music lessons.

The willingness of teens to share the financial burden shows that they are very aware of rising college costs, Young said.

More than 80 percent of teens reported that they consider education to be essential to future success, compared with 56 percent of adults surveyed who say they felt that way as teens.

"We've become more conscious of the opportunities that are out there for us and the competition that's out there," said Megan Partridge, 17, a student at Voorhees High School in Glen Gardner, N.J.

1. What percentage of teens surveyed are saving money for college?

2. What percentage surveyed are saving money in total?

3. Name three savings plans for college mentioned in the article. Write down one detail about each.

4. Do you have a savings plan? (Saving can be any way you save; cash at home, with your parents, at the bank, etc.) What are you saving for?

MAKING CENT$ OF IT

The best way to understand how to budget is to do it yourself. Predict how much you think you will spend the rest of today and tomorrow. Keep a spending diary for the next two days (or longer if you can). Then, go through each of the steps for creating a budget. Answer these questions about your spending habits:

1. How much did you spend on things without thinking about their cost? Circle them on your diary.

2. How much more did you spend than you predicted? Find the total.

3. While making your budget, plan for a week at a time. How much do you need every week? What are your expenses? Categorize the budget in a way that works for you, and try to add your diary's information into it.

4. Is your budget suitable for your income? Why or why not?

Make Smart Spending Decisions

You can reduce your expenses and find more room in your budget for saving if you make smart spending decisions. Here are a few ways you can be a more conscientious spender:

Avoid impulse spending. Ever walked into a store intending to buy one thing, only to walk out with that and five other things? It's called *impulse shopping*. And it's the sort of thing that harms budgets across America. To avoid this, you need to be systematic. Make a list before you go shopping, and try to stick to it. Carry around only a limited amount of cash in your wallet—say $20—to buy what you have already planned on buying for that day, to prevent you from buying things that cost more. Try thinking about any item you're interested in buying in terms of how many hours of work it would take you to earn it. (For example, say you were thinking of buying a $300 surf board. If you earn $10 an hour at your job, it would take you over 30 hours—perhaps two to three weeks of work—to earn back the money.) These tips will help you decide whether it's really worth it for you. What if you're sure you can't live without an item you see? Put it through the "one week test." Hold off buying for one week, and if you still want the item, you can consider buying it.

Learn to tell when you're being marketed to. Advertising is *meant* to motivate you to buy stuff—stuff you may not need at all. To accomplish this, the people who write the advertisements tell you what you want to hear, knowing it will activate your buying desire, even if it means stretching or completely ignoring the truth. Recognizing marketing strategies can help you to notice when you are being marketed to. The following are some of the most common tactics companies use to promote their products. Watch out for them.

Technique	How It Works	What You Might Hear
Bandwagon	Taps into your desire to have the same things your peers have	"Teens lo-o-o-ve X!"
Endorsement	Uses an expert or celebrity to pitch the product, in the expectation that you will trust the person's opinion	"I'm Serena Williams, and I use X."
Promotional	Offers you a discount when you buy the product	"Buy X now, and get Y free!"

Technique	How It Works	What You Might Hear
Facts and figures	Appeals to your sense of logic by offering information about the product	"X has proven to be 99% effective in laboratory studies."
Name-calling	Tries to one-up the competition by saying how the product is better	"X is faster and stronger than Y"
Emotional	Taps into your fears and desires to make you interested	"Worried about zits? No need to be with X."
Association	Attempts to connect the product to something you have positive associations with	"X product is as soft and cuddly as a new puppy!"
Urgency	Makes you feel as if you have to act now	"Buy X in the next 10 minutes—it's going fast!"

There are other ways businesses market products. For example, stores put small items by the cash register hoping you will be inspired to add these to your purchase as you're checking out. Retailers may put complementary items near each other—like ice cream and chocolate sauce, or iPods and headphones—hoping you'll buy both. They may also create special displays for products they're trying to push.

You want to become a conscious consumer, and try to be aware of when you become interested in something just because you are marketed to.

Do your homework. If you are planning to buy something big—say, a camera—don't just go to the store and try to pick one out there. You don't need the pressure of a pesky salesperson, who might have incentive (like a commission) to lead you to an expensive product. Instead, before you leave home check out reviews of camera brands, from the objective product-testing magazine *Consumer Reports* (*www.consumerreports.org*), or check other online sites to see what consumers have said about the product. The point is to make sure you select a quality product you'll be satisfied with.

Once you choose a brand you like, there's another step before you're ready to buy: comparison shop. Especially when you're going to buy something that costs more than the amount you typically carry in your wallet, it's wise to comparison shop—to see how this product is priced at other stores.

Sales Tax Adds to the Price!

When you buy certain items in most states, you won't just pay the price marked on the tag. Your final bill will be higher due to sales tax, which states use to collect revenue on purchases made. Sales tax is expressed as a percentage of the bill; a 5% sales tax equals 5 cents tax for every $1 spent. To calculate the tax added to the item, you multiply the tax rate (expressed as a decimal) by the subtotal, and then add the subtotal.

So for example, if your state charges a sales tax of 5% on a new computer hard drive system that costs $120, the total you pay would come to $126.

($120 × 0.05) + $120 = $126

Wait for sales, but don't get wooed by them. Prices are not inherent. They are based on demand—the higher the demand, the higher the price. If you want something and it seems too expensive, wait it out. Inevitably, demand will fall, and as it does, the price will fall. With clothes, it is seasonal; in August, people are no longer thinking about buying summer clothes, yet stores must get rid of their inventory to make room for fall. Thus, you should start to see sales. With technology, sales may come about when a newer model has been released. Or an item may go on sale during a slow time of year for the store.

Whatever the reason, a sale can pay off in a big way. If you can get 20% off on a $300 surf board, you're saving $60, which is not insignificant. That's money that you can put toward another purchase, or better yet, that you can put in your savings account, and have it grow. It pays to wait for the sale. Your best friend may have the newest board, but he's inevitably paying for the privilege.

You must remember that sales are also used as a marketing tactic, meant to get you into the store and to buy when you otherwise would not. You have almost certainly gone into a store at some point, noticed they had a sale, and been tempted. Sometimes stores purposely discount one thing in order to get you to buy another that's more expensive. This is true for cell phones—you get the phone for free or at a fraction of the "price" because you're signing up for the service, which is much more valuable. So the key is to ask yourself (and be honest!): Do I really want this? Would I be interested in buying it even if it weren't on sale?

MAKING CENT$ OF IT

Go through some magazines, newspapers, Web sites, or watch TV and collect or record examples of the advertising strategies listed on pages 91–92. Bring at least four in to show the class, and write an explanation of which category each belongs to and why.

3.2 Understanding Banks and Bank Products

TERMS TO KNOW

retail bank	debit card
liquidity	savings account
Federal Deposit Insurance	money market deposit account
Corporation (FDIC)	APY (annual percentage yield)
credit union	nominal interest rate
checking account	real interest rate
ATM (automated teller machine)	fee schedule

Getting Started

Budgets are all about cash flow: money in and money out. That money has to go in and out of somewhere—and piggy banks aren't usually big enough to hold a full paycheck's worth of cash. Besides offering limited space to store money, that change jar isn't protected from theft, fire, or other disaster. Also, it's hard to track where the money goes.

These are among the reasons people start putting their money in a **retail bank**, a financial institution that takes deposits and makes loans to everyday citizens. Bank accounts are the best place to store cash for both current expenses and short-term goals, not to mention emergencies.

What Banks Offer Individuals

Some 90 percent of Americans have money on deposit with banks, according to the Federal Reserve. This is what they get:

Accessibility. Money in most types of bank accounts is almost as easy to access as if it were in a piggy bank. You can withdraw money at ATMs, by using checks, debit cards, or going to the bank. You can typically take the money out without paying any fees or penalties. In other words, bank accounts are very liquid. **Liquidity** refers to the ease of converting an investment into cash. Because of the liquidity bank accounts offer, they are a good place to store money you are likely to need within the next six months or so, including the funds to pay for the expenses you budgeted in the previous section. Accounts offer various ways for you to transfer funds to other people or businesses.

Security from loss, theft, and disaster. If you keep all your money in your wallet, you run the risk of losing it or that someone will steal it. If your house burns down, your cash might turn to ashes. In most retail banks, your money is better protected against such things. (Just consider the fire-proof vaults and the security cameras and guards.)

Theoretically, storing cash in a bank could present its own risks. If the bank fails, or goes out of business, your money could go with it. Thankfully, the government has taken steps to make sure that customers won't lose anything if that happens. The **Federal Deposit Insurance Corporation**, or FDIC, is a government agency that will guarantee deposits—up to $250,000 per person—if a bank goes bankrupt. The FDIC was founded during the Great Depression, when many banks failed and left their customers suffering devastating losses of savings. (While most banks are covered by FDIC, not all are. Check with your local bank before depositing.)

Penny and Nick

"Nick! I got my first paycheck!" Penny exclaimed.

"That's awesome Pen," Nick said. "Glad babysitting for the terrible twosome has some benefits. What are you gonna do with the money?"

"Probably just have my mom cash it at the bank, then put it in my desk drawer at home. Try not to spend it right away," Penny sighed.

Pretend you're Nick and explain to Penny the reasons why she might want to open a bank account.

Guaranteed growth. Banks actually pay depositors—people who have accounts—to store their money, in the form of interest. In Chapter One you learned about interest, and how it's paid to a lender of money by the borrower. As a depositor, you are the lender. So why does a bank want to borrow your money? The profitable part of the bank's business is writing loans, such as home mortgages, auto loans, and business loans. The bank needs to have money to provide these loans. Depositors provide the money. This is profitable because the bank charges borrowers of loans more interest than it pays depositors.

Because you are guaranteed a specific interest rate on most basic bank accounts (usually savings), you can never lose money in a bank account; your deposit will only grow in value. The rate of growth, however, can be much lower than other investments, (low risk means low reward), and it may fall behind the rate of inflation. To state it another way, the reward of a guaranteed rate must be weighed against the chance that you might do better elsewhere.

Ability to manage spending. In doing the exercise at the start of this chapter, you may have found that you did not know what happened to the dollars you most recently had in your wallet. With bank accounts, you get monthly or quarterly statements of where your money has gone. You can also look at your account online to get information between statements. You also have proof that bills were paid. Thus, bank accounts are an important tool in the budgeting process: they help you track your spending to see how it lines up with your projections. Also, since you usually have to take some action to access cash that's in a bank account, it's just a tiny bit harder to spend money—which is a good thing. Money that isn't spent thoughtlessly can be thoughtfully applied to a goal in the future.

Types of Banks

When people say "banks" they typically mean traditional retail banks, which operate as for-profit institutions and have branch locations where you can go to make transactions. These can be either national (think Chase, Bank of America, Wachovia, or Citibank) or local (La Jolla Bank or Bank of Hawaii). Aside from these, however, there are a few other types of banking institutions at which you can make deposits. Here are the ones you need to know about:

Credit unions. **Credit unions** are non-profits that are owned by their members, who typically have a common interest. That interest may be an industry (Actors Federal Credit Union), a neighborhood (WATTS United Credit Union in Los Angeles), or a church (Florida Episcopal Federal Credit Union). Some credit unions restrict membership; others allow anyone to join, for a fee.

Credit unions offer the same types of accounts as banks (though they have different names), and also write loans. In both cases, they are often able to offer better rates than big banks, which typically have higher overhead. Just like banks, credit union deposits are insured for up to $250,000 per person; but the National Credit Union Administration, not the FDIC, is the insurer. You can find a credit union near you by searching the Credit Union National Association online at *www.cuna.org*; or the National Credit Union Administration at *www.ncua.gov*.

Savings and loan associations. Also known as thrift institutions or *thrifts*, these came into being in the early nineteenth century specifically to promote the availability of home loans. Historically they offered only one type of account—a savings account—and used these deposits to make loans. The ones that still exist resemble retail banks—they're even insured by the FDIC. Among the bigger differences are: they are still required to do more home mortgage business; they tend to be local institutions; and they are often owned by their depositors (like credit unions).

Online banks. These institutions, which have popped up in recent years, don't have storefronts that you can walk into. Instead, they operate solely through the Internet. You can mail in deposits, and get money through ATMs (some even reimburse ATM fees from other banks, since they may not have their own ATMs). Online banks sometimes pay slightly higher interest rates than commercial banks because they have lower expenses, like not paying for stores or as many employees.

Types of Bank Accounts

Banks may write loans and issue credit cards. They may offer investment brokerage services. Our focus in this chapter, however, is on their savings and money management functions. The following are the primary savings tools offered by banks, from lowest interest rate to highest:

Checking accounts. **Checking accounts** are the most liquid type of account; they offer many ways to access cash. For example, customers can write checks or use an *ATM card* (a plastic card that can be used at the **Automated Teller Machine** or **ATM**) to access their money. Often, the ATM card also works as a **debit card**, meaning you can use it at ATMs as well as at a store cash register; the purchase amount will be automatically withdrawn from your account. Checking accounts typically offer the most withdrawals free per month of any bank product. In some cases, you can make unlimited transactions. The drawback is that you also lose out on interest: such accounts pay the least of any bank product. Many pay no interest at all.

"Yes, we offer no-fee checking accounts. For a small fee."

In this cartoon, the bank manager has just answered the customer's question. What do you think the question was? What is the cartoonist saying about bank services?

Savings accounts. **Savings accounts** allow fewer free transactions than checking accounts—typically less than six withdrawals or transfers a month—but typically pay a higher interest rate. Unlike a checking account, you do not have access to the money via checks or debit card, though you may be able to make infrequent withdrawals at an ATM. You can usually open a savings account with a first deposit of under $100.

Money market deposit accounts. Similar to savings accounts, these accounts combine some of the features of savings and checking, usually with higher interest rates. Like a savings account, the number of transactions allowed is limited. Unlike a savings account, you can often write checks against the account balance. These accounts sometimes require a higher deposit to open, usually $1,000 to $10,000, and a higher balance to be maintained, which is why the bank is willing to pay more.

Certificates of deposit. CDs, as they are known, are savings vehicles that require larger deposits, often $1,000 or more, and longer commitments. You promise to keep your money in the CD for a fixed period—common terms are six months, one year and five years—during which time you will not be able to withdraw from the account or otherwise access it. A CD has a date of maturity at which point you can withdraw the money without fees, but if you take it out before the maturity date, you will have to pay a penalty. Because the bank is getting guaranteed access to your money for that period, it is willing to pay you a higher interest rate than with other savings vehicles; one-year CDs have paid out 4.9% on average since 1984.

Comparing Interest Rates

With any type of bank account, the higher the interest rate, the faster your money will grow. Since rates vary from bank to bank, you'll need to shop around for the best offerings. This can seem confusing, however, since interest on bank accounts can compound monthly, quarterly, or annually. It may be obvious that an account paying 2% that compounds monthly will end up paying more than an account that pays the same percent and compounds annually. It's harder to tell, however, when it's 2.1% compounding annually vs. 1.9% compounding monthly.

To make it easier for consumers to compare rates, the Truth in Savings Act of 1991 required that banks calculate and demonstrate to consumers a standardized **APY** or **annual percentage yield** for an account. This is an effective yearly rate that factors in compounding in order to allow you to compare accounts. If Account A and Account B pay the same interest rate, but B compounds more frequently, B will show a higher APY, since your money will end up growing faster in B.

As you learned earlier, interest rates on bank accounts often lag behind the rate of inflation—and when they do, it will mean your money will not be able to buy as much in the future as it can now. The APY is a **nominal interest rate**, meaning it doesn't consider inflation. To see if your money will keep pace with inflation in order to maintain the same purchasing power, you need to look at the **real interest rate** of your account, the interest rate after inflation. You would use this formula:

APY – rate of inflation = real interest rate

So, if your account pays 2% APY and yearly inflation is estimated at 2.5%:

2% − 2.5% = −0.5% real interest rate

(Your money is losing half a percent of value per year.)

In this case, inflation is winning. If your account were paying 5%:

5% − 2.5% = 2.5% real interest rate

(You're winning. Your money is growing faster than inflation.)

Because banks pay so little, it's unwise to keep all your money at the bank once you start making a full-time income. Even if you lose some to inflation, banks are still an ideal place to store money for current needs, as they allow easy access to cash. They are also the best place to save for the short term and for emergencies. Once you have money to save beyond these, however, you should probably consider investing it (as you'll learn in Chapter Four).

MAKING CENT$ OF IT

It's important to be able to compare rates on bank accounts so that you can get the best deal. Bank A and Bank B both offer money market accounts.

Bank A	Bank B
$1,000 minimum balance	$1,000 minimum balance
2.75% APY	3.38% APY

1. Which of these money market accounts would you choose? Why?

2. What is the real interest rate on the account you chose, if the inflation rate is 2.2%?

3. What is the real interest rate on the other account, assuming the same circumstances?

Shopping for a Bank

If you don't already have bank accounts, you may want to consider opening both a checking and a savings account—as having them will help you manage your current expenses and start setting aside money for future goals. It's beneficial to have these at the same institution, since you can then transfer money more easily between them; you can get both accounts on one statement; and you can often access both online or through an ATM card.

When comparing banks, you'll likely find great variety in terms. Interest rates will vary a little, but then there are fees, and they can vary a lot. Because of these variances, you want to shop around to find the best deal. Narrow your options to the best banks for your location, and then either go into the branch or do some research online. Here are some of the key questions you should get answers to:

- What is the APY?
- Is there a branch or an ATM near my home? (It's best if there is, so that you can avoid other bank ATM fees.)
- Are my deposits FDIC insured? (Make sure the answer is yes.)
- What is the minimum deposit required to open the account?
- Is there a monthly maintenance or service fee? If so, what is it, and how can I avoid it?
- If there is a minimum balance requirement, what is it?
- Can I manage the account online?

You should also ask to see a copy of the **fee schedule**, a complete list of account fees that banks are mandated to create and provide to customers per the Truth in Savings Act.

Ask the bank if it has special accounts for teens or students—many do, and these usually have no monthly fees or requirements for either checking or savings accounts. If you can't find such a deal locally, you'll want to know your minimum balance requirement and possible monthly fees, and make sure to allow for those in your budget.

MAKING CENT$ OF IT

Visit the Web sites of three local banks (start by typing their names into a search engine), and look for information about a basic savings account offered by each. Take notes on each bank regarding the six pieces of information listed here. When you have all the information, choose a bank. Write a paragraph in which you explain the reasons for your choice.

1. Name of the bank
2. APY on their basic savings account
3. Minimum first deposit
4. Minimum balance
5. Maintenance fee
6. Other fees

Using and Protecting Bank Accounts

> ### TERMS TO KNOW

signature card	nonsufficient funds fee
emergency fund	check register
safe deposit box	fraud
bank statement	identity theft
PIN (personal identification number)	Federal Trade Commission (FTC)
overdraft/overdrawing	

Getting Started

When you have chosen a bank, you can bring in cash or a check (like your paycheck) to open the account; it will be your first deposit. You should also bring ID (a driver's license if you have one) and your Social Security card. They will likely run your name through a system called ChexSystems, which is used to verify that you have not previously been irresponsible with an account. You will be asked to sign a **signature card**, which is kept on file. This allows the bank to compare the signatures on future transactions to make sure it's really you and not a criminal trying to access your money. It should take less than an hour to set up an account, and when you're done, you will likely get a packet of information about your new account to take home.

What to Save in Savings

Because bank deposits gain little interest and can sometimes fall behind inflation, you won't always want to save all your money at the bank. Nevertheless, savings accounts are necessary to start building your savings.

A savings account is a good place to set aside money you're likely to need within the next few months to a year—for short- to medium-term goals. It's good to keep this money out of your checking account, as you'd be tempted to spend it. On the other hand, you don't want to invest it in something that has the potential to lose value; you want be sure it is there when you need it. The bank offers this security. You might put money for these purposes in a savings account, a money market account, or a CD.

This savings account, sometimes known as an **emergency fund**, can be dedicated to paying for unexpected expenses. If your car's muffler gives out, or your computer's hard drive crashes, you may have to pay a lot of money all at once to fix the problem. An emergency fund is a cash cushion that you build so that you won't have to go into debt when a crisis strikes. Job loss, for most adults, presents the biggest potential for financial loss, since it means losing income and the ability to pay for necessary expenses. The average job search takes between four and six months at any time, according to the Bureau of Labor Statistics (BLS). That means that if you were on your own, you would figure out how much to put away by adding up your necessary spending per month— housing costs, utilities, food, insurance costs, and loan minimums—*and multiply by six*. That is how much you might want to have set aside for the possibility of emergency. Until you get to the point of supporting yourself, of course, you may want to have, say, $500 set aside for the unexpected. The bank is a good place to store funds for this purpose because of the liquidity it provides; you need these funds to be easily available in the moment a crisis hits. Generally, you're best off keeping that money in a money market or savings account.

 ## Safe Deposit Boxes Offer Safe Keeping

Banks also offer the opportunity to store important documents and small valuables onsite in a **safe deposit box**. These rented boxes within the bank's vault are similar to safes and are meant to resist theft, fire, and water. People who don't have a place in their home that offers such protections may use a safe deposit box to store jewelry, a will, deeds to a home, marriage certificate, passports, birth certificates, and insurance policies.

Using Your Checking Account

Of all the account types, a checking account (known as a *share draft account* at a credit union) allows you the easiest access to your money on deposit. It also offers several ways of depositing new money. Because of the ease of withdrawal and deposit, checking accounts are the best accounts from which to pay your regular and day-to-day expenses. The following are some of the ways you might withdraw or deposit via a checking account. As you're making these transactions, keep in mind the account's minimum balance requirement, if there is one, and do your best to stay above it to avoid paying fees. You can make deposits, payments and withdrawals with your checking account in all these ways:

At bank branches. During bank business hours you can make a deposit, withdrawal or transfer between accounts directly with a teller (a bank employee) at a bank branch (or location). Usually, you have to fill out a transaction slip for each of these, which note your account number and the amount of money in your transaction, among other information. You can withdraw only up to your account balance.

By using checks. It's not always convenient to carry around large amounts of cash. It's also not ideal to send cash through the mail, as someone could intercept that envelope and keep the money for themselves. That's where checks come in. Checks allow you to give money to another person or business without it being in cash. They are made out to a certain person or business, and can only be deposited by that party (unless signed over to someone else). For these reasons, they are often used to pay bills by mail.

Routing Number   Account Number   Check Number

 What is a routing number? Who is authorized to sign a check from a checking account?

To write a check, use a pen to write the date, the name of the payee and the amount the check is for. The amount will also have to be spelled out in words below the name of the payee. Then you must sign it at the bottom right. In your monthly **bank statement**, which shows your transaction history, your bank may provide digital images of checks you've written that have been cashed.

To deposit someone else's check paid to you, you must sign the back (which is called "endorsing" it) and write the number of the account to which you are depositing it. Be sure to deposit it promptly: Most checks are invalidated after 90 days. Also, an endorsed check can be cashed by anyone who gets a hold of it; so avoid signing it until you're at the bank to deposit it.

One thing to be aware of when using checks (whether you are depositing or writing): they won't "clear" right away. That means the funds deposited will not be available immediately. Typically, it takes at least a few hours or a few days after a check is deposited for it to clear. As a result, on your deposit receipt, you may see "available balance" and "present balance" as two different numbers. Thus, you must be aware of what checks you have that are still being processed, either coming or going from your account.

At the ATM. Many checking accounts come with the option of an ATM card. This option is very convenient: since automated teller machines are open 24 hours a day, you can do your banking well after bank hours. Your card will even work in other cities, states, and countries, assuming the ATM is part of a network your bank participates in.

When you get your ATM card, you'll have to choose a **PIN**, or **personal identification number**, four or more digits used as a security feature to verify your identity. You'll enter this code when using the ATM. Don't tell anyone your PIN, as that plus your card will allow them to get money from your account.

Using an ATM is convenient, but it's not always cheap. While you can use your own bank's ATMs for free, you're typically charged fees for using ATMs from banks other than your own. Avoid such fees by using your own bank's ATM when you need cash. You may want to pick a bank that has ATMs near your home, school, or job so that it will be convenient for you. Also, since your own bank may limit the number of ATM transactions you can make for free, you may want to think about how much cash you'll need for the week.

With a debit card. Some ATM cards also serve as debit cards. Debit cards are similar to credit cards in that they can be used to pay for things at the store or online. They may also have the familiar Visa or MasterCard logo on them. While they may look similar, *debit cards are very different from credit cards.* The biggest difference: With a credit card, the issuer is loaning you money to buy an item—you are taking on debt to buy something. With a debit card, the money is withdrawn from your checking account directly. It's a good alternative, because you can spend only up to what's in your account, whereas credit cards allow you to spend beyond your means.

Most stores today accept debit cards. To pay, you may have to enter your PIN—the same PIN you use at the ATM. Or you may have the option of choosing "credit" and signing for the purchase instead of entering your PIN. Whether you put in your PIN number or choose "credit" and sign, the money is still withdrawn (debited) from your account in the same way. So you can use it just like a credit card at the store, but it acts like a check on your account.

When you are making a purchase, you may have the option to get cash back as well. This is like using the store as your ATM. So, if you spent $15 at the pharmacy, and you chose to get $40 cash back, it would show up as a debit of $55 from the store. You typically do not pay any fees to withdraw money in this way.

It's worth noting that debit purchases may take a few days to process (just like checks), so you need to be conscious of how much money you really have left.

Online. These days, most banks allow customers to transfer funds between accounts or make bill payments via the bank's Web site. You need to enter an ID and password to access these features. Once you do, you may get a screen that lists all your accounts at the bank. If you click through to each, you can see individual transactions up to the moment. It's an easy way to check whether transactions have processed, if your checks have been cleared, or what your available balance is.

Online banking can be useful if you want to transfer money between checking and savings accounts. In fact, you can set up automatic transfers, which will do this on a regular schedule without your having to initiate anything. Online banking features are becoming more and more sophisticated each year. Be sure to check with your bank, and utilize these services (most of which are free) as they can make your banking experience much easier.

Overdrawing on Your Checking

If you try to use your debit card for an item that costs more than what is in your account, or you try to draw more than your account balance from your ATM, you are **overdrawing** your account and the transaction will typically be denied. If your transaction is denied on the spot, nothing will come out of your account, and you will not be charged any fees. If the transaction is accepted, or cash withdrawn from the ATM, what usually results is an "overdraft fee" on your account from your bank. Customers can opt into these overdraft programs, in which the bank will allow the excess withdrawal, pay it for you, and then charge you the amount you have exceeded your balance plus a flat fee of around $30. It's basically a short-term loan.

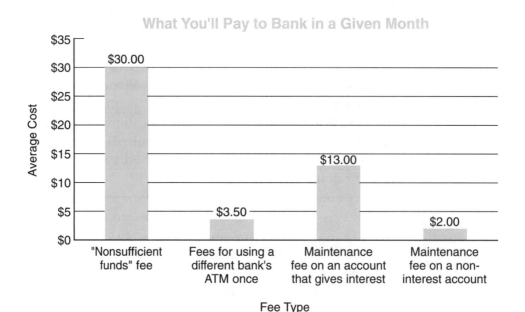

Source: Bankrate.com "2009 Checking Study."

Based on the previous graph, if you used a non-bank ATM twice in one month from an interest-paying account, those fees plus maintenance fees would cost you how much that month?

Furthermore, if you accidentally write a check in excess of your balance or have an automatic bill payment go through when you don't have the funds in your account, the payment will "bounce," meaning it will be returned to your bank unpaid. As a result, your bank may charge you a bounce fee or **nonsufficient funds fee** (also, on average, $30); and the other bank may charge you a fee to return the check, too. You may end up paying something like $50 in fees if you just go over your balance by $5!

Instead, avoid these fees entirely by making sure you have enough money in your account before paying for something or withdrawing money. In the next section, you will learn how to stay on top of your account balance by recording all your transactions.

 *Using a Check Cashing Store Will Cost You!*

Perhaps you've passed by storefronts that advertise that they will cash checks for you. Using the services provided by such establishments is often very, very costly: The stores make money, in part, by taking a percentage of your check. The percentage ranges from one to 10%, which means that on a $1,000 check you might pay $100 in fees! Ouch! Meanwhile, if you have a checking account, you can usually cash checks for free at the bank that holds your account. It makes more sense to have a bank account. (In Chapter Five, you'll learn about another steeply priced service offered by the same establishments: the payday loan.)

Balancing Your Checkbook

As noted above, it can take days for deposits, checks, and debits to be processed. For example, you may deposit $300 on Monday, and write a $200 check on Tuesday. On Wednesday when you go to withdraw money at the ATM it looks as if you still have $300 in your account, even though you really have $100 available. If you withdraw over that $100, when the check goes through you'll be hit with fees. To avoid fees, you need to stay on top of your finances.

So how do you do this? You can use the **check register** in your checkbook to record every transaction, so that you know how much money you actually have at any given point.

To fill out a check register, start by entering the beginning balance (or if you already have an account, the balance at the end of the last statement). Then enter every single transaction, as shown here, including withdrawals, deposits, checks, and interest payments as they happen. (If you don't want to carry your checkbook around with you, save your receipts, bring them home, and enter them as soon as you can.)

A Check Register With a Month of Transactions

Trans. Type or Check #	Date	Description	Debit/ Payment Amount (-)	Fees (-)	Deposit Amount (+)	Balance
	1/1	Balance				$1,000.00
101	1/3	Rent	$400.00			$600.00
ATM	1/6	Cash	$40.00	$2.00		$558.00
debit	1/10	Starbucks	$10.16			$547.84
102	1/12	My-Tell Wireless	$40.00			$507.84
ATM	1/14	Cash	$40.00			$467.84
deposit	1/15	Paycheck (XYZ inc.)			$110.12	$577.96
ATM	1/22	Cash	$40.00			$537.96
interest	1/25	Interest			$0.26	$538.22
debit	1/25	Chic Boutique (gift)	$25.11			$513.11
ATM	1/29	Cash	$40.00			$473.11
deposit	1/30	Paycheck (XYZ inc.)			$110.12	$583.23
fee	1/30	Bank Service Fee	$10.00			$573.23

Even if a transaction has not yet processed, you can turn to your check register to see what the effective balance is on your account.

At the end of every banking cycle, you will get a statement, either on paper or online, that lists every transaction during the period (typically a month) for your account. On it, you will see your beginning and ending balance for the period, and an inventory that will look a lot like your check register. You may also receive the actual *canceled* (deposited or cashed) checks you've written, or images of them. You can—and should—reconcile all this with your checkbook register to make sure they match. Your ending balance for the period should be the same in your register as it is on the statement.

But don't be surprised if it isn't! This is common. There are many reasons for this, including these possibilities:

- a check you wrote hasn't been cashed yet
- a check you deposited hasn't cleared
- a debit purchase you made hasn't cleared
- you made deposits or withdrawals between the statement date and the day it came in the mail
- you earned interest during the period that you didn't account for

Start with those canceled (cleared) checks, and make sure you have all of them listed in your register. Vice versa, you should also check to see if all the checks you listed in your register have been cancelled. Look at the list of deposits and other transactions, and do the same. You might put a check mark on your register and the statement once you have confirmed that they appear the same in both places.

As for the things that appear in your register but not in your statement, usually there is a form on the back of your statement to help you check your math regarding things that haven't yet cleared. On this, you can make a list of transactions on your register that do not appear on the statement, something like this:

Deposits not appearing on this statement (date/amount)	Withdrawals not appearing on this statement (date/amount)	Check #
12/22 $45 from Chris	12/19 $102 My-Tell Wireless	101
	12/28 $40 ATM	
TOTAL $45	TOTAL $142	

Then do the math to reconcile (balance) the two:

1. List the statement's end balance
2. Total the deposits that are on the register but not on the statement
3. Add them together (line 1 + line 2)
4. Total the withdrawals that are on the register but not on the statement
5. Final total: subtract the withdrawals from your total (line 3 – line 4 = actual balance)

This result should match your register balance. If it does not, you might go back over your numbers with a calculator.

Go back to your statement to see if there were transactions there that did not appear in your register, it's possible you just left something off. If there are transactions and they do not look familiar, it's possible there was an error on someone else's part (for example, your card was double swiped at a store, or an ATM incorrectly processed your transaction). It's also possible that you have been the victim of **fraud**, intentional deceit for the purpose of gain. If you have double-checked your math and the error doesn't seem to be on your part, you'll want to follow the steps in the next section.

 ## Don't Throw Out That Paperwork!

For budgeting purposes, and for financial planning as a whole, you'll need to hang onto some paperwork. (Some files you should keep for tax and legal purposes as well.)

Keep a "one-month" file in which you put all your receipts for stuff you've bought. At the end of the month, when you get your bank statement, you can reconcile it against the receipts to ensure that there are no fraudulent charges. Then you can trash these if they don't contain any other valuable information.

Keep a "one-year" file for every statement you get from your bank, your pay stubs and your receipts for important items. At the end of the year, go through it. You'll want to make sure your pay stubs equal what's listed on your Form W-2, or the document your employer sends stating your earnings and tax paid for the year. Keep receipts on big items for the length of any warranty, just in case you need the item fixed.

Keep a "forever" file for your income tax returns. These you'll keep indefinitely; and anything supporting them for up to six years (that's how long the Internal Revenue Service has to audit a tax return).

MAKING CENT$ OF IT

Alexis had the following transactions in June:

- Balance as of 6/1 was $452
- ATM withdrawals of: $60 plus a $2 fee on 6/11 and $80 (no fee) on 6/20
- Deposits of: $989 on 6/2 and 6/16
- Check #201 written on 6/4 for $650 to M&K Realty for rent
- Check #202 written on 6/4 for $75 to Nevada Power Authority
- Debit of $24 from Galangal Restaurant on 6/12
- Maintenance fee of $10 on 6/11

Make a table with the following headings, then fill in the transactions on the check register in the order they are dated. When you have completed the register, answer the questions.

Trans. Type or Check #	Date	Description	Debit/ Payment Amount (–)	Fees	Deposit Amount (+)	Balance
	6/1	Balance				$452.00

1. What was Alexis's balance on 6/5?
2. What was her balance at the end of this period?
3. Could Alexis have written a check for $800 on 6/5 without overdrawing her account? What about on 6/17?

What to Do if There Are Transactions You Don't Recognize

If there's a rogue transaction on your bill—say a debit charge you don't recognize—you need to do something about it, so that you get your money back.

Under the Electronic Fund Transfers Act, or EFTA, consumers have the right to dispute transactions they believe are in error and can have the bank investigate them. While you may initiate this by phone, it's best to send a written letter and keep a copy, so that you will have proof of the communication. The letter should note the date and amount of the transaction you are disputing, and the reason. You must send the letter within 60 days of the date on the statement on which the error appears. Otherwise, you are not entitled to an investigation or any money back.

Depending on the type of transaction, the bank must investigate, and it may be required to credit you the amount in dispute while it investigates. After the investigation is concluded, the bank is required to communicate to you the resolution.

The transaction may have resulted from a mistake by someone with whom you've done business. It may be an error on the bank's part. Or, it may be that someone has gained access to your account, and made fraudulent charges. The first two are more easily fixable; the latter is a serious crime that may take some time to resolve.

Because fraud is often initiated with theft of ATM or debit cards, there are some protections from the EFTA to cover you against these risks. As long as you report the transaction within 60 days of the statement date, you are left bearing only a small portion of the charges; the bank must reimburse you the rest. If you don't report it, you're responsible for all of it.

If your card is lost or stolen, you must tell the bank immediately, because the amount that you have to bear of unauthorized transactions depends on when you report the card missing and how it was used. If the card was swiped and processed as "credit," you'll have to bear no charges made fraudulently as long as you report it missing before the card is used; you'd be liable for just $50 if it was used before you reported it.

If the card was used as debit and you inform the bank within two business days of learning that the card is missing, you're liable only for $50 of fraudulent transactions. The bank will bear the loss of the rest. If you report it after two business days, however, you could be responsible for as much as $500 of fraudulent charges. If you don't report the transaction within 60 days of the date of the statement upon which it appears, you will be 100% responsible. (These rules change throughout the years, so ask your bank or check the FDIC Web site at *www.FDIC.gov* and browse "consumer protection" as these laws may apply to you one day.)

That's a good reason to monitor your accounts online and review your statements every month. The sooner you report a suspicious charge or charges, the less of it you will be responsible for, and the faster the problem can be fixed.

Protect Against Identity Theft and Fraud

DETER·DETECT·DEFEND

AVOID THEFT

www.ftc.gov/idtheft

Anyone who accesses your accounts without your permission is committing **identity theft**—the unlawful use of your personal information. Identity theft can occur when someone uses your account numbers, checks, or debit cards, as well as a credit card or Social Security Number, among other things. Using these, singularly or in combination, an identity thief can drain your accounts, open loans and build debts in your name, apply for government benefits in your name, and even commit other crimes while posing as you. According to the **Federal Trade Commission (FTC)**, the branch of the government responsible for consumer protections, eight million Americans were victims of identity theft in 2006.

In many situations, victims get back any money "lost" to such crimes, thanks to protections from laws like EFTA. Even so, you can expect that trying to correct the situation will involve lots of your time and energy. So, you want to try to prevent it. If your accounts are compromised, you should be ready to act promptly. As you just learned, when it comes to bank accounts, the sooner you recognize fraud, the less liability you have for losses. The FTC suggests a three-pronged approach to fighting identity fraud: Deter, Detect, and Defend.

Deter

Guard important numbers. Don't carry your Social Security card in your wallet, and give out the number only when it's required. (Among the situations it might be necessary: you're starting a new job, you're opening a new account with a bank or credit card company, you're filing your taxes.) This ID number—together with other identifying information—can be used to take out loans in your name or to access your account. Try to memorize this number, and keep the card in a secure place at home. Also, when buying things online, shop only from stores with good reputations and make sure the page address where you actually make the payments starts with *https*. The *s* indicates that the site is secure and your information will not be intercepted by hackers.

Shred trash that that includes personal information. That includes your address, account numbers or Social Security Number. Some identity thieves get their information by going through the garbage. If you don't have a shredder, make sure you cut or tear these papers up in a way that would make it difficult for a thief to piece together the numbers.

Never respond to e-mail requesting personal info. Identity thieves use a tactic called *phishing*, which means sending e-mails that try to get you to reveal important data about yourself. Many of these e-mails look very legitimate; they may even appear to be from your bank, your favorite Web sites, or even the IRS. Don't respond to unsolicited e-mails or click on links in them. If you doubt at all that the e-mail is legitimate, call the company the e-mail is purportedly from (but don't use the phone number in the e-mail, use the one on the company's Web site).

Watch your wallet. Not all thieves use technologically savvy approaches—they don't have to. They can simply take your wallet and have access to a lot of necessary information, from your driver's license to your bank card. So, zip your purse, and try not to keep your wallet in your back pocket. Be especially attentive in crowded public areas, when you might not feel someone steal into your things as easily.

Protect your passwords. Don't tell anyone your log-in information for your bank, your credit card, even for something like Facebook. Also, avoid using the same password more than once; use something a savvy thief would not be able to guess (not your initials or your date of birth); and try to use a combination of numbers, letters, and punctuation symbols.

Detect

Monitor your accounts. Go over statements for all financial accounts when they arrive, and keep an eye out for any transactions that you do not recognize, as this could be a sign of fraud. Call up the institution to get more information about any transaction that is in question. Other causes for suspicion: you get a bill for an account you don't recall having signed up for; your credit report isn't as good as it should be. You want to act on any suspected identity theft—following the steps listed under "defend"—as quickly as possible so that the situation does not get worse.

Defend

Close infiltrated accounts. If you notice something unusual in an account, immediately notify the banks or creditors, by phoning their customer service lines and asking to speak with someone in their fraud division. Explain that you would like to close the account and why; send a letter reiterating this point. If there were fraudulent charges made, tell the customer service person that you would like to initiate a dispute on these.

Inform the authorities. Identity theft is a crime, punishable with jail time. Informing the police will help them catch and prosecute the offenders. It also will help protect you. Ask for a copy of the police report, as you may need to send this to creditors or banks to help them investigate the dispute. Also, let the FTC know. Go to *www.ftc.gov* or call 1-877-ID-THEFT to file a complaint. The agency maintains a database of identity theft crimes and criminals.

CHAPTER REVIEW

Master the Vocabulary

Use the personal finance terms from the start of each section to complete the following sentences.

1. A(n) _____ helps you balance your current expenses and future goals against your income.

2. _____ income is the portion of income you have left over after expenses and taxes.

3. _____ is the act of helping charities financially or by volunteering.

4. You have a budget _____ if your expenses are less than your income; you have a _____ if your spending exceeds your income.

5. Some states levy _____ tax on purchases as a way of making more revenue.

6. Bank of America, Wachovia, and Chase are examples of _____ .

7. _____ refers to the ability to access money in an account and turn it into cash.

8. The _____ is a government agency that protects bank depositors' money, up to $250,000.

9. A(n) _____ is a banking institution owned by its members, who typically share some common interest.

10. A(n) _____ is the most liquid bank product as it offers the most ways to access your cash.

11. Two types of accounts designed for savers that offer limited transactions are _____ and _____ .

12. _____ is a standardized way banks are required to represent the interest rate on their accounts.

13. The _____ interest rate does not consider the effect of inflation, while the _____ interest rate factors in inflation.

14. When you go to open an account at a bank, you should ask to see the _____ so that you know what charges you might have to pay.

15. You'll have to sign your name on a(n) _____ in the process of opening an account at the bank, so the bank can identify your signature on future transactions.

16. A(n) _____ is a rented, locked space within a bank's vault where you can store things like deeds to property, birth certificates and jewelry.

17. A(n) _____ lets you withdraw cash from your account at any hour, even when banks are closed—but you must enter your _____ on its keypad to do so.

18. When you use a(n) _____ to make purchases, the money will be withdrawn straight from your checking account.

19. A(n) _____ occurs when money withdrawn from the account exceeds the account balance.

20. A check bounces when there is not enough money in your account to cover it; in such a circumstance, you'll pay a(n) _____ fee.

21. It's important to fill in every transaction from your checking account on the _____. That makes it easy to reconcile your account once the bank statement comes.

22. _____ is the unlawful use of your personal information by someone else; it is a form of _____, or intentional deceit for the purpose of gain.

Apply What You've Learned

1. Avi graduated from college a few months ago, and now would like to create a monthly budget. His take-home, disposable income from his job is $2,000 a month, and he's identified the following monthly expenses: Rent on his apartment will be $600 a month, and utilities (including cell phone, Internet, electric/gas, and cable) will cost him $300 a month. He spends $300 on groceries. His car insurance is $125, and he spends $100 a month on gas. He also owes $100 a month on his student loans. Create a spending plan outline like the one below, and fill in those numbers under "Budget."

Avi's Monthly Budget

A. Income	Budget	Actual
	$	$
A. Total	$	$
B. Giving/Saving		
	$	$
B. Total	$	$
C. Expenses		
	$	$
	$	$
C. Total	$	$
A − (B + C) Total	$	$

a. His short-term goal is to buy a new $1,500 laptop, but he'd also like to have some money left over for entertainment. Help him determine an amount to save each month, and an amount he could put toward entertainment. Fill these numbers in, and reassess Avi's spending plan under the "Actual" column.

b. With the amount you're having him save each month, how quickly might he reach his goal of saving for the computer?

2. Match up the five types of advertising techniques below with examples of how they might be used. Write an example of each.

A. Name-calling

B. Emotional

C. Urgency

D. Bandwagon

E. Facts and figures

1. "This is the latest trend, everyone wants one!"

2. "This has been proven 87% effective in laboratory tests."

3. "This is your last chance to get this price!"

4. "Angry over those high prices? Come see us!"

5. "Our product is faster and better than our competitor's."

3. Calculate the sales tax on the following purchases:

a. A $200 purchase in a state with a tax rate of 4.25%

b. A $42 shirt and a $25 tie in a state with a tax rate of 6%

c. A $42 shirt and a $25 tie in a state with a tax rate of 7%

d. A $12 book in a state with no sales tax

4. Explain why people might want to open bank accounts instead of keeping cash at home.

5. a. If the inflation rate is 2% and a savings account you're looking at is paying 4% APY, what is the real interest rate?

b. If the inflation rate is 4.5% and a savings account you're looking at is paying 4% APY, what is the real interest rate?

6. Rank these accounts in order by liquidity, from most liquid to least liquid.

• Money market deposit account

• CD

• Checking

7. Rank these accounts in order of interest rates you might expect, from highest to lowest.
   - Savings account
   - Money market deposit account
   - CD
   - Checking

8. Which of these would make a good PIN number?
   A. your birth date
   B. a random number
   C. your mother's birth date
   D. the house number from where you used to live

9. How might you avoid the following?
   a. ATM fees
   b. Maintenance fees
   c. Overdraft fees

10. Across the top of a piece of lined paper, fill it out with headings from a check register, like the one below. Fill in the transactions below in order of their occurrence.

Trans. Type or Check #	Date	Description	Debit/ Payment Amount (−)	Fees (−)	Deposit Amount (+)	Balance
	9/1	Balance				$120

   - A starting balance on 9/1 of $120.
   - Check 101 for "homecoming dance fees" for $12 on 9/21
   - Check 102 for "art club dues" on 9/26 for $10
   - ATM withdrawal of $40 on 9/16
   - Debit card transaction of $60 at *Debbie's Books* on 9/29
   - Paycheck deposit of $86 on 9/24
   - Transfer to savings of $25 on 9/17
   - Maintenance fee of $10 on 9/30

   a. What is the balance on 9/22?
   b. Say you want a $70 sweater that you saw on 9/29. Could you have bought it?
   c. What is the ending balance on 9/30?

11. Look at this bank statement below and answer the questions that follow it.

   a. What is the account number?

   b. For what period is this statement reporting?

   c. How many total withdrawals were made (checks, ATM withdrawals, debits)?

   d. What was the total withdrawal amount?

BANK OF U.S.A.

John Doe
333 Main Street
Anytown, USA 67543

Account number 123455-4321
Statement date 4/1 to 4/31

Checking account

Beginning balance	$250.00
Deposits	$534.01
Withdrawals	$424.62
Fees	$ 12.00
Ending balance	$347.39

DEPOSITS

Date	Description	Amount
4/15	Direct deposit from Wheelies Skate Shop	$262.65
4/20	ATM check deposit	$75
4/30	Direct deposit from Wheelies Skate Shop	$196.36
	Total	$534.01

CHECKS PAID

Date	Check #	Description	Amount
4/16	165	National Car Insurance Co.	$86.86
4/18	166	Cell Tell	$65
		Total	$151.86

ATM/DEBIT

Date	Description	Amount
4/2	ATM at 12 Main Street	$100
4/12	Card Purchase at Video Game Garage	$25.14
4/14	Purchase at The Lunch Box	$7.62
4/16	ATM at 12 Main Street	$100
4/28	ATM at 12 Main Street	$40
	Total	$272.76

OTHER

Date	Description	Amount
4/28	Service fee	$12
	Total	$12

e. The balance on this person's check register says $290.39, and doesn't match the statement's balance on the previous page. Here is what is missing:

- A deposit was made 4/29 for $25 that doesn't show on the statement
- check #167 mailed on 4/26 for $62
- an ATM withdrawal of $20 on 4/30

Reconcile the register to the statement on a piece of paper with the headings shown here.

Deposits not appearing on this statement (date/amount)	Withdrawals not appearing on this statement (date/amount)	Check #
Total:	Total:	

Adding and subtracting these transactions from the statement, does the statement balance now match the register's balance?

CHAPTER 4

Investing for the Future

Chapter Objectives

Students will:

✔ Learn the risks and rewards of investing
✔ Discover what investment options there are, and which are right for which goals
✔ Know the taxes paid on investment earnings
✔ Recognize signs of investment fraud in order to protect themselves from becoming victims

> **Personalize It!** *Imagine you have $300 in savings and are given the opportunity to take a chance with it, a chance that would make it equally likely to gain $20 as lose $20—that is, you'd be just as likely to end up with $320 as with $280. Would you do it? Why or why not? What if it was the chance of either losing five dollars or gaining ten?*

Introduction

In the last chapter, you learned how to allocate money for savings by means of a budget. You also learned that you have to sacrifice some spending today in order to have money to set aside for use tomorrow.

Saving money is the first step to reaching the financial goals you set for yourself in Chapter One. *Saving* traditionally refers to putting money aside in the bank (in savings accounts, money market accounts and CDs), where it will earn relatively little. The low interest rates banks pay means the depositor's money grows slowly. There is almost no risk in keeping money at a bank, and the low interest rate is essentially the cost of having that security.

Hoping that their money will grow faster, many people **invest** some of their savings. Investing means buying different types of financial products that have the potential to provide more substantial growth; but the chance of taking a higher reward brings with it a chance of losing some money as well. In this chapter, you will learn more about the risks and rewards of investing. You will study common types of investments, and follow some of them to see how they perform. You will determine an appropriate investment strategy for your goals, as well as learn some universal objectives. Finally, you will learn how to identify an investment that's too good to be true.

4.1 The Risks and Rewards Investors Face

TERMS TO KNOW

return	volatility	portfolio
growth investing	capital gains	diversification
income investing	capital losses	asset allocation
security/securities	dividends	dollar-cost averaging
capital appreciation	capital preservation	

Getting Started

In "Personalize It," you were asked to consider what kind of risks you would be willing to take in order to increase your money. Knowing the upside and the downside of how you would invest that money helps in navigating between the risks you are willing to take, given the reward you might receive. This is a simplified way of understanding the kinds of decisions investors face. Investing involves real risk. As a rule, the greater the risk you take the greater the possible reward.

The Rewards of Investing

The potential for investing is, of course, increasing your capital (money). The gain or loss on invested capital is known as the **return**. Just as with interest, the return is typically expressed as a percentage of gain or loss as compared to the original investment. As an example, a $16 gain on a $200 investment in one year is equal to an *8% annual return*. Over the long term, returns on most investments tend to be higher than the interest paid on bank accounts.

As an investor, you have two general strategies for making money on your money. You can invest for money growth, or for money income; called **growth investing** and **income investing**, respectively. Your investment plan may include one or both strategies, and may change over time.

Growth investing. This involves buying a **security** (or **securities:** financial instruments that represents value) or an object (a house, a painting) in the hopes that it will appreciate in value, so that you can sell it for more than you paid. Perhaps you've heard the phrase "buy low, sell high"? Growth investors live by this motto. They seek out **capital appreciation**, meaning an increase in the value of the security in which they invested.

When investing for capital appreciation, you don't make money until you sell the item you have purchased. You may *see* prices on the asset increase while you own it, but these gains are only on paper, since you don't have the money in your pocket until you sell. Typically you will have to wait some time to experience significant increase in value. The capital appreciation you may receive depends on the going price for the investment, and this price can go up or down during the time you own the item or security. (The extent of an investment's price fluctuation is referred to as its **volatility**.) Investments with the potential for capital appreciation are bought and sold on financial markets, where prices fluctuate in response to supply and demand for each particular security. When there are more people who want to buy the item than those willing to sell it, prices go up. When there are more sellers than buyers, prices go down. Depending on how far down prices go, you may find yourself unable to sell the investment for as much as you paid for it.

If your investment appreciates and you sell it, the difference between the price you sold for and the price you bought for is called **capital gains**. (You have gained money on top of the *capital* you initially invested.) On the other hand, if you sell it for less than you paid, you will have **capital losses**.

Income investing. Some people use investments to increase their current cash flow rather than waiting for future capital appreciation. These investors invest with an income strategy. They buy certain investments that pay out money on a regular basis. Some of these are fixed-income investments, meaning they pay out a set percentage or amount at set intervals. Other investments vary in the income they provide.

The payout may be in the form of interest—as with bank accounts—or in the form of **dividends**, which are a share of a company's profits. A 3% annual yield of dividends or interest on $1,000 comes out to $30 a year. The money received from any income investment fits into the category of unearned income, which you learned about in Chapter Two.

As an investor, you should be comfortable figuring out the annual return on an investment. This can be calculated for both growth and income investments. It is a way to measure either price increase of the asset or annual yields. Here is the formula:

$$\text{Annual return} = \frac{(\text{end-of-year value} - \text{beginning-of-year value}) + \text{dividends}}{\text{beginning-of-year value}} \times 100$$

MAKING CENT$ OF IT

Using the annual return formula, what is the return on the following?

1. An investment bought on January 1 for $100 that is worth $200 on December 31, with no dividends.

2. An investment bought on January 1 for $100 that is worth $200 on December 31, with $10 in dividends.

3. An investment bought on January 1 for $200 that is worth $100 on December 31, with no dividends.

4. An investment bought on January 1 for $100 that is worth $100 on December 31, with $5 in dividends.

The Risks of Investing

Alas, there's no such thing as a free lunch. To grow your capital—whether by way of a growth or income investment strategy—involves taking certain risks. As the diagram here shows, not all investments present the same potential for loss:

 List three reasons why the investments at the bottom of the pyramid are labeled "low risk, low reward." What makes them safe?

Later in this chapter, you will learn about some of these investment choices. For now, it's enough to say that the risk of loss increases as you approach the top of the triangle.

Many of the investments at the peak of this pyramid are *growth investments*. Growth investments tend to be volatile, meaning they may shift in price significantly within the course of a week, a day, or even a few minutes. An investment that was appreciating may suddenly lose value or vice versa. Thus, a commonly repeated axiom of investing: past performance does not guarantee future returns. You can't predict how an investment will do just by looking at how it's done before.

Losing money is a risk you face with any investment, but with growth investments in particular the value of the investment can drop below the purchase price. If you bought something for $100 and it's now selling for $50, for example, choosing to sell means a loss of $50. (Later in the chapter, you will learn some factors that may cause specific investments to lose money.) On the other hand, since high risk goes with high reward, the riskier investments have the possibility to produce the greatest growth. So, investing in these, you would have to be willing accept the chance of losing significantly, in order to have the chance of gaining significantly. Because of the risk of loss, investing for growth makes sense for money goals that are three years out or more; that time affords you the ability to be patient through the bad times in the market, and to wait for the better times to sell.

Those investments at the bottom of the pyramid, on the other hand, present the least risk of loss, but also the least potential for gain. Most of the investments toward the bottom are *income investments*. As you can see, bank accounts are at the very bottom. Bank accounts are fixed income, because they pay a set interest rate. Since income investments are less risky than growth investments, this type of investing does not have the potential to do as well. Still, many people—especially retirees—want the certainty of the income, so the security of income is worth giving up the potential greater gain. One thing to be aware of though, with income investments, is that the lowest returns can present exposure to another type of risk: namely, that your money will not keep up with inflation.

How much risk would you be willing to take with your money? Not all individuals have the same tolerance for risk, which explains why there are different answers to the question at the chapter opening. These different levels of aversion to risk may also explain why one of your friends prefers to ski the steepest black-diamond trails while another sticks to the smooth bunny slope. The fact of the matter is, however, that you will need to take some types of risk if you want to grow your money.

When (and When Not) to Invest

Because there are risk and time constraints involved, investing doesn't make sense for all of your savings. Some money you cannot afford to take risks with. That includes funds needed in the short term—for current expenses and for goals within the next year or so—as well as for emergencies. When it comes to money for these purposes, you need **capital preservation**, or protection from loss. Bank accounts provide this, since they will never lose value except to inflation. They also offer another important component: liquidity—it's relatively quick and easy to access your money. Many investments are *illiquid*, because you have to sell them before you can turn them into cash, and this takes time. Illiquid investments don't make sense for money you're likely to need soon, because you may not have the resources or ability to sell on short notice.

For these reasons, all investors should have a certain percentage of their savings in the bank. When it comes to money for current expenses, short-term savings, and emergencies, then "low risk, low reward" wins.

When it comes to longer-term goals, however, you don't need to worry as much about liquidity, and you can take more risk in your investment choices. In fact, goals that are more than five years away may be a good match for growth investments, as you can ride out periods in which volatility is unfavorable to the price of the investment. In other words, there will be more time to choose when to sell, and wait for the best gains.

Higher risk means the possibility for higher reward. Most investments have historically earned more, on average, than bank accounts. The difference of even one percentage point above what you can do at the bank is significant. If the bank pays 3% and you save $100 a month, you will have $14,009 in ten years. If you were able to average an annual return of 4% in a certain investment, you'd have $14,718. If you were able to average an annual return of 9%—a realistic estimate for some investments—you'd have $19,109. Such growth can help put major goals like a house, a small start-up business, a wedding, travel, or even your retirement within your reach.

Penny and Nick

"I really want to be rich someday," Penny said to Nick as they headed through the hallways to their next class. "I'm wondering if I should start investing my allowance."

"Weren't you paying attention in class when Mrs. Buck explained what money you're best off investing and what you're not?" Nick asked.

"Uh, I guess I was thinking about last night's *American Idol*," she confessed.

Pretend you're Nick and explain to Penny why she might not want to invest her allowance.

Managing the Risk of Investing

You can't completely eliminate the risks of investing. In fact, often by reducing one you accentuate another. (You may fight inflation risk with risk for higher reward, but that higher reward is the risk of capital loss, or illiquidity.) There are certain investment strategies, however, that you can employ to reduce risks through tradeoffs:

Investing based on the time you have. Time is a major factor in deciding what risks can be taken in your investment strategy. As you just learned, you want to be extra cautious with money for current needs and expenses, emergencies, and goals within a year—these funds you want to keep liquid, usually in the bank.

For goals between one and five years out, you may be able to take more risk and purchase income-producing investments. These usually guarantee a set percent return over a preset time limit. With a still relatively short period before you need the money, you can't afford the risks of tying money into growth investments, you may not have time to recover from any market losses.

A growth strategy is better for goals that are five years or more off, as time allows you to weather the market downturns more easily. You also have time to adjust your strategy. You take the bigger risks when you have many years to get to your goal, then you reduce the capital appreciation portion of your **portfolio,** or all of your investment holdings, in favor of capital preservation as you start approaching your deadline. In other words, you give yourself time to build wealth early on, then transition to maintaining what you have built.

Below are two model portfolios for retirement funds. One is for a 25-year-old and the other is for a 57-year-old. As you can see, the person who has more time until retirement can afford to employ more of a growth strategy. They have more time to gain back any losses they encounter, and reinvest money they gain for more growth.

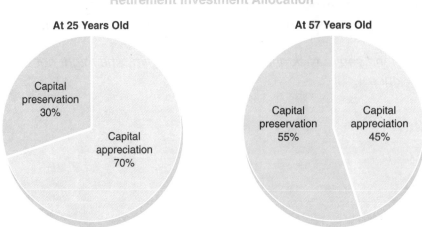

Retirement Investment Allocation

At 25 Years Old

Capital preservation 30%

Capital appreciation 70%

At 57 Years Old

Capital preservation 55%

Capital appreciation 45%

Diversifying. If your investment strategy involved putting all your money into one type of investment, you could see everything lose value all at once. You can reduce this risk with a **diversification** strategy, which means including in a portfolio different kinds of investments, with varying risks, return potential, and market exposures. The idea is that holding a broad enough variety of investment types means some will increase when others don't, so there's never one point in time where major losses are accrued.

There are two ways to diversify: in terms of the investment types held, known as asset classes, and then within those asset classes.

Diversifying between asset classes is known as **asset allocation**. It is usually illustrated with a pie chart showing the variety of asset classes you own and what percentage of the portfolio makes up each. Each of the investments listed on the risk pyramid is an asset class: stocks, bonds, options, mutual funds, CDs, T-bills, etc. are examples of different classes of assets. Below is an example of a diversified asset allocation:

Investment Portfolio Allocation

Checking/Savings
5%

CDs
5%

Corporate bonds
10%

Treasury bonds
10%

U.S. stock market mutual funds
55%

Individual company stocks
5%

International stock market mutual funds
10%

How much of this portfolio is devoted to capital preservation vs. capital appreciation? Do you know which investments make up each of these portions of the portfolio?

As an investor, it's wise to have a plan for asset allocation, and then make purchases based on that plan. It can be difficult and costly to make changes to asset allocation once investments have been bought, so it's not advised to rearrange frequently. (Some accounts do allow you to re-balance, or reset your allocation. It's advisable to do this once per year.) The right allocation goes back, in part, to the last section: the farther out the goal, the more of your portfolio can be in riskier growth invest-ments.

The second part of diversification means making sure that your invest-ments are not all in one industry or sector. For example, you would not want to hold onto just technology industry stocks in the stock part of your portfolio (growth investments), so that you don't end up losing everything in stocks, as many investors did when the "Dot-Com Bubble" burst in 2000. If an entire industry suffers major loss, like the Internet did in 2000, all of those stocks suffer. Even if stocks are only a 20% por-tion of a portfolio, it can cause serious loss if not diversified within itself. (We will go over the stock market in the next section).

Dollar-cost averaging. One risk, previously mentioned, is timing risk: You know that the aim of investing is to buy low and sell high. It is im-possible to predict with certainty whether an investment's price will in-crease or decrease from its current price; so it can be difficult to tell if you are buying at a low point (when it's relatively cheap) or a high point (when it's relatively expensive). That's what **dollar-cost averaging** aims to lessen.

This method involves investing over time in an asset, rather than all at once. You allot equal amounts of money to buy into a certain invest-ment on a regular schedule. The market will be moving up and down during this time, and your money will be able to buy more shares of the investment when they are cheap and fewer when they are expensive. As a result, you average out the number of shares you get, so that you don't buy only when prices are highest. As a comparison, think about how you would not want to buy all the toilet paper you need for the year at one time. There's a chance it could go on sale, and you'll have spent more than you needed to.

Let's say, for example, you invested $1,200 in a year and were buying shares (stock) of a certain investment that fluctuates in price.

Dollar-cost Average Investing

	Investment Amount	Cost per Share	Number of Shares
January	$100	$12	8
February	$100	$9	11
March	$100	$7	14
April	$100	$5	20
May	$100	$10	10
June	$100	$14	7
July	$100	$16	6
August	$100	$10	10
September	$100	$10	10
October	$100	$7	14
November	$100	$10	10
December	$100	$12	8
Total	$1,200	$122	128

First of all, to determine how many shares $100 buys each month, you divide the investment amount (in this case $100) by the cost per share during that time.

$$\frac{\text{Investment}}{\text{cost per share}} = \text{shares purchased}$$

For January:

$$\frac{\$100 \text{ investment}}{\$12 \text{ per share}} = \text{about 8 shares}$$

Looking at this chart, you can see how you end up with fewer shares of the investment when the price per share is higher, and more shares when it is lower.

Purchasing this way gives you the benefits of diminishing risk, and the chance that the average cost you pay overall for the shares over time will come out to be less than the average market cost per share over that time. You could determine the *average market price* for this investment over the time period by adding up the cost per share for every month ($122) and dividing by the number of months (12): $10.17.

Now you can compare this to the average cost you paid per share by dividing the money investment by the number of shares you ended up with:

$$\frac{\$1,200 \text{ investment}}{128 \text{ total shares}} = \$9.37$$

So, your *average cost per share* in this case would be $9.37. As you can see, you ended up paying less per share than the actual average market price per share over the year. For comparison, let's imagine you'd invested the entire $1,200 in one average month (the average market share price being $10.17). You would have ended up with only about 118 shares.

$$\frac{\$1{,}200 \text{ investment}}{\$10.17 \text{ cost per share}} = \text{about 118 shares}$$

That's compared to the 128 shares with dollar-cost averaging. Of course, more shares are better because it means the return is worth more to you. It won't always work out that your average cost per share is less than the average market price per share, but you will reduce the risk of having invested the entire lump sum at a more expensive point.

MAKING CENT$ OF IT

Imagine that you invest $50 a month in a security that has the following prices per share. Calculate how many shares you would have at the end, the average price you paid, and the average market price over that time.

Dollar-cost Average Investing

	Investment Amount	Cost per Share	Number of Shares
January	$50	$5	10
February	$50	$2	25
March	$50	$5	10
April	$50	$5	10
May	$50	$10	5
June	$50	$8	6
July	$50	$6	8
August	$50	$2	25
September	$50	$10	5
October	$50	$10	5
November	$50	$10	5
December	$50	$6	8
Total			

1. Calculate the total shares purchased.
2. What is your average cost per share?
3. What is the average market price per share?

4.2 Where to Save and Where to Invest

TERMS TO KNOW

bonds	default	bull market
stocks	equities	bear market
mutual funds	shares	Net Asset Value (NAV)
real estate	public companies	prospectus
U.S. Savings Bonds	initial public offering (IPO)	sales load
par value	stock exchanges	brokers
coupon	ticker symbols	investment club
maturity	indexes/indices	

Getting Started

As you learned in the previous section, a diversified asset allocation involves a variety of different investment types. Among the options most commonly available to individual investors are:

- bank accounts: savings accounts, CDs, and money market deposit accounts
- **bonds**, or loans to companies and governments
- **stocks**, which represent ownership stakes in companies
- **mutual funds**, which pool investors' money to buy an assortment of stocks and bonds
- **real estate**, commercial or residential property
- art and collectibles, such as paintings, baseball cards, or antiques

In this section, you will learn about how these investments work, what risks are involved with each, as well as when they might and might not be appropriate to invest in. Some of them can be used for income, some for growth, and some for both.

Income and Capital Preservation Investments

Savings accounts, money market accounts, and CDs. In the last chapter, you learned about savings accounts, CDs, and money market deposit accounts. These are the safest places to save. They are also fixed-income, meaning they guarantee a set rate of return. You won't get much

"MY FIRST PIECE OF ADVICE IS NOT to PUT ALL YOUR EGGS IN ONE BASKET."

Diversification works no matter what you may be investing.

for your money, however. One-year CDs have paid out 4.9% on average since 1984 (with rates under 1% in the late 2000s) and five-year CDs have averaged 5.8% APY. Savings accounts rarely return 1% APY. What these products do offer is capital preservation and liquidity. Most investors keep some of their savings—particularly for emergencies and short-term goals—in these products.

U.S. Savings Bonds. Bonds, in general, are loans that the investor makes to a government or corporation. **U.S. Savings Bonds** are a type of bond issued by the U.S. Treasury, and were originally designed as a way for the government to raise money to pay for World War I. They are very safe investments—as safe as bank accounts—guaranteed by the federal government.

Savings bonds are known by their serial number prefixes. Currently you can buy only Series EE bonds and Series I bonds, which both gain interest for up to 30 years. You can only buy $5,000 worth of each per year. On both types of savings bonds, interest compounds twice a year. In general, however, savings bonds tend to pay relatively little compared to other investments; in some cases you may get less than you might at the bank. They do have one significant advantage over bank accounts, however, because you do not owe state or local tax on the interest. These bonds do present liquidity risk; if you redeem the bond before five years, you may owe a penalty. Because of this, savings bonds make better sense for goals more than five years out, where money security is a plus, like money for retirement. On the other hand, you may miss out on higher-returning investments by being tied up in them. It's a tradeoff between security and reward.

Corporate and government bonds. When people use the word "bond," they're typically not referring to savings bonds, but to another type of bond that works a bit differently. There are three primary types of these bonds:

- U.S. Treasury bonds, notes and bills, which are issued by the U.S. government
- Municipal bonds, issued by state and local governments
- Corporate bonds, issued by companies

These types of bonds also pay interest, and like bank accounts, they are considered fixed-income investments. Unlike with savings bonds, interest on these bonds does not compound; it is simple interest. The **par value**, or face value, is what you will pay if you buy them when they are issued, and each promise an interest rate based on that par value, also known as the **coupon**. Bonds also have a **maturity** date upon which the borrower has agreed to return the principal—and the period to maturity can be as short as a few months or as long as 30 years. A bond with a par value of $1,000, a coupon of 5%, and a maturity of ten years will pay $50 a year, or $500 in total.

The yields on government and corporate bonds are greater than the yields on bank accounts and savings bonds. Within the category, the yields are higher as you increase in risk and maturity. The risk with bonds is **default**, or that the issuer (or borrower of your money) will be unable to pay back your principal because they have no money to pay, they have defaulted on their "loan." As for maturity, longer maturity bonds tend to pay more than short-term bonds, though it means sacrificing liquidity and the possibility of better returns elsewhere.

In general, bonds are less liquid than bank accounts because you must either wait until maturity or find someone to buy the bond in order to turn your investment into cash. For investors who have enough other liquid funds, bonds can be a useful part of a diversified portfolio. As fixed-income investments, bonds help provide capital preservation.

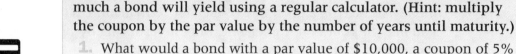
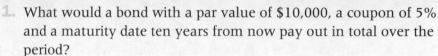

MAKING CENT$ OF IT

Interest on most bonds is *simple interest*, so you can figure out how much a bond will yield using a regular calculator. (Hint: multiply the coupon by the par value by the number of years until maturity.)

1. What would a bond with a par value of $10,000, a coupon of 5% and a maturity date ten years from now pay out in total over the period?

2. What could you expect in total from a bond with a par value of $1,000, a coupon of 2%, and a maturity date of one year?

3. From a bond with a par value of $500, a coupon of 3.5%, and a maturity date five years from now?

Stocks and the Stock Market

When buying stock, you are actually buying a piece of a corporation. That's why stocks are also called **equities** or **shares**, since you're buying a share in the ownership of the company. Companies that issue stock are known as **public companies**, in contrast to companies that are privately owned. Companies "go public" as a way of raising money. They break ownership of the company into small pieces and sell those to the public. (Abercrombie & Fitch, for example, has 87 *million* shares of the company on the market.) Even if they own little stock in the company, every shareholder gets some say in how the company is managed, which includes voting on certain issues.

Selling stock gives firms more freedom than a bank loan or a bond, because they can raise money they need without being required to repay anything back if they do not do well. As a shareholder, therefore, you will also be accepting the risk that the company could fail (known as *default*), and you will not be able to get your money back. The possible reward for taking such risk, however, is that if the company is successful the benefit from price appreciation in its shares means selling for a profit. Large company stocks might also pay dividends (a portion of its profits); since these companies are already big, they may have little room to grow and can't necessarily offer investors the potential for capital appreciation. So they offer the potential for income through dividends.

The first time a company sells stock is called an **initial public offering** (IPO). For the IPO, the company decides how many shares it will sell and at what price. When Google "went public" in August 2004, for example, it offered 19.6 million shares at $85 each. After the IPO, if you want stock, you will usually have to buy it from another investor.

Such trades of these shares on the market can only happen on **stock exchanges**, marketplaces where stocks are bought and sold. Two of the largest in the United States are the New York Stock Exchange (NYSE) and the National Association of Securities Dealers Automated Quotations (NASDAQ).

Those who buy and sell through these markets must have a special license and must be registered members of the exchange. So if you want to own stock, you will have to have one of these brokers working on your behalf. A broker puts in an order for you, for a fee.

Traders busy at work on the New York Stock Exchange floor.

Stocks are identified by **ticker symbols**, those three- or four-letter codes that identify the company on the stock market. Abercrombie & Fitch Co., for example, is ANF. To see how a certain stock is currently trading, you can look at the business section a newspaper for information from the prior day's closing stock prices. Or you can look online for real-time info, at sites like *yahoofinance.com*, *WSJ.com*, *cnnmoney.com* and others.

The share price of a stock at any given time is based upon supply and demand. Each company issues a limited supply of shares, and not all the people who own the stock are looking to sell at one time. If more people are willing to sell than there are people willing to buy, the prices will trend downwards; if there are more buyers than available shares for sale, the prices will move higher. One of the more important factors driving demand is the past growth and expected future growth of the company. In part, this is measured by the company's earnings, or profits. Companies must announce earnings four times a year, and the stock price usually fluctuates around this time as investors buy and sell in response to the information.

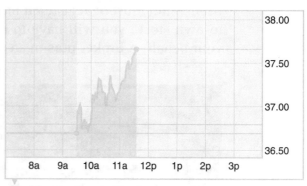

Abercrombie & Fitch Co.

NYSE ANF

$37.64

Change	+0.84 +2.28%
Volume	**730,423**
	Jul 26, 2010 11:34 a.m.

Previous close	**$36.80**

Day low	Day high
$36.66	**$37.64**

52-week low	52-week high
$27.20	**$51.12**

1d • 5d • 3m • 6m • 1y • 3y • 5y

Note the following on the stock snapshot above:

1. Current selling price: That moment's price
2. Change and percentage change: The difference between yesterday's end of day price and the current price
3. Previous close: The price on the last trade yesterday (also called "closing price")
4. Volume: The number of shares traded so far that day
5. High and low: The lowest and highest price trades for that day
6. 52-week high and 52-week low: The highest and lowest trades within the past year

There's plenty besides earnings that can have an impact on demand, and therefore stock prices. The stock price is said to reflect all known public information about the company. So, investors may pay attention to the company's annual report to investors, usually found on their Web site, as well as other announcements the company is legally required to make. Investors may also pay attention to news related to the company or changes in that company's industry. (For example, Abercrombie & Fitch might change in value following changes in other clothing company stock prices.)

Despite their volatility, however, U.S. stocks have produced an average annual return of 9.6% from 1926 to 2008, (according to Ibbotson Associates, an investment research company)—this is almost double the return of bonds over the same period.

How Investors Use Stock Market Indices

You've probably heard mention on the news that "the stock market" was up or down on a given day. The newscasters are really referring to **indices**, which track the performance of a representative selection of stocks. Among the more frequently cited indexes are the Dow Jones Industrial Average, which tracks 30 of the largest public companies in the United States, and the S&P 500 which tracks the 500 largest U.S. traded companies.

Dow Jones Industrial Average
DOW JONES GLOBAL INDICES: DJIA

10,494 ↑

Change	+68.95 +0.66%
Volume	55.25m
Jul 26, 2010 11:34 a.m.	
Previous close	**10,424**
Day low	Day high
10,414	**10,497**
52-week low	52-week high
9,007	**11,258**

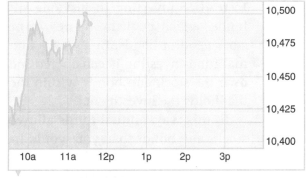

The points, shown in the upper left, depend on the average values of the stocks in the index. The Dow Jones index is price-weighted, meaning each company stock in the index makes up a fraction of the index in proportions based on their quoted prices.

When investors are feeling assured that their investments will appreciate and therefore are buying more stocks, the indexes are generally gaining points, and it's called a **bull market**. When the market is trending downward over a period of time, because investors are thinking negatively about the market, and selling in response, it's called a **bear market**. Investors often look to the performance of the indices to benchmark performance of their own investments: the goal is to do as well as or better than the index.

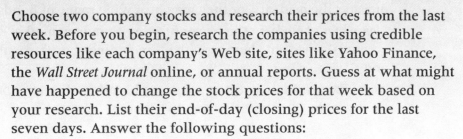

MAKING CENT$ OF IT

Choose two company stocks and research their prices from the last week. Before you begin, research the companies using credible resources like each company's Web site, sites like Yahoo Finance, the *Wall Street Journal* online, or annual reports. Guess at what might have happened to change the stock prices for that week based on your research. List their end-of-day (closing) prices for the last seven days. Answer the following questions:

1. Did the stocks do what you thought they would?

2. Would you buy them now, given what you know?

> 3. Every day the percent change is noted. Average those for the week; what was the week's average percentage change? Did the stock "trend" (move) up or down?

Mutual Funds

Instead of investing in just one stock, many investors turn to mutual funds, which pool the money of many investors to buy a selection of stocks and/or bonds. In a way, a mutual fund is a portfolio in itself. Mutual fund investing is considered indirect investing—you do not directly own the stock and bonds within the fund. You own a share of the fund that holds the investments.

In this way, mutual funds allow you to have access to more types of stocks and bonds than you would have been able to afford yourself—for example, if you only had $250 to invest, you may be only able to buy a few shares of a certain stock. If you invested instead in a mutual fund, you'd be investing in all the things the fund is investing in, which may be, for example, 50 different stocks. Another benefit: your money has a better chance of growing than if it were in just one stock because it is in multiple investments. If one stock in the fund goes down in value, you have the chance that another may be going up to balance it out. Because of the *diversification* mutual funds provide, many investors prefer them to individual stocks and bonds. In fact, mutual funds are the predominant investment choice in many retirement accounts.

Mutual funds come in many varieties. Some are passively managed, which means they automatically invest in correlation with a major index (such as the Dow Jones Industrial Average or S&P 500). These are called index funds. Others are actively managed, meaning that a manager or management team chooses what to invest in and when. There are four main categories of funds, and within them many different types.

- *Equity funds* invest primarily in stocks.
- *Bond funds* invest primarily in bonds. They may invest only in bonds of a specific maturity, or they may be a wide range of bonds.
- *Money-market funds* (not to be confused with money market deposit accounts) invest in short-term debt, including some Treasury bonds and CDs.
- *Asset-allocation funds* invest in some combination of stocks and bonds— for example, 60% equities and 40% bonds.

Most mutual funds have minimum initial investment requirements, of a few hundred or a few thousand dollars. How many shares you will be able to buy depends upon the demand for the investments within the funds. The price per share of a mutual fund is known as **NAV**, or **Net Asset Value**, per share. Funds calculate this, typically on a daily basis, on the closing prices of all the holdings.

Like stocks, mutual funds also have ticker symbols (for example, Vanguard's Total Stock Market Index Fund is VTSMX). That means you can find a mutual fund's NAV on finance sites like those mentioned in the section on stocks. On a given day, a site like one of those might show the following:

Vanguard Growth & Income (VQNPX)

Jul 23: **23.43** ⬆ 0.19 (0.82%)

Net Asset Value:	23.43
Trade Time:	Jul 23
Change:	⬆ 0.19 (0.82%)
Prev Close:	23.24
YTD Return*:	−6.18%
Net Assets*:	3.98B
Yield*:	1.88%

*As of 30-Jun-10:

VQNPX — Jul 23, 2010

2006   2008   2010

3m 6m 1y 2y 5y max

What you see:

- Net Asset Value: The current NAV at that time
- Change: What happened between the previous day's close and the current NAV
- YTD return: is how the fund has performed since January 1 (or a specified date acting as the start of that fund's "year")
- Yield: What you receive in dividends or interest as a percentage of investment

In researching a fund, you also want take a look at the fund company's own materials. All mutual funds are required by law to publish an annual **prospectus**, an explanatory document about the fund's intentions. You can find it online or request it by calling the fund directly. Several pages long and often in tiny type, a prospectus can be intimidating. Once you understand the key parts, it gets easier to navigate. Every prospectus will include:

- Investment objectives: Different funds have different goals. For example, one fund may be focused on capital preservation; another might be focused on growth.

- Investing strategy: Here, the fund managers will explain how they intend to get to their goal. This may include an explanation of the asset allocation of the fund.

- Investment risks: The fund will disclose what risks you might face by buying in.

- Past performance: The fund is required to show a bar chart of its annual returns for the past ten years, as well as a table showing the returns for last one, five and ten years.

- Expenses and fees: The prospectus must include a fee table that shows what fees the fund charges. It will also give an example of how those fees might affect a $10,000 investment. The lower the fees the better, since these can lower your overall returns.

You will want to pay particular attention to the fees. With mutual funds, there are two types of fees: sales loads and operating expenses (assessed throughout the life of the fund). A **sales load** is a commission paid to the person who sells you the fund. Operating expenses, expressed as a percentage, will be assessed annually on the amount you have in the fund and taken as payment.

Just because a fund has a sales load and high management fees does not mean it will perform better than a less expensive fund; the fee is unrelated to the performance. Sales loads and management expenses will definitely take some of your returns. It's always better to search for lower fees.

MAKING CENT$ OF IT

Before you buy any mutual fund, you want to do some research on it to see how it invests and whether it aligns with your goals. Take a look at the prospectus for a mutual fund found on *www.vanguard.com*, under "What We Offer," "Mutual Funds." The bottom of the page will have a link to the prospectus. Pick a fund, and answer the questions about that fund below.

1. Who is the fund's manager?

2. What is the fund's investment strategy?

3. How did the fund do last year?

4. What is the sales load of the fund?

5. Looking at the past performance, was it very successful over the past year? five years? ten years?

6. Now head to a Web site that follows that fund on the market (sites like *WSJ.com* or Yahoo Finance, mentioned in previous sections). List the closing price NAV of the fund for the last week.

Real Estate

Many adults have invested in real estate by buying a home. Homebuyers may primarily be looking for a place to live, but most are also hoping the property *appreciates* over the years, so that they can sell it for more than they paid later on. During the real estate "bubble" of the mid-2000s, homes in some areas were experiencing appreciation in excess of 20% a year—meaning that if you bought a house before then, you could make a pretty good profit when you sold. Of course, by 2008 home prices nationally were down over 18%. That's why it was called a bubble; it "popped" under its own pressure.

Profiting from real estate is not a sure bet, though many people have made considerable returns on investments. Here too, price is based on demand. Real estate demand is very much a factor of location: a home in one city may appreciate faster or slower than a comparable home in another. The same is true of different parts of the same city, or even the same street. Property in areas with better school districts, lower crime rates, and better job prospects tends to be priced higher than similar property in areas with the less desirable features.

The average home in the United States cost $164,000 in 2010, according to the National Association of Realtors. With such a high cost, buyers can't afford to pay the entire purchase price from their savings. Instead they make a down payment, or a percentage of the property's price upfront (usually ten to 20%), and take a mortgage to pay for the balance. You own the amount you paid for with the down payment; the bank that gives you the loan owns as much of the house as is mortgaged. Every month when you send in a check to pay your mortgage bill, you build your equity, or ownership in the home.

If later you are able to sell the house for as much as you paid for it, you get back all the equity you've built (the money you've put in) and the mortgage is paid off. For example, let's say you bought a house for $200,000 several years ago and have made a down payment and mortgage payments equaling $150,000, and are left with a mortgage of $50,000 when you are ready to sell. If you sell for the same price you paid, the bank gets $50,000 to cover the mortgage and you get back the $150,000 that you have put it in. If you are forced to sell for less than what you paid, you must pay off the loan first before taking your share. So a sales price of $175,000 means you'd only get $125,000 of the $150,000 you put in. If you sell for more than you bought it for—the best-case scenario—you still pay the bank only what's left of the mortgage, $50,000, and you get to keep the amount you invested plus the profits. So if you sell for $300,000, you get $250,000 back (your investment of $150,000 plus a $100,000 profit).

Besides the possibility of capital gains, there is a tax benefit to owning a home: you may qualify for a deduction on mortgage interest paid.

Of course, there are plenty of non-financial advantages to having a place to call your own. It's nice not having a landlord who restricts your decorating choices.

Some investors also buy real estate that they don't plan to live in, either for growth or income. In terms of growth, they may buy residential (like a house) or commercial (like an office building) properties, with the hope of reselling when the value increases. During the housing boom of the mid-2000s, prices were rising so quickly that many investors were buying homes and selling them within months for more than they paid. Some people buy secondary real estate with the aim of renting it out to make extra income. This can provide the investor with a steady cash flow—though it can take a long time before the down payment has been recouped and the mortgage is paid off.

After the housing boom of the mid-2000s came the housing crisis, where people were losing their homes to banks in *foreclosures.* Houses were depreciating (decreasing in value) because there were so many more houses on the market than people able to buy them.

Real estate investors and homebuyers face several risks. Of course there is market risk, heightened by the fact that they are investing in a single asset (they lack diversification). Also, there's the risk of not being able to bear the monthly mortgage payments—if a homebuyer loses a job and is not able to pay, he or she will have to surrender the house to the bank holding the mortgage. There's also significant liquidity risk. Depending on the market, they may not be able to sell the house as quickly or for as much money as they would like.

Art and Collectibles

Some people buy collectibles (items like antiques, stamps, baseball cards, or dolls) or art (such as paintings or sculpture) as an investment. These, as investments, can be very risky.

For one thing, it all depends on the whims of potential buyers, which can change overnight—so there isn't necessarily the long-term growth potential as with stocks, bonds, or CDs. As a collectibles investor, therefore, you end up having to guess at the future consumer demand for the item, which, of course, is a gamble.

Because you're completely dependent upon another person's interest in your item, collectibles are fairly *illiquid*, or not easily converted into cash. You have to find someone else who is interested enough in the item and willing to pay the right price before you can sell for a profit. Finally, collectibles also represent only one aspect of production from one company, so your investment is even less diversified than holding a single stock. For example: would you rather hold one Batman comic book and hope it goes up in value, or own a share of Marvel Comics stock (Ticker: MVL), which produces many comic books each year, creates products based on its characters, and licenses its characters to other companies? Obviously, the latter presents less risk. In reality, it's probably best to think of collectibles as something to buy for personal appreciation, rather than for capital appreciation.

How to Buy Investments

Basically, there are two ways to acquire investments:

Buying from the seller. Some securities can be purchased directly from the institutions that issue them, and you typically do not have to pay any fees to do so. For example, U.S. Treasury Bonds can be bought from the Treasury. Mutual funds can be purchased from the fund company. A few hundred stocks on the market can be purchased directly. Your employer, if it is a public company, may also allow you to purchase its stock directly. Otherwise with stock, you will probably need a broker.

Through a broker. Investment **brokers** are people who are licensed to act as go-betweens for buyers and sellers of investments. As noted earlier, only brokers can make trades on the floor of a stock exchange; so typically you would need a broker to buy stock. People also use brokers to buy mutual funds and bonds.

There are different types of brokers: A full-service broker not only buys and sells for you, but also provides research and guidance, helping you choose investments. A financial advisor or planner may also be licensed as a broker, or will work with a broker on your behalf. A broker may get a commission from the investment companies every time they buy or sell investments, they may get paid by the client, or both.

Not all brokers offer this type of service, or charge these types of prices. Discount brokerages, which include online brokerage sites (such as E*TRADE and TD Ameritrade), don't give you personalized advice. These types of brokers—whom you will never meet—merely make transactions as per your directions. You do your own research and make your own investment decisions; the company just puts them into action. For this reason, the commission on these is lower—from five to 20 dollars per trade or a monthly fee for a certain number of trades.

 **An Investment Club Can Help You Learn More About Investing**

Just as people in your school's Spanish club may come together to educate one another on the customs of Spanish-speaking countries, people in an **investment club** share a common interest in investing and come together to educate one another on investments. Some of these clubs are meant solely to help members build specific awareness (for example, each person presents data about a stock or fund they are interested in). Other groups create a portfolio of investments that they think would work well together, and without buying them, track the returns to their "mock portfolio." It's good to practice investing and portfolio strategies in such a way. If you are interested in starting an investment club yourself at your school, ask your personal finance, economics, or math teacher if he or she would be willing to sponsor and advise it.

MAKING CENT$ OF IT

Think of one short-term (within the year) and one long-term (five or more years out) savings goal, and write them down on a piece of paper. Using all that you've learned about different investments, their risks, and the ways to reduce the risks, give two detailed investment plans or strategies for each goal.

How Taxes Affect Investment Returns

TERMS TO KNOW

basis	529 college savings plan	traditional IRA
short-term capital gains	tax-deferred	Roth IRA
long-term capital gains	IRA	

Getting Started

Unfortunately, money made from investing is not completely free—the government requires taxes on what you've gained. How much the IRS will want depends on how the money was acquired.

Taxes on Interest, Capital Gains, and Dividends

The taxes you pay on these three types of unearned income depend on what *tax bracket* you fall into. We mentioned these brackets in Chapter Two. The tax bracket you fall under (once you are an independent adult) depends on both earned income and unearned income.

Interest. Interest income—that is, money from bank accounts and bonds—is taxed like ordinary income. You must list it on your Form 1040, and add it to your earned (salary or wage) income. It is subject to your tax rate, as little as 10% or as much as 35%. That means that if you earned $1,000 in interest, you may have to pay anywhere from $100 to $350 of it to the government. The financial institutions that pay you interest will send you a Form 1099.

Capital gains. When you sell an investment, you are taxed on the difference between the **basis**—the price at which you bought it minus commissions or fees—and what you sell it for, *if* you sell for over the basis. How much you will be taxed depends on how long you owned it: A year or less and the money is considered a **short-term capital gain**, and it is taxed like ordinary income. Over a year and it's considered **long-term capital gain**, and usually it's taxed at less than ordinary income. Because of this difference in tax treatment, it's wise to try to hold an investment for at least a year before selling.

The other thing to note is that if you sell an investment for *less* than you paid for it, you can take capital losses on your tax return, first to off-set any current capital gains, and then what's left can be used to reduce your regular taxable income up to a certain amount per year.

Dividends. Most dividends are taxed at 15%. Required taxes on dividends and other investment income are subject to change over time, so do some research or ask a financial planner about these taxes once you start to plan your investment strategies.

MAKING CENT$ OF IT

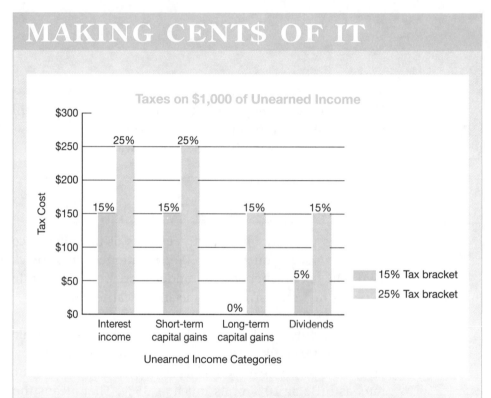

You should know how much taxes will lower your investment returns. Imagine you are in the 25% tax bracket, and answer the following questions:

1. If you have $600 in interest income, how much will it be after taxes?

2. If you have $600 in short-term capital gains, how much will it be after taxes?

3. If you have $600 in long-term capital gains?

4. If you have $600 in dividends?

Investing in Tax-Advantaged Accounts

To encourage people to save up for important goals like college or retirement, the government has allowed for the creation of certain tax-advantaged investment accounts.

College costs. The average cost of tuition, room and board for a four-year state college could be as high as $27,000 per year according to the College Board. In total, a college education might cost you or your parents $108,000 or more. The less you can afford to pay outright, the more you will have to take out in loans. Loans cost money (interest is expensive!), and the interest compounds in the same way interest compounds in a savings account. So basically, it pays to save as much as you can now to minimize what you have to borrow later. It's not too late to start saving or adding to your parents' savings. Even if you're a senior, it's not too late; there are four years of tuition ahead of you to pay.

A **529 college savings plan** is an account meant for college savings, named after the section of tax law that allows it. There are two types of 529s: savings plans and prepaid plans. Within these, you or your parents can choose mutual funds from a limited selection offered by the plan. You can use the money from a savings plan at almost any college or university. Prepaid accounts are a way to prepay tuition at an in-state public college specifically. On both, growth on your investments is **tax-deferred** (you pay taxes once you take money out to use, but you do not have to pay taxes on your money before then) and you can take the money out free of federal taxes if you do use it for college costs. Some states will also allow a tax deduction on contributions.

Each state offers one or more plans. You do not have to choose your own state's plans; in fact, it may be better to go out of state—as some state's plans have higher fees than others. You should know what your state's tax benefit is first, as you may have to make contributions to an in-state plan to get the break on state tax. Check out *www.savingforcollege.com* or *www.finaid.com* for more information.

Expenses in retirement. "Wait!" you say, "I haven't even started working yet. Why must I think about retirement?!" Your golden years may seem a long way off, but retirement *is* something you should start saving for when you're young. The younger you are when you start, the more time your money has to compound and grow.

You are likely to need savings to help fund your lifestyle during the later years when you no longer have an income from a job. While you may collect Social Security in retirement, this government subsidy—which averages $14,000 a year—probably won't be enough to provide the life you might like to live. As you learned in Chapter Two, some companies provide pensions to long-tenured employees. These days, however, most do not; and even if you are lucky enough to get a pension, it still may not be enough to cover your costs. That means you will need to build a retirement fund. To be able to draw just $40,000 a year from your savings, and have a good chance of doing so for your entire retirement, you will likely need a "nest egg" of around $1 million. *That's* why you need to think about retirement while you're young.

There are several types of tax-advantaged accounts designated for retirement savings. (Just be aware that if you withdraw the money before age 59½ you pay a penalty of 10% of the value.)

Employer-sponsored retirement savings plans such as 401(k) or 403(b) accounts, which you learned a little bit about in Chapter Two, allow you to save a certain percentage of salary and invest it in the mutual fund options your employer has decided to offer. The money you elect to stash is pretax (you don't have to pay income taxes on it). Since you're postponing taking this portion of compensation to your retirement years, you reduce your taxable income for the year. The accounts are tax-deferred, so you will owe tax on withdrawals in retirement. In addition to your own contributions, your employer may match a certain amount of your contributions dollar for dollar. If you don't contribute, you're leaving free money from being put to good use. Once you've vested (stayed within your company for a set amount of time), you get to keep the money your company has put in on your behalf even if you leave that job. If you stay for less than the vesting time, though, you will forfeit all or part of the employer contribution.

Because of all these advantages, it's wise to join these plans as soon as you can. (Not all companies offer a 401(k) or 403(b) plan.) As you start your career, you may not be able to contribute much, since you likely will not be earning a copious salary. You should still try to invest at least a little. (Remember the effects of compound interest from Chapter One?)

A personal way of investing for retirement is also available, through an IRA. **IRA** stands for Individual Retirement Account, a kind of retirement account that anyone who has income can set up through a bank, brokerage or investment company. In general, IRAs are used by people who do not have an employer-sponsored plan, or who cannot save as much as they would need to in their 401(k) or 403(b). Like the 401(k) or 403(b) plans, IRA growth is tax-deferred. What's different is that you have the freedom to choose any investment you want (instead of choosing from a limited list).

With a **traditional IRA**, those who earn under a certain income can deduct contributions on their taxes. That means the money you put into one of these accounts is pretax. With a traditional IRA, however, you will have to pay taxes on withdrawals, at your ordinary income tax rate, in retirement. Another type of IRA, called a **Roth IRA**, does not offer a tax deduction up front, but instead allows you to withdraw tax-free after age 59½. The reason people invest in Roth IRAs is because they think they might be in a higher tax bracket at retirement than they are now.

As you invest in any of these accounts your choices of securities should align with the amount of time you have until retirement, with the majority of your investment in stocks (capital appreciation) when you are in your 20s moving to a majority bond allocation (capital preservation), as you near retirement. At a younger age, you can afford to take risk for the potential of growth, but as you get older you need to focus on preserving what has been saved.

MAKING CENT$ OF IT

Answer the following questions about retirement.

1. Contrast two differences between the traditional IRA and the Roth IRA.

2. Imagine this scenario: You plan on retiring at age 64 and assume you will live until about 91. You expect that all the living expenses you will have during retirement will be $40,000 per year. You expect to get only $13,000 a year from Social Security and $16,000 a year from your 401(k). How much more money will you have to have saved by the time you are 64 in order to cover all the rest of your expenses? (For simplicity, assume your money doesn't grow during retirement.)

4.4 Protecting Investments

TERMS TO KNOW

Securities and Exchange Commission (SEC)
advance-fee fraud
fake-check scams

pyramid schemes
Ponzi schemes

Getting Started

While nothing can be done to completely eliminate the risks involved in investing, the U.S. government does take certain actions to either limit the risks or make you more aware of them. This role is overseen by the **Securities and Exchange Commission** (the **SEC**), a government agency that provides regulation and law enforcement actions on behalf of investors. The SEC was founded in 1934, during the depression and not long after the great stock market crash of 1929. Before the crash, many Americans put money in the stock market blind to the risks they were taking. Even if they had wanted to get more information about what they were really investing in, they may not have been able to trust what the companies were telling them. Many people lost the bulk of their life savings, and were financially devastated. They also became less willing to trust the markets, so the government intervened in order to put faith back in investments. The government formed the SEC to help restore confidence.

What the SEC Does

One important role of the agency is to guarantee access to certain basic information about investments, so that people can be knowledgeable on what they buy and own. It's because of the SEC that public companies must file quarterly reports and annual reports about their stock, and they must send out annual reports to shareholders; it's also the reason mutual funds must write prospectuses. The purpose is so that individual investors can better understand what they are getting into.

Besides requiring certain filings, the SEC also polices investment companies to make sure they are not purposely providing incorrect information or participating in other unfair practices. Doing so would be considered fraud.

The agency also requires companies that sell investments, people, and firms that trade investments to comply with inspections. Enforcing securities laws, the SEC takes administrative actions against wrongdoers, such as assessing monetary fines or revoking a person's right to sell securities. It also has authority to take cases to civil court to seek injunctions that prohibit the person or firm from continuing illicit activities, helping to initiate criminal charges where appropriate.

The financial industry also regulates itself: FINRA, the Financial Industry Regulatory Authority, licenses investment professionals and helps support the SEC in its functions.

CAUGHT IN A SCAM

Even trying to sell your car isn't safe from becoming a victim of a scam. Read below about how credible businesses, the Internet, and friendly demeanor are all used to con everyday people out of their money.

"Omahans Caught in Scam"
By Joe Ruff
The Omaha World-Herald

Matt and Angie Larson have their car back, but they don't have the $10,500 they hoped to get by selling their 2005 Toyota Corolla.

The Omaha couple were victims of a scam after Matt Larson, a 33-year-old environmental engineer who will attend law school in Illinois this fall, listed their car for sale on Craigslist.

Here's what happened leading up to the car's recovery, according to the Larsons and Omaha police:

A woman who appeared to be in her 20s, whom Larson described as a "sporty type girl," called the couple's home on July 30 asking about their ad on Craigslist. She said she had been in a car accident, received some insurance money and needed a car quickly.

She showed up the next day in a pickup truck that she said was her boyfriend's and asked to take the Corolla for a test drive. The young woman chatted amiably with Larson, who was holding his newborn son, Grant, about having a 3-year-old daughter.

She returned from the test drive saying she liked the car and returned later with what appeared to be a cashier's check from Allstate insurance company. The check even had Allstate's logo and the company's motto, "You're in good hands."

"It looked official," Larson said. "Not that we were questioning that much, but if it had been a personal check we would not have given the car until the check cleared."

The woman said that she was from Eugene, Ore., and that her boyfriend was working construction in the Omaha area. She said she received $12,000 from the insurance company, so the $10,500 the Larsons were asking for the car was within her budget.

The Larsons deposited the check in their bank on Aug. 2. Two days later, the bank told them it was fraudulent. Larson reported the incident to police last Friday.

Allstate spokeswoman Joanna Augustunski said people need to be on guard for such scams.

"We're urging consumers to be really careful, as a lot of these scammers use well-known brands to lend credibility to their schemes," Augustunski said.

Allstate doesn't issue cashier's checks, Augustunski said. Most of the company's checks to settle claims are made out to the person who suffered the damage, she said.

Augustunski said people with questions can call Allstate at 800-255-7828.

Susan MacTavish Best, a spokeswoman for Craigslist, said the company tries to prevent scammers from using their ads. Most fraud can be avoided by dealing only with people who live nearby, and people should be aware that fake cashier's checks and money orders are common, she said.

Tips from the Federal Trade Commission include knowing the people with whom you deal. If you accept a check, ask for one drawn on a local bank and visit the bank before accepting the check to ensure that it is valid.

Angie Larson said she and her husband are glad to have their car back and they might try to sell it again, even on Craigslist. But their strategy will be different this time, she said. They won't be taking a cashier's check.

1. What made the girl's scam seem legitimate?
2. What did she say or do to earn trust? List three examples.
3. Next time, what should the Larsons do with a check they receive, according to the Federal Trade Commission?

Recognizing Financial Fraud

Not surprisingly, there are devious people out there; people who want to get their hands on others' money, and they will tell all sorts of stories to get it. Often they pose as investment representatives or brokers, selling some "great" investments with "guaranteed returns." In spite of the SEC's best efforts, it sometimes can't catch up fast enough with scam artists. One study from the Federal Trade Commission showed that one in ten people have been victims of financial scams. Watch out for the following types of scams.

The scam: **Advance fee fraud.**
The story: The scammer promises to get you something; a loan, a job, or access to some kind of "shopping club" that offers discount prices. Some scammers have even posed as people looking for someone to adopt their cuddly cat or dog.

The catch: All you have to do is pay a fee upfront. Of course, the person disappears with your "down payment," and you never get the thing that was promised.

The scam: **Fake check scams.**
The story: A Nigerian prince or long-lost cousin you've never heard of writes saying they need your help transferring millions of dollars out of their war-torn country. You will be rewarded handsomely.

The catch: The "prince" sends you a check, which he instructs you to deposit into your account; and then to wire a certain amount of it back to him. You can keep the rest. That check bounces, but the money you've wired from your own account is gone—and so is your dear cousin.

Watch out, too, for sweepstakes e-mails, which work in a similar way (you have to return some of the money for "fees"); and beware, if you sell things over the Internet, of buyers who "accidentally" write you a check for bigger than the amount necessary, and ask for some of it back.

The scam: **Pyramid schemes**, multi-level marketing and chain letters.
The story: Just invest a small amount—say $10—which you send to the person who recruited you. Then all you have to do is recruit ten more people to invest—and supposedly you get the $100 they put in. That's a return nine times over your initial investment!

The catch: The people you recruit also have to recruit ten people, and eventually, there just are not enough people to sustain this operation. That means somebody won't get his or her money. The farther you are down the pyramid from the originator of the scam, the greater chance you will lose money. This scam is also what's behind the "Work at home! Stuff envelopes!" ads you may see on bulletin boards, on electric poles, or in newspaper ads around town. You will be asked to pay for the information about working from home, and what you get instead are more flyers to post—then it's your number on the sign, meaning you're abetting the scam artist.

The scam: **Ponzi schemes.**
The story: Someone promises that you can earn some high rate of return—say 30%—on your money risk-free with a great investment opportunity. Your money will go toward hedging currency or some other vague investment.

The catch: There's no such thing as a risk-free investment. Actually, this type of investment is not even an investment. Those who partake in scams like this are originally lured in with short-term promises—say, earning 25% in a month. They put in a small amount of money and make the return promised, so they believe it works. They invest more, and tell others. Problem is, there is no actual investment. The money some people get back initially actually comes from what other investors put in. The rest of the money goes to pay for the scammer's new Ferrari. Ask to get your money back, and guess what? Your money is gone, your investment "lost" on the market.

Just knowing these scam types can help you stave off some of the more common trickery. There are also a few other red flags to help you determine if an investment offer isn't legit. One is a high level of secrecy. Legitimate investment companies *must make disclosures about their investments,* thanks to the SEC. So if you're told not to tell anyone about something, be suspicious. Also be wary if you're told you must act fast. With a real investment, there is time for you to think and research. Finally, remember that when something sounds too good to be true—like your having a rich cousin you've never heard of—it probably is. You can't have a generous reward without having to take any risks.

CHAPTER REVIEW

Master the Vocabulary

Use the personal finance terms from the start of each section to complete the following sentences.

1. Saving is the process of setting aside money for future use, typically in a bank account; _____ involves using the money you've saved to buy securities or objects that may provide greater earnings.

2. The gain or loss on the money you have invested is your _____. It is often expressed as a percentage of your principal investment.

3. _____ investing means buying securities or objects with the aim to buy low and sell for more money later; _____ investing means buying certain investments that pay out interest or dividends on a regular basis.

4. An investment's price uncertainty is known as its _____.

5. If you sell an investment for more than you paid, you will have _____; if you can't, you will have _____.

6. _____ are a share of profits that stockholders of certain substantial companies may be entitled to.

7. Banks provide _____, or protection from loss, as opposed to capital appreciation.

8. Your entire collection of investment holdings is known as your _____.

9. _____ is a way to reduce risk exposure, as it involves making sure your investments are spread among a wide group of asset classes.

10. _____ refers to the specific mix of the investment types within your portfolio.

11. _____ is a way of buying into an investment over time so that you are not buying only when prices are highest.

12. _____ can be thought of as types of loans made to governments or corporations; _____ are shares of ownership of a company; and _____ are collective investments that contain both of these.

13. People who invest in _____ buy property either with hopes that it will appreciate in value or will provide income through renters.

14. _____ are issued by the U.S. Treasury that gain interest for 30 years and are known by their serial number prefixes.

15. The _____ of a conventional bond is its cost when it was issued; its _____ is the rate of return; its _____ is the date at which the borrower has agreed to return the capital.

16. The risk with bonds is _____, or that the borrower will not be able to return your capital because of significant loss or bankruptcy. This

risk is highest with so-called junk bonds, and lowest with those issued by the federal government.

17. Companies that issue stock are called _____.

18. Another word for stocks is _____, since shareholders own a piece of the company whose stock they own.

19. A stock is identified by its _____, which is a three- or four-letter code such as GOOG (for Google).

20. The first time a company offers stock for purchase is called its _____. After that, stocks are available for trade on a(n) _____ like the NYSE.

21. _____, such as the S&P 500, track the performance of a certain illustrative selection of stocks.

22. If investors are confident and buying stocks with an expectation of growth, you might have what is called a _____ market; if investors are selling stocks, it is called a _____ market.

23. The price per share of a mutual fund is called its _____.

24. When you shop for mutual funds, you should look at the information in the fund's _____, an explanatory document that the company is required by law to publish.

25. Many people buy investments through a _____, a person licensed to act as a go-between for buyers and sellers.

26. Investments in which you do not pay tax on gains until withdrawal are _____.

27. A(n) _____ is a tax-advantaged retirement investment account that you can open at a bank or brokerage.

28. The _____ is a government agency that oversees the investment industry.

Apply What You've Learned

1. Explain the relationship between risk and return.

2. Name and explain some ways of reducing investment risk.

3. You own stock that had been trading for $10 a share as of January 1. What would your return be if you sold at the end of the year when it was:

   a. trading for $12 a share at the end of December?

   b. trading for $16 a share at the end of December?

   c. trading for $9 a share at the end of December?

   d. trading for $9 a share at the end of December, and also had $1 in dividends for the year?

4. Imagine you invested $50 a month in a mutual fund this year, and the cost per share varied as follows:

Dollar-cost Average Investing			
	Investment Amount	Cost per Share	Number of Shares
January	$50	$6	8
February	$50	$8	6
March	$50	$9	
April	$50	$10	
May	$50	$10	
June	$50	$10	
July	$50	$7	
August	$50	$7	
September	$50	$5	
October	$50	$4	
November	$50	$5	
December	$50	$8	
Total			

a. What is the average price per share you would have paid? (Note: round to whole shares each month, and divide total investment by total shares.)

b. What price per share would you have paid if you invested all the money in October instead?

c. What price per share would you have paid if you invested it all in April?

d. What was the *average market cost* per share over the year?

5. Draw up a list of the types of investments covered in the chapter. Answer the following questions regarding investment choices:

a. If your main goal was liquidity, which investments might you choose?

b. If your main goal was income, which might you choose?

c. If your main goal was growth, which might you choose?

6. Which of these provides the greatest potential for long-term growth?

A. CDs

B. stocks

C. municipal bonds

D. money market accounts

7. Hank, age 26, has just started working at a job that has a 401(k) account for employees. He intends to allocate $150 of his paycheck monthly to his contribution, and he needs to decide which investment strategy to choose given the companies options. Which of these seems like the more appropriate allocation?

A. 65% bonds, 35% stock

B. 12% bonds, 88% stock

8. Anchali receives a $500 check from her grandmother for her 18th birthday and to celebrate high school graduation. Rather than spending it, she decides she will keep the money to use toward a new car that she predicts she will need in one year. Should she invest the money? How? Or should she save it in the bank?

9. How much would a bond with a par value of $1,000, and a coupon of 3%, and a maturity of five years pay per year? How much in total?

10. A headline in the newspaper reads "Government considering new tax breaks for homebuilders." What types of company or industry stocks might be affected by this news?

11. Look at the following stock snapshot, and answer the questions that follow:

a. What stock is this?

b. What price did it close at the day before?

c. Is the price now up or down from the previous day? By how much?

d. What was the high and low selling price for this stock in the last 52 weeks?

Bank of America Corp.

NYSE BAC

$14.10 ⬆

Change	+0.36 +2.62%
Volume	**59.77m**
	Jul 26, 2010 12:14 p.m.

Previous close	**$13.74**

Day low	Day high
$13.71	**$14.10**

52-week low	52-week high
$12.51	**$19.86**

1d • 5d • 3m • 6m • 1y • 3y • 5y

12. Name and explain the four categories of mutual funds.

13. What are some of the benefits of investing in mutual funds over individual stocks?

14. Refer to the bar graph on page 148 to answer the following questions:

    a. If you are in the 15% tax bracket and earned $540 in interest, how much interest do you get to keep, after taxes?

    b. What if you had the same earnings in short-term capital gains?

    c. If you had earned that $540 in long-term capital gains, how much would you really get, after taxes (still in the 15% tax bracket)?

15. Refer to the section: "Recognizing Financial Fraud" on page 154, and answer the following questions:

    a. Name two financial scams; give one real-life example of each.

    b. Imagine you were the scammer for one of the scenarios: what are you telling the "customer" about your available offer? What emotions do you appeal to? Write a paragraph, create a scenario of the scam and dialogue to go with it.

CHAPTER 5

Using Credit Wisely

Chapter Objectives

Students will:

✔ Analyze the costs and consequences of using credit
✔ Learn how to read a credit report and manage credit history
✔ Manage the responsibilities of credit card use and misuse
✔ Read about the kinds of credit and loans available

> **Personalize It!** *Imagine something you want to buy but cannot afford right now. Your parents offer to lend you the money, but they will charge you a small percentage extra added onto the loan every month until it's paid off. What would you think about before accepting this offer?*

Introduction

"Buy now, pay later!"

Have you ever seen a sign advertising this offer? It may sound tempting. There are probably many items you would like to buy but can't afford right now. (A car, maybe? That new surf or skateboard?) The stores that display these kinds of signs are offering you a way to take that expensive item home now, and pay for it over time. In other words, to buy it on credit.

Credit is basically an advance of money to a customer, with the understanding that the customer will pay it back later. Credit cards are a form of credit; so are home mortgages, student loans, and auto loans.

Credit can be a valuable and useful financial tool. It can help you to pay for investment items like a college education, a home or a start-up business. By using credit, you can pay for these over time rather than all at once. Credit cards also offer the convenience of being able to buy things without having to take out specific loans for each of the purchases made with them.

Borrowing has costs and risks, however. For one thing, it is not free money. You usually owe interest on what you borrow, so you will end up paying more—sometimes much, much more—than the actual cost of the item. Also, if you rely too heavily on borrowing, you may owe more than you can afford to pay back—and be stuck paying off debt for a very long time. That can have serious consequences on your current and future finances. In this chapter, you will learn how to use credit to your advantage.

5.1 The Cost of Credit

TERMS TO KNOW

lenders	closed-end credit	delinquent
principal	amortization	forbearance
annual percentage rate (APR)	open-end credit	default
prime rate	credit limit	collection agency
finance charge	minimum payment	repossession
installment loans	balance	foreclosure
revolving credit	promissory note	bankruptcy

Getting Started

While there are sometimes benefits to using credit, you must also understand that **lenders**—those that extend credit, typically banks—have significant financial incentive to *offer* you credit: they will make you pay interest on the money you borrow.

As a saver, you are paid interest; but as a borrower, you pay it. So what's good news for the lender is bad news for the borrower.

Because you will have to pay interest, buying with credit is typically more expensive than paying with cash. Just how much more expensive depends on several factors.

Understanding APR

The higher the interest rate on a loan or credit card, the more you will pay to borrow. The interest rate on a loan is expressed as an annual percentage of the **principal**, or amount you are borrowing, and is called the **annual percentage rate**, or **APR**. On a certain loan, the APR might be 7%, for example. While interest may be charged daily or monthly, the APR is the yearly rate, meant to create uniformity for consumers in understanding loans (just like APY on bank accounts). The *actual* interest rate is called the periodic rate, or the APR expressed over the period in which the interest is applied. To get the monthly periodic rate, the formula would be:

$$\frac{APR}{12} = \text{monthly percentage rate}$$

So for a loan with a 12% APR, the monthly rate is 1%, because

$$(12 \div 12) = 1$$

The rate banks charge their best customers, usually corporations rather than individuals, is known as the **prime rate**, and this is often used as a reference point for *consumer* loans. This rate is affected by the state of the economy and government fiscal policy. How much above prime you will pay depends largely upon your previous behaviors with credit. We get into this in greater depth later in the chapter; but for now, let's just say that if you have taken on a high amount of debt, or missed several payments, it will cost you. The greater the risk that you seem to be, the higher your rates will be. That is, the more you will pay to borrow a certain amount of money.

The APR can be either fixed or variable. *Fixed* means it will stay the same for the life of the loan. If it is *variable*, it means it will shift, reassessed at times by the bank given both economic factors and your personal behavior with the loan. Still, with both of these types of APRs, the interest on loans is compound interest. As you know, compounding means faster growth; so compounding can be a detriment to borrowers, because it means a loan costs more.

The cost of credit in dollars is known as the **finance charge**, which is both interest owed and also any fees on the loan besides interest that the lender may charge. The finance charge represents the *opportunity cost* of using credit. If you had used cash and paid right away, you'd have that extra money to save, invest, or spend.

Understanding Types of Loans

The type of credit makes a difference, too, in how much it will cost. There are two main categories of credit: **installment loans** and **revolving credit**.

An installment loan, also called **closed-end credit**, is a one-time advance of a sum of money that you agree to pay back over a predetermined length of time (called a term). Examples of this type of loan include mortgages, car loans, and student loans.

The term on such loans may be a number of weeks, months, or years. Payments on the loan are for a fixed amount, usually due monthly. These monthly payments pay off both interest accrued, and principal owed. The lender will give you what is called an **amortization** table, which shows how payments are applied over the loan term (dividing each payment into paying interest, and paying principal), and how that leads to paying off the loan.

The other type of credit is revolving credit. Credit cards fall into this category. Revolving credit is also known as **open-end credit**, in part because there is no term to the loan; you can take as little or as much time as you want to pay back what you borrow. Also, instead of a set loan amount you are given a maximum amount you are allowed to borrow at any one time—called a **credit limit**, or credit line. You're allowed to add charges on a continuous basis, up to the limit. So if you have a $10,000 credit limit, and you charge $8,000, you will have $2,000 in available credit to use. As you pay that $8,000 off, your available credit climbs back up to $10,000.

While the creditor (lender) does not set the terms of repayment, they do typically require a **minimum payment** each month, which is the lowest amount of money you can pay to keep the line open. Usually a minimum payment equals 2 to 5% of the balance owed, or a set amount like $25.

With revolving credit, if you were to pay off the full amount you have charged by the end of the same billing period for those charges, you would not be assessed any finance charges. Basically, you get up to a one-month loan for free. If you don't pay off what is owed at the end of the period, however, then interest is applied. It continues to be applied for every billing period in which there is a **balance**, or any outstanding debt. Typically, the interest charged on credit lines is a much higher rate than with closed-end loans.

The Cost of Closed-End Credit

With installment loans—or closed-end credit—there are a few factors that ultimately affect how much you will pay to borrow: the amount of money you are borrowing (or *principal*), the APR, and the loan term.

The first of these, the total principal, has obvious ramifications. The larger the amount of money you borrow, the greater the interest charges—for example, 7% of $10,000 is always going to be more than 7% of $5,000.

The APR matters to the cost because a higher or lower interest rate means faster or slower compounding of interest charges, respectively. Let's consider an example: say you are borrowing $10,000 and the bank offers you an annual rate of 7% for a loan that you have to pay back over 36 months, or three years. That comes to monthly payments of $309, and a grand total of $11,116 paid over those three years.

As you can see, by borrowing the money, you pay $1,116 in interest. That's the cost over paying in cash up front. The opportunity cost of borrowing, then, is that you lost $1,116 that you could have done something else with.

 Let's say you shop around a bit for APR rates—and when you do, you find you can qualify for loans at 5% and 6%, respectively. These calculations can be made online at *www.bankrate.com/calculators.aspx* or by searching for a "loan payment calculator" in Google or Yahoo.

Loan Principal	APR	Term	Monthly Payment	Total Payment	*Premium,* or total cost over principal
$10,000	7%	3 years	$309	$11,116	$1,116
$10,000	6%	3 years	$304	$10,952	$952
$10,000	5%	3 years	$300	$10,790	$790

If you have loans with the same terms and different interest rates, the one with the lowest rate is cheapest and has the lowest payments and the lowest total interest costs. The lower the rate, the cheaper the loan, so it pays to shop around for the best rate.

Lastly, to see how the term can affect the cost, let's imagine that the banker is offering the same APR rate for two different terms: three or four years.

Loan Principal	APR	Term	Monthly Payment	Total Payment	Premium
$10,000	7%	3 years	$308	$11,116	$1,116
$10,000	7%	4 years	$239	$11,494	$1,494

Q: Ms. Yiwen Wu took out a $10,000, 4-year term loan to fix her car, buy a new computer, and buy a few suits and work clothes necessary for her new job. She has $3,500 left over after her expenses. What would you advise her to do with the extra money? What effect would that have on her premium?

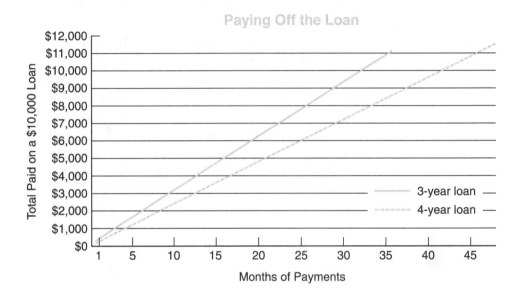

By increasing the length of the loan, you decrease your monthly payment, but you increase your total cost, because the APR is applied to more payments than with the first loan. The lesson: if you have two loans with the same rate and different terms, the one with the longer term will have cheaper monthly payments, but higher ultimate cost. Obviously, it's better to pay less in total for a loan, so you might lean toward the shorter loan—but it comes down to what you can afford on a monthly basis. If you could not afford the $308 each month, then the 4-year loan would be a better option. If you take out the longer-term loan, and discover you can pay above the monthly payment, you may increase your payments, paying more when you can. This will decrease your interest charges, and overall total cost. Still, you will always be responsible for at least the amount of your monthly payments.

In sum, the amount borrowed, the APR, and the term will all affect the cost of the loan.

MAKING CENT$ OF IT

1. a. You take out $10,000 in loans each year to cover your tuition. Your school loans accrue interest at 6% per year. On graduation day (four years of college finally over!), how much interest has accrued?

   b. What is your total loan balance (principal plus interest)?

2. One student college loan gives you a one-year grace period before payments are due (that is, you don't have to start paying until a year after you graduate). Another says that you have to start paying right out of college, but so long as you're in school there will be no interest charged on your principal (interest begins to be charged the day you graduate). Which loan would you choose and why?

The Cost of Open-End Credit

Using revolving debt—such as credit cards—won't cost you anything if you pay off what you have charged at the end of each billing cycle. If you *don't* pay it in full, the amount of interest you ultimately pay depends on the APR, the amount you charge, and how long you take to pay it off.

To see how much revolving debt might cost, say you charge (borrow) $10,000 on a line of credit. For comparison's sake, it has the same rate as the earlier installment loan of 7% yearly. Unlike an installment loan, revolving credit has no set term by which the total must be paid back. Instead there is a minimum payment that is set per month. You can pay anywhere from the minimum to the total owed each month. We will assume you only make the minimum required payments, which in this example is 3% of the balance owed. Check it out for yourself using the credit card calculator at *www.bankrate.com/calculators.aspx*.

Credit Charge	APR	Monthly Minimum Payment	Time it will take to pay it off	Total Payment	Premium
$10,000	7%	3% of balance	160 months	$12,371.53	$2,371.53

Behold the power of compound interest! That's right, it would take 160 months—over 13 years!—to pay off that debt completely. In the process, you'd pay $2,371 in interest. Pretty expensive! It is significantly more expensive than an installment loan at the same interest rate. With

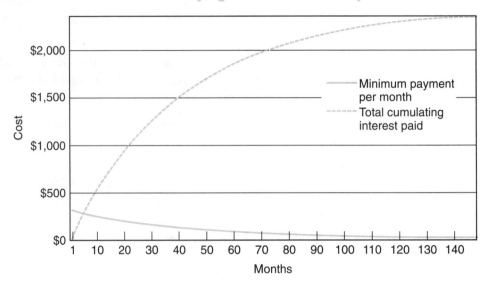

Paying 3% of the balance per month, as you see, means you slowly owe less and less per month. During that time, however, interest keeps accruing on what you don't pay off! This means you end up paying more and more and more for your credit card purchases.

the installment loan, that set payment per month means you pay off more and more of the principal balance, and interest costs actually decrease monthly as you pay the balance. With credit where you pay only the minimum, you pay so little each month that interest is added on higher balances for longer periods, so you continue to owe more interest, and it takes that much longer to pay off the loan. That's not to mention that it's unlikely the credit card rate would ever be as low as this; usually revolving credit comes at higher rates than an installment loan (anywhere from nine to 20%). In reality, the credit card would be *even more expensive* than this example and take even longer to pay off. Probably by the time the debt is paid, you'd have long ago forgotten the thing you bought—yet you've just finished paying it off.

As you can see, the minimum payment that lenders require is something of a financial trap; by paying only that much, you end up taking a long time to pay off the charge and paying *a lot* of interest in the process. The more you can pay per month, the better. See below how setting your own *dollar* minimum can speed up the payoff.

Credit Charge	Monthly Minimum Payment	Time it will take to pay it off	Total Payment	Premium
$10,000	Set at $305	37 months	$11,131.38	$1,131.38

Faster, and cheaper, besides. Still, even that comes out to three years before you've paid off that debt. Over that time, the balance can cause stress and get in the way of other goals.

Really, its best if you can pay off the balance on open-end credit in full at the end of every billing period, as you will never owe interest charges. Since that is not always possible, you should at least have a plan for paying off what you charge before you charge it. That way, it won't become an obligation and a high cost for you.

MAKING CENT$ OF IT

1. You've charged $5,000 on an 18% APR credit card.
   a. If your minimum payment is 3% (you owe 3% of your balance each month), how much is your first minimum payment? (No interest owed yet, remember.)
   b. You pay the minimum; with your new balance, how much will your interest charge be after the second month?
   c. If you pay the minimum again (this time on balance and interest), how much are you paying the second billing period?
2. Let's say you decided to pay $200 a month instead. After the first month's payment, what will the second month's interest accrued come out to?

Good Debt, Bad Debt

You know that debt is money owed. You learned a little about debt in Chapter One, in which you discovered that any money you owe is a liability that counts against your net worth. Because of the costs of borrowing, there are some general guidelines about when taking on debt is a good idea and when it's a bad idea.

No doubt you have heard the word debt used in a negative context, but it's important to note that not all debt is bad. Some should be thought of as good debt, and that usually includes mortgages and student loans. What makes these good is that the borrowed money is used to invest in something that may provide future wealth. Houses and college educations, for example, often provide future wealth which outweighs the costs of the loans. These particular loans also tend to come with interest rate charges in the single digits, and you may get a tax deduction for interest paid on them. Finally, it would take you a long time to save up the cash to pay for these in their entirety, even if you were a diligent saver. Borrowing allows you to gain the benefits of the house or the education now, and pay for it over time.

On the other hand, borrowing money to buy something that would *not* gain value might be considered bad debt—you continue to pay more for it, even while it is worth less and less. Assuming you won't pay it off in full by the billing date, the balance on a credit card after buying, say, a flat-panel TV or a new wardrobe could be considered bad debt. These are *wants* rather than *needs*, disposable goods that will likely lose value almost immediately. Beyond that, however, you will end up paying well over the store's price once you figure in all the interest.

It's also considered bad debt when an item bought on credit is completely used up by the time you have fully paid for it—a dinner paid for with a credit card, for example, will be eaten and forgotten by the time the bill comes. In general, credit card balances carried past the first billing cycle are usually thought of as bad debt because credit cards have such high APRs. You are paying a very high price to borrow.

Any kind of debt—even good debt—has the potential to be bad for you if you take on more than you can handle. If you end up with more debt than you can afford to pay off, it can jeopardize your future financial goals, as you will have to redirect a lot of your income to this rather than savings. Debt can have negative effects on your physical health and mental health; it can cause stress in your relationships. Thus, you must also think about whether debt is good or bad in relation to your budget. You don't want to take on more credit (debt, loans, etc.) than you can financially bear. One common guideline is the 20-10 rule, which says that a reasonable amount of debt that you could take on should be no more than 20% of your annual income, and your monthly payments should be under 10% of your monthly income.

The Long-Term Consequences of Misusing Credit

If you do take on more debt than you can handle, or are irresponsible in paying down the debt you have, you may end up doing serious damage to your personal finances and your chances at future loans. To illustrate this, let's imagine that our friend Mark finds himself unable to make his car loan payments for a few months due to job/income problems. Let's follow the storyline, to see what happens to Mark.

When Mark applied for his loan, he most likely had to sign a **promissory note**—like a contract with the lender—stating that he would repay the amount borrowed. This contract entitles the lender to pursue certain recourse (retaliatory action) if Mark does not live up to his end of the bargain.

Once Mark misses just one payment, the loan is considered **delinquent**, and at that point, the lender will probably start charging late fees *on top of* the interest due. If the cause of Mark's delinquency was a medical issue, lost job, divorce, accident or other tragedy, he might have called his lenders immediately to request **forbearance**. That is, a relaxed payment schedule that would help him get out of economic hardship. During the forbearance period, interest may still accrue, and would be added on in a lump sum when the period is up.

For now, let's assume he does not ask for forbearance. He continues to miss payments, and after a few more months, the lender determines that his account is in **default**, meaning he has not abided by the loan terms.

This is where the idea of "pursuing recourse" comes in. As for the promissory note, the lender now can take action to get the money back. The lenders may start to call Mark frequently to check up on the payment. Or they may turn the matter over to a **collection agency**, a company that tracks down delinquent debt in exchange for a commission. The collection agency will do everything in its power to get the money, including calling Mark frequently and sending him formal letters. (The Fair Debt Collection Practices Act prevents bill collectors from using deceptive, abusive, or harassing tactics to get their money.)

The company to which the debt is owed may pursue **repossession**, in which it claims ownership of the item Mark borrowed money to buy; with a house this is called **foreclosure**.

The lender may send a "repo" man—short for repossession—who doesn't even have to let delinquent borrowers know in advance that he's coming to get their things. He may tow, or even hotwire Mark's car!

In a desperate case, the creditor may sue, asking a judge to freeze Mark's bank account or have up to 25% of his wages redirected to paying off the loan.

At a certain point, Mark might be interested in filing for **bankruptcy**, a last resort in which a debtor declares an inability to pay in court in order to be freed from debt. First, by law, he would have to go through a credit counseling program. A credit counseling agency would help him try to work out a repayment plan, and to negotiate with the lenders for better terms. The agency may also try to consolidate multiple debts into one account, or get the lenders to accept a lesser sum. If he went through the program and still could not come up with a way to pay the creditors to their satisfaction, Mark could *then* file a petition in U.S. Bankruptcy Court to declare bankruptcy.

The two types of individual bankruptcy are called Chapter 7 and Chapter 13, named for the section of the legal code under which they fall. Under Chapter 7, a person appointed by the court would sell off most of Mark's assets and distribute the money to those he owes. His debts would be discharged. Many people have to file for Chapter 13 bankruptcy. Under Chapter 13, Mark would keep his assets, but be assigned a three-to-five year repayment plan.

While bankruptcy may provide some relief psychologically, the downside is that it would seriously impair Mark's ability to get credit in the future—if he is even approved, he would have to pay some of the highest interest rates.

Given the serious consequences that credit/loan misuse can have, you want to give serious consideration to whether you can afford a certain debt before you take it on. If you do decide to take on debt, you need to be sure to manage it responsibly.

MAKING CENT$ OF IT

You have a loan out for your car. Then the unexpected happens. Answer the following questions:

1. If you lost your job and were unable to make loan payments, you should call your creditors and ask for a _____ on your loan.

2. If you don't ask for one, and keep missing loan payments, your loan will eventually go into _____ .

3. List three things a creditor has the right to pursue, and may do to you or your car once this happens.

5.2 Being Creditworthy

TERMS TO KNOW

capacity	credit reporting agencies	FICO
secured loan	(or bureaus)	credit score
collateral	joint account	subprime
credit report	tax liens	

Getting Started

Imagine a friend asks to borrow 50 dollars. You probably would pause before saying yes or no. In your head, you may be thinking back on your friend's past behavior. Does he or she have the means to pay you back? If your buddy ever borrowed from you in the past, did he or she quickly repay the loan? Does he or she tend to be responsible in general?

Creditors ask the same questions about people who are applying for loans. They don't want to be left holding the bill for a borrower's debt. Before they even extend money to you, banks and other loan companies want to get a sense that you are responsible, and that you can afford to pay back what you borrow. In other words, they're looking at your creditworthiness. Your creditworthiness also helps determine the interest rate you are charged.

What Factors Lenders Consider

To get a loan or other form of credit, you first must apply. The issuer will then consider several factors in deciding whether or not to approve your application—and subsequently, how much to charge you for the privilege of borrowing. The factors the lenders consider are often called the three Cs: capacity, collateral, and character.

Capacity. Clearly, a lender does not want to be left unpaid for a borrower's debt. So when you apply for a loan, the bank may first look at your income and other debt obligations to see if you would have the money to make the payments on the credit you are applying for. To prove **capacity**, or the ability to pay the loan, you may be required to show the lender proof of income, assets, and other debt (for example, pay stubs and account statements).

Collateral. Creditors may want to mitigate (lessen) their risk even further. Particularly with big loans, they want to know that they have insurance of sorts if you are unable to pay back what you have borrowed. So some loans must be **secured**, meaning that you must guarantee them with **collateral**, an asset worth as much as or more than the amount you are borrowing. (If you are borrowing money to buy a house or car, that house or car typically will be the collateral.) The agreement is that the bank can take ownership of the asset if the loan is not paid as planned.

Character. Creditors will also consider your previous and current use of other forms of credit in order to get a sense of how much risk you pose as a borrower. The lenders can look back on your credit history through a **credit report**, or a document that chronicles your borrowing over the past several years. The report shows every loan or credit line you have taken out over a certain period, as well as payment history on that loan. Companies known as **credit reporting agencies** (or **credit bureaus**) prepare these reports for lenders. Wondering how the bureaus get info on your past credit experiences? Well, each time you get new credit, the issuer informs the bureaus, which will then link your history to your new account. Once the loan is active, the issuer and the credit reporting agencies remain in touch about your handling of that loan, and the reporting agencies keep track of this on your credit reports. Good behavior will buy you a low interest rate on loans, better borrowing terms and access to more loan types. Creditors aren't the only ones who can access credit reports; insurance companies, employers and potential employers, landlords and certain government agencies can also request them.

It's also important to note what lenders will *not* consider: The Equal Opportunity Credit Act prohibits lenders from discriminating on the basis of sex, race, religion, marital status, ethnicity, age or the fact that a person receives income from public assistance. Creditors may ask about these, but they cannot base a decision on them.

A Credit Report: The Basics

The biggest three credit bureaus are Equifax, Experian, and TransUnion. Though each one prepares its credit report in a slightly different way, the information included is generally the same.

Personal information. The report will give your name, Social Security Number, address (and previous addresses) as well as employer (and previous employers). Note: because this information gets reported by the creditors, it may be out of date, or it may show up in a few different versions. Watch out for errors.

Inquiries. Anytime a business or agency requests your credit report, that request will be listed. These inquiries can stay on your report for up to two years, and whenever they are the result of you applying for credit (applying for a mortgage, say) they are called hard inquiries. Soft inquiries, on the other hand are report requests that didn't begin with you applying for credit—situations like a credit card company looking to send you a preapproved card solicitation, or you viewing your own report.

Account summary. This is an abridged version of the account history (see next). Usually, it gives the reader an overview of which types of accounts you have, your total balances by category, and the types of credit.

Account history. This is the long version. Every installment loan or revolving credit you've had in the last seven to ten years should be listed here, with the account number, name of the issuing institution (like the bank's name), date it was opened and date of last activity (like, paying your bill or charging something). It will say whether the account is individual or a **joint account**—meaning you share responsibility with someone else—and what type of credit it is. It will also give any credit limit, the highest balance on the account, and the balance as of the last time the credit reporting agency was updated. It shows the current status of the account, and whether it is in good standing or not. Delinquencies will be noted here. If the account went into default, it will say so; and this can stay on the credit report for seven years.

Public records. Here the bureau lists any piece of public information that may be relevant to a financial history. That includes bankruptcy—Chapter 13 can stay on record for seven years, Chapter 7 for ten years. Some other things that might be noted in this section: judgments made against you in civil court, and **tax liens**, or claims by a state or federal government on something you own in order to secure money for unpaid taxes.

As a result of the 2003 Fair and Accurate Credit Transactions Act, you are entitled to receive a free copy of your credit report from each of the three bureaus once a year. You can get them via *www.annualcreditreport.com*. Experts recommend that you request one copy from each at least once per year so that you stay up-to-date on changes in your credit history. Any report, after your free copy of each, will cost you $10, unless you were denied credit in the last two months—in which case the bureau that provided the information to the creditor must give you a copy on request.

What Your Credit Score Means

Lenders may also look to third-party agencies—chiefly a company called Fair Isaac Corporation, or **FICO**—to help them interpret credit reports in a standard fashion. FICO turns the information in people's credit reports into a numerical assessment of creditworthiness, known as a **credit score**, which it then provides to interested lenders. Lenders use credit scores to determine who should get better loan rates.

In the United States, FICO credit scores range from 300 to 850, with the highest scores representing those who are the lowest-risk borrowers. Scores of 760 and above will usually earn lenders' best interest rates. The term **subprime**, from the mortgage crisis of the late 2000s, refers to risky credit borrowers with under "prime" credit scores, typically those with credit scores 620 and below. These borrowers are considered at high risk of defaulting on their loans, and often will either be denied credit or assessed at the highest interest rates.

In calculating your credit score, FICO looks to your credit report for the following factors, which are listed from those that have the most influence to those that have the least.

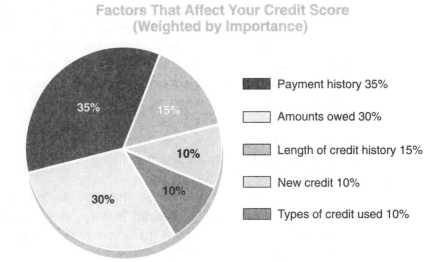

Factors That Affect Your Credit Score
(Weighted by Importance)

- Payment history 35%
- Amounts owed 30%
- Length of credit history 15%
- New credit 10%
- Types of credit used 10%

Your payment history (35%) This represents the greatest portion of your score. The creditor is looking for delinquencies (late payments), accounts sent to collection, and bankruptcies. The ideal credit candidate pays on time all the time. The impact of certain negative incidents on a credit score can be as much as 100 points per incident.

Amounts owed (30%) The score considers the total amount you owe, but also how much you owe compared to the credit you have available, to determine if you are overextended. So for revolving debt, the scoring agency would look to see what your balances are in relation to your credit line. On installment loans, the scoring agency might look at how much you have left to pay off, against the original loan total.

Length of credit history (15%) Someone with a long credit history of good behavior should score better than someone with a shorter history of the same behavior, because FICO looks especially carefully at your oldest account. FICO also looks at the average time on all accounts.

New credit (10%) According to FICO, a person who opens several forms of credit in a relatively short period of time may be more of a credit risk than someone who does not. They are looking to see that you haven't gone on a credit spree lately. The company will also pay particular attention to your newest account.

Types of credit used (10%) The credit score also takes into account the different kinds of credit you have—auto loan, mortgage, credit cards—and how well you are handling them. In general, lenders like to see that you have been successful at managing various types.

You have to pay between $7 and $15 to get your credit score. Since your credit score is based on the information in your credit report, which you can get for free, you need not get your score unless you're planning to apply for credit in the next six months.

Your score may not be high starting out, since you won't have had many (if any) credit experiences. Your first credit card can be an important tool to helping you build a good reputation, which is why later in the chapter you learn how to use this wisely.

Errors on a Credit Report

According to a study conducted by the nonprofit U.S. Public Interest Research Groups, one in four credit reports contain an error serious enough to result in the denial of credit. You don't want a mistake to ruin your chances of getting a loan or of getting a better interest rate.

When you get your report, you want to review it carefully to make sure there are no inaccuracies. Start by making sure your name, address, and Social Security Number are correct. Then look at the accounts to make sure that any account you closed shows as such, that there aren't any accounts listed that are not yours (this sometimes happens if you have the same name as someone else), and that the actions listed happened as it says they did.

The Fair Credit Reporting Act set up a procedure for consumers to file disputes regarding credit report information, and for the bureaus to respond to these disputes. You must send a letter to the bureau that created that specific report, explaining the error. Make sure you include with the letter copies of any relevant documentation. You can check out more at *www.ftc.gov/bcp/consumer.shtm* under "Credit & Loans."

The bureaus then have 30 to 45 days to investigate with the creditors, and respond to you in writing with the findings. If changes are made to your report based on your dispute, a new copy of your report will be sent with the letter. On request, the bureau will notify anyone who pulled your report in the last six months of the changes.

Should the agency find against you, you have the right to include a personal statement that will appear on your credit report. This might say: "Due to a serious medical illness between June and December 2011, I had been unable to work and was thus unable to pay my Visa bills during that time. In January 2012, in better health, I returned to a full-time job and have been making regular payments on this account; it is currently in good standing. Please consider this an anomaly in an otherwise responsible credit history." The bureau may charge you a fee for this. If you dispute something on one report, you may want to check the other reports, just to make sure they haven't included the same error.

 **Not All "Free Credit Reports" Are Actually Free**

The only place to get truly free credit reports is at *www.annualcreditreport.com*. Avoid other sites that promise a credit report for free. Usually such sites are just credit monitoring services, which would go periodically through your reports looking for any negative incidents or possible identity theft. You pay for the monitoring—a service most people don't need. With just the monthly fees for monitoring, that credit report could cost you $100 or more a year.

MAKING CENT$ OF IT

1. List the five things commonly seen on a credit report.
2. Name the most important piece of information taken into account in creating a credit score.
3. Who do you turn to when you want to dispute or correct an error on your credit report?

5.3 Using Credit Cards Wisely

TERMS TO KNOW

average daily balance   cash advance   authorized user
grace period   balance transfer   rewards cards
penalty APR

Getting Started

Credit cards are likely to be your first introduction to borrowing. If you don't have a card already, you will probably get one within the next few years. A credit card can be a very useful tool. It can also put your other financial goals in jeopardy, if used unwisely.

A credit card is a form of revolving credit, and as you learned earlier, this type of debt has no predetermined payoff period. Thus, how much you pay to use the card, and how much of a benefit—or detriment—it will ultimately be is up to you. In this section, you will learn to use credit cards wisely, so that you stand to gain more than lose in your credit experience.

Credit Cards: the Good and the Bad

There are many benefits of using credit cards—chief among them, convenience. With a credit card, you can buy things even when you don't have cash in your wallet. That's especially handy in emergencies. Credit cards also allow you to buy something and pay for it over time, which can be helpful when you need a more expensive item like a sofa set for your new apartment, or a plane ticket to visit a friend far away. Buying with credit, you get to make use of the item before you fully paid for it.

There is also safety in using plastic, because you don't always need to carry around cash. If your wallet were stolen, you'd have no way of re-

"What's your not-quite-so prime rate?"

What is the definition of the prime rate? What does a credit score have to do with loan interest rates? Use your understanding of the prime rate and credit scores to explain the cartoon.

trieving the cash. With cards, because of the Fair Credit Billing Act, if someone uses your card without your authorization, your maximum liability is $50, and it may be zero if you inform the issuer (the lender) that a card is stolen before it is used.

Another advantage: your credit card issuer will act as your advocate and representative in disputes with a seller. If, say, you ordered something online and it's not as advertised, you can issue a dispute with the creditor, who will take up the problem. You would not have to pay for the purchase until the creditor has investigated, either. Finally, credit cards, when used wisely, can help you build a solid credit history that will allow you to get low rates on future borrowing.

On the other hand, credit cards can have some serious drawbacks.

Whenever you "carry a balance," as it is called when you don't pay off the debt within one billing cycle, you end up paying interest. The starting interest rates on credit cards tend to be between nine and 25%, which is high compared to other forms of credit—so the longer you take to pay off an item you've charged, the more expensive it becomes. So credit cards can be a particularly costly way to buy something. Imagine paying an added one-fourth of an item's purchase price per month—it's like the opposite of buying something on sale! Many cardholders carry a balance, which is why credit card companies make so much money.

By vastly expanding your purchasing power beyond the limits of your checking account balance, credit cards can also tempt you to buy more than you can afford. Creditors are especially eager for *your* business because they know young people often impulse shop, and don't understand the consequences of charging more than they can pay off. Some 82 percent of college students carry a balance—*an average of $3,173*, according to lender Sallie Mae. Meanwhile, students with credit card debt are more likely than debt-free peers to drop out of school due to financial pressure. Plus, those who start their credit history carrying a balance may grow into adults who carry an even bigger balance: the average U.S. household has about $10,000 in credit card debt, according to 2009 surveys.

Finally, keeping a big balance or missing payments can do serious damage to your credit score, making it harder and more expensive for you to get other credit in the future. In sum, whether or not credit cards will be an advantage to *you* comes down to how you use them.

WHY SOME PEOPLE REJECT CREDIT

Many adults have chosen not to have credit cards at all. What is their motivation and what are they missing? This article attempts to find out.

"More consumers just say no to credit cards"

By Sandra Block
USA Today

Emily Maddox, 24, of Knoxville, Tenn., is the kind of customer credit card companies covet. She has a good job as an Internet marketing coordinator, and she lives within her means. But she's never had a credit card, and she has no plans to apply for one.

Credit cards, she says, "make me really nervous, and I've never felt comfortable having one."

In a country where the average consumer owns five credit cards, Maddox may seem somewhat quaint, like an Amish farmer who drives a horse-drawn buggy. But proponents of a no-credit-card lifestyle say there's nothing old-fashioned about their choices. And they're convinced that their numbers will grow as consumers become increasingly disenchanted with credit card industry practices.

Reasons consumers are opting to live without credit cards:

Desire for a simpler lifestyle. Two years ago, Adam and Courtney Baker decided to reduce their debts, sell most of their stuff, and spend a year or two traveling around the world. By selling their small business and a rental property, they were able to pay off more than $11,000 in credit card debt.

Initially, they planned to use an American Express card during their travels, says Adam Baker. But once the couple wiped out their debt, they decided to stick with debit cards and cash. Going without credit cards helps them keep a handle on their spending and suits their stripped-down lifestyle, says Baker, 25, a freelance writer whose blog about his family's experience is titled Man vs. Debt (*www.manvsdebt.com*).

"We enjoy not having them (credit cards) in our lives," says Baker. "Getting 1.5% cash back for using four cards and juggling them is just not something that interests us. We have bigger and better things we want to focus our attention on."

Louis Rosas-Guyon, 37, a business technology consultant in Miami, says his life has become less stressful since he stopped using credit cards 10 years ago. His epiphany came after he plugged his $18,000 in balances into an Excel spreadsheet and learned that, at the rate he was going, it would take him 180 years to pay off his credit card debts.

Instead, he went into what he calls "aggressive debt-payment mode." He negotiated with his lenders, consolidated his debt and borrowed money from a relative, eventually paying off the balances.

"I have far fewer bills and headaches and fears about that monthly billing cycle," Rosas-Guyon says. "My life has gotten substantially easier because I've offloaded 10 to 12 different credit cards that I no longer have to make a payment on."

Increased acceptance of debit cards. A decade ago, consumers who didn't want to use credit cards had two choices: carry a lot of cash or write checks and hold up the supermarket line. Today, debit cards blend the discipline of cash with the convenience of plastic and are accepted by most merchants that accept credit cards. In recent years, their popularity has soared.

A July 2009 survey by Auriemma Consulting Group found that 28% of consumers had shifted the way they pay for purchases in the past year, with an increase in debit card usage coming at the expense of credit cards. Forty-six percent of consumers surveyed said they believed debit cards helped control their spending.

"There's quietly been a debit card revolution," says best-selling personal finance author Dave Ramsey, who urges fans of his radio and Fox Business TV show to cut up their credit cards. Now that debit cards are broadly accepted, he says, using a credit card "with all its fees and interest rates and traps with customer service is really stupid."

Scott Talbott, senior vice president of government affairs for the Financial Services Roundtable, says the shift reflects a desire by consumers to get a better handle on their spending, rather than a rejection of credit cards.

1. What are the reasons the people in the story gave for not using credit cards?

2. In what ways might not having a credit card harm their credit? In what ways might it help?

3. What are your thoughts about using credit cards now that you've read this?

What to Look for When Getting a Credit Card

Making sure a credit card will be more of a benefit for you than a detriment starts with selecting the right card. Fortunately, there is an easy way to identify a card's stipulations and compare it to its competition. As a result of the Truth in Lending Act, card issuers are required to disclose certain important terms in the application. These will be listed in what's called the Schumer Box—named after the senator that pushed for the legislation. In it, issuers are required to disclose the following:

APR. Most credit cards offer a variable APR, meaning that the rate will change periodically, typically with the prime rate. The box should say if the APR is an introductory rate, meaning that it will expire within a period of time and be reset to a higher number. This permanent APR will also be noted—and this is the more important number. The lower the permanent APR, the better. You could check in at *www.bankrate.com* to see what the average APR on credit cards is currently. You may not necessarily get approved for a card at the APR that is advertised.

Method for calculating the balance. Issuers can determine the balance to which they apply finance charges (which are applied as percentages) in several ways. The most common one is by taking an **average daily balance**. With this method, the card company averages out what you have to pay on the card from each day of the month. This method automatically figures in any payments and any purchases you make. To understand this, consider the example: in January you owe a balance of $1,000, and then pay off $600 of it on January 15. (You owe $1,000 from the first to the 15th, and then only owe $400 from January 16–31.)

The issuer would add up the balances, and divide by the number of days to arrive at the *average daily balance*, as follows:

$$\frac{(\$1,000 \times 14 \text{ days}) + (\$400 \times 17 \text{ days})}{31 \text{ days}} = \$671$$

Then the card company would apply the monthly rate charges based on that averaged amount of $671.

Annual fees. Some issuers charge yearly membership fees to their cardholders. As you're starting out, it's best to look for a no-fee card.

Grace period. The **grace period** is the time between the statement date and the due date, which you have to pay off purchases made during the period; no finance charges accrue.

Late fees. This is what you will be charged if you do not pay your bill by the due date.

Penalty APR. This is what your interest rate will go up to if you violate the terms of your credit card agreement. Usually, there is an asterisk on this section that will explain below what triggers this rate—often it's paying your bill late or going over the credit limit. **Penalty APR** rates can top 30%, so it pays to know—and abide by—the terms.

Other APRs and fees. Here, the box will state costs for other uses of the card. For example, most cards will let you withdraw money directly from an ATM, a transaction known as a **cash advance**. Doing so, however, means you pay a much higher APR than if you made a purchase; plus it costs a one-time transaction fee, often 2 to 4% of the advance. Thus, you are better off just paying with the card. Another feature some cards offer: an appealingly low rate if you make a **balance transfer**, or move what you owe from another card to this one. Often, that appealing rate—sometimes as little as 0%—is a teaser that lasts only a few months. Also, many people who use this feature don't understand that while they may not pay interest on that transferred balance, they will still pay the regular APR on new purchases.

The wrong card can cost you hundreds of dollars more in interest per year. You want to shop around for a card. (Try using sites like *www.cardratings.com* and *www.cardtrak.com.*) Look for the types of terms mentioned here, giving greatest importance to a low APR.

MAKING CENT$ OF IT

Look at the following two credit cards and decide which gives the better deal:

Terms	Card A	Card B
APR	8.75%	10%
Method of Calculating the Balance	Using an average daily balance	Using an average daily balance
Annual Fee	$40	$0
Grace Period	15 days from statement	10 days from statement
Late Fee	$25	$20
Penalty APR	26.50%	19.25%

How to Get a Credit Card

If you have a card before age 18, it often means you are an **authorized user** on your parents' card. You are allowed to use it but the charges go towards your parent's statement. At age 18, you can get a credit card in your name if a parent or guardian cosigns—meaning he or she agrees to share responsibility for the charges—or if you can prove you have sufficient income to pay the bills yourself. By the age of 21, you can apply for a card on your own.

A credit card application may ask for a driver's license number, Social Security Number, and address; as well as information about employment, income, and debt. The creditor will then check credit reports and the FICO credit score to determine whether or not to approve the application; it will also use this to determine what APR and what credit line to offer.

If you do not have sufficient credit history or have a low credit score, you may not qualify for unsecured credit. You might instead have to begin by taking a *secured credit card.* Secured just means they might require putting money on hold with the issuer as collateral, or having one of your guardians sign as a guarantor.

 **Not All Cards Are the Same**

If you've been studying this book in order, you have already learned about debit cards, in Chapter Three. Also, you may have already had experiences with prepaid (stored-value) cards, which are like gift cards for specific amounts of money, but issued by credit card companies and useable almost everywhere. Knowing the distinction between these three types of cards will keep you aware of what debts you owe, and in what ways you spend your money.

Reading a Credit Card Statement

For these purposes, let's say that you just got your unsecured first credit card—with an APR of 14% and a credit limit of $1,000. To celebrate, you decide to get that shiny new electric guitar (price: $400). On August 15, you head to the store, tell the clerk you are taking the guitar, and slap down your new card. You will be asked to authorize the purchase by signing the receipt—then the guitar is yours.

Basically, the guitar was bought on loan. At the end of the billing period (which is typically 30 days long), you get a statement in the mail or by e-mail. The statement will show the beginning and ending balance from the billing period, as well as any purchases and payments within the period. The guitar will appear as a purchase, along with the date it was purchased and the store from which it was purchased.

The bill will also state the APR for purchases—here 14%—as well as the periodic rate. (You can divide the APR by 12 to get the periodic rate for the month.) Your statement will also show the minimum amount due and the date by which it is due. The time between the statement closing date and the due date is called the grace period, and it is typically about 15 days.

If you pay in full by the due date, you will not owe any interest. If you make a payment by that date, but your payment does not cover the charges in full, the issuer will start to apply interest to the balance, using the appropriate periodic rate. As you learned earlier in the chapter, paying only the minimum can get you into trouble because it will take you a very long time to pay off the balance, and the creditor will keep adding interest. If you are charging other purchases in the meantime, you are extending the payoff period—and the ultimate costs—even further.

If you do not make *any* payment by the end of the grace period, you will owe a late fee, typically around $39 a month. The creditor may also report your late payment to the credit bureau, which can seriously harm your score. It may also decide to punish you with a penalty APR on new transactions.

Charging the Smart Way

Whether a card will be a positive or a negative in your life will be determined by the way you use it. There are a few well-known guidelines for credit card use that can help you to make the most out of one.

Stick with just a few cards. You can better curb temptation to spend, and manage payments if you are dealing with one or two cards, especially when just beginning to use credit. In general, you want to avoid department store cards; though these often come with a sign-up discount (like "20% off your first purchase!"). These often have much higher rates than regular cards however, and can hurt your credit score.

Choose cash over credit. Using cash or a debit card will help you stay within your budget. You will be more conscious about whether you can truly afford something when the money has to come straight from your account. Avoid charging everyday expenses like groceries or gas to a credit card. Your groceries will be eaten, or you will need another tank of gas before the bill even comes. Plus, you don't want to get too used to relying on credit for expenses that you should have budgeted for in your checking account.

Think before you buy. Credit cards increase the likelihood of impulse spending. Without a credit card, if you don't have cash for something, you can't buy it; but with a credit card, you may feel that you *can* buy it, and then pay it back later. Before you purchase something on credit, ask yourself these questions: Is it a want or a need? Can I wait to buy it until I've saved enough cash? If I charge it, when will I be able to pay for it? The answers can help you refrain from impulse buys. So can referring back to the budget you created in Chapter Three.

Pay in full, or at least pay more than the minimum. As you have learned, making only minimum payments will have you paying for the item for years to come, and it will be far more expensive than the item's actual price. Besides, carrying a balance can have consequences on your mental health (debt can be worrisome), and your credit rating.

Penny and Nick

"You won't believe the amazing snowboard I found online today, Pen," Nick told Penny.

"Sounds great," she replied, thinking more about badminton practice that night than a silly snowboard.

"Only one problem," he said. "It costs $500. I wish I had a credit card! I'd buy it right away!"

Penny hears this and immediately begins to tell Nick about the pros and cons of credit use for this type of purchase. What would she say?

Initiating a Dispute

You should carefully read your monthly statements and reconcile them against receipts for the things you've charged. This should help you notice billing errors, such as a charge in the wrong amount, a charge for something you never received or didn't purchase, a lack of credit for a payment you made. Or you may discover fraudulent transactions (charges made by someone using your card without your permission). As noted earlier, you have limited liability for fraudulent transactions when using a credit card. Still, you should contact your card issuer if you see an unexpected transaction on your statement, as you may lose your protection if you do not report these within 60 days.

Should you see an unusual transaction—be it human error or real fraud—you should call the card issuer, and follow up with a letter to the "billing inquiries" address on the bill, within 60 days of the bill on which the error first appears. In the letter, include your name, account number, and an explanation of the error along with any necessary photocopies of documentation or proof that you may have. The FTC recommends following the format given at *www.ftc.gov/bcp/* (click on the "ID theft" link, and look under "Facts for Consumers").

Under the Fair Credit Billing Act, you are not required to pay an amount in dispute, or any applicable finance charges, until the issue has been resolved. The company must send you a letter in explanation, either stating that they will make a correction (including any relevant fees and finance charges) or they have found no error and what they will be charging you (with finance charges during the dispute).

The most you would have to pay for a fraudulent transaction is $50. If you realize your card was lost or stolen you should call the issuer immediately, doing so could reduce your liability to nothing if you report the loss before the card is used.

MAKING CENT$ OF IT

In the section "Charging the Smart Way" (page 186), four ways of smart credit card use are listed. List them in order of importance *to you*, and explain why each one falls where it does on your list.

Example: 1. *Pay with cash over credit. Not using the card means not accidentally accruing fees that I can't afford.*

2. *Have fewer cards. I don't want to have many cards anyway, so this is important to remember.*

3. . . .

4. . . .

Fast Facts *Rewards Cards Encourage You to Charge More*

You might see card offers that promise things like cash back, airline miles, or points earned. Many card companies offer rewards programs, through which you earn these miles, points, or money back on each dollar you spend. **Rewards cards** can be a good deal for some people. For others, however, it is just temptation to earn more "points" by spending more money. These cards also often come with higher interest rates. Before you sign up for one, make sure you're the type who will pay the bill in full every month. These cards also have annual fees, so you will want to make sure the rewards benefit will balance out the overall cost of the card for you.

Other Forms of Credit and Loans

TERMS TO KNOW

financial aid	Stafford Loan	security deposit
grants	unsubsidized student	rent-to-own
scholarships	loans	in-store financing
work-study	PLUS loan	payday loans
Free Application for Federal	private student loans	overdraft protection
Student Aid (FAFSA)	refinance	line of credit
Perkins Loan	closing costs	pawnshops
subsidized student loans	lease	pawnbroker

Getting Started

Credit cards will probably be one of your first introductions to borrowing, and you will likely use these throughout your life. As your life proceeds, you will also find need for other forms of credit—to pay for college, to buy a car, or to buy a house. So in this section, you will learn more about student loans, auto loans, and mortgages. You will also be introduced to some forms of credit you might want to steer clear of, such as in-store financing, payday loans, overdraft protections, and rent-to-own agreements.

Borrowing for College

The average tuition and expenses for four years at a public college is $60,000, according to the College Board. So even if you and your parents have been diligently saving for your education, you might need **financial aid**, or assistance from other sources. Financial aid can include **grants** (free money from the government or school, typically given to those with financial need), **scholarships** (free money given based on criteria like academic ability or athletic skill), **work-study** (a job that will provide you with money for college expenses), and of course, loans.

Obviously, the first three are better options because they need not be paid back, but not everyone qualifies for them. Fifty-three percent of full-time college students take out loans to pay for school, according to the National Postsecondary Student Aid Study. The average graduate with loans comes out owing $20,098, according to the Project on Student Debt. You may have to take on some loans, too.

Getting financial aid usually begins with filing the **FAFSA**, or **Free Application for Federal Student Aid**. This form asks you and your parents for information on your finances in order to determine your *expected family contribution*—or the portion of college costs that you are expected to be able to pay out of pocket—as well as your eligibility for grants, work-study and loans. You can file this as early as January first of the year you plan to enroll in college, and you have to file again each subsequent year you attend.

There are three types of student loans you might hear about: federal loans to students, federal loans to parents, and private loans. Students are generally advised to commit to loans in that order, as the federal loans—which are guaranteed by the U.S. government—tend to come with the lowest rates.

The cheapest government loan to students is the **Perkins Loan**. These are given to students with exceptional financial need. Undergrads can get up to $4,000 per year, for a maximum of $20,000 in total. The interest rate on these installment loans is fixed at a very low rate. Perkins Loans are **subsidized student loans**, which means they don't accrue interest until you finish school. There is then a ten-year repayment period, but first a nine-month grace period after graduation before you need to start paying back the loan.

The other fixed-rate government loan to students is called the **Stafford**, and the interest rate on this is usually one or two percentage points higher than the Perkins but still lower than most other college loans. Some Stafford Loans are subsidized, but many are **unsubsidized student loans**, meaning the interest accrues while you're in college. The subsidized kind is given to students with financial need who don't qualify for a Perkins or who need more than a Perkins can provide. *Any* student is eligible for an unsubsidized Stafford. This is the best available loan for many students from middle-class families. The amount you can get depends on your year in school (juniors and seniors can borrow more than freshman and sophomores) and whether your parents are helping you pay for school. You have to start paying the loans back nine months after graduation, and the term length is usually ten years.

Your parents can take out a **PLUS loan** ("Parent Loan for Undergraduate Students"). These have much higher borrowing limits—in fact, these can usually cover the rest of tuition. The rates are a bit higher than on the Stafford Loan, and these are not available subsidized. Payments are owed on the loan almost right away.

Private student loans are usually advised only as a last resort. These are issued by banks, and are not regulated by the government. There are no limits on how much you can borrow, but these loans also typically come with high rates. The rates are also variable—meaning they can go up or down over the term of the loan—whereas federal loans are fixed. Unlike federal loans to students, the rate you get on private loans is based on your credit history, and that of your parents if they are cosigning. You typically need a credit score of 650 or more to get approved.

These loans may come with a grace period after graduation, meaning that repayments won't have to start until six or 12 months after you finish school.

Borrowing to Buy a Car

In the next few years, there's a good chance that you will need to buy a car. If you buy a car used, you may be able to pay for it out of savings. If you buy new—or if you buy a relatively new used car—you may have to take out an auto loan. This will be a standard installment loan in which the car you buy serves as collateral.

Before buying a car, it pays to start by looking at your budget to see how much you can afford to spend each month on an auto loan, when adding in new expenses like insurance and gas. That way, you are less likely to fall in love at the showroom with a car that's outside your budget. Once you have an estimate on what you can afford, you can research car options and prices (on sites like *Edmunds.com* or *KBB.com*).

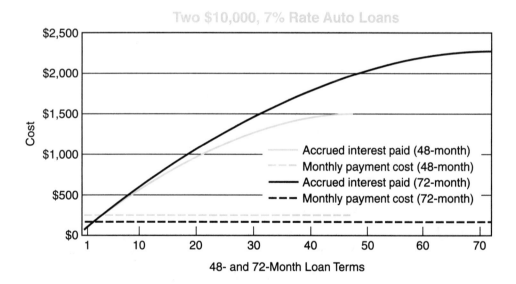

Two $10,000, 7% Rate Auto Loans

Legend:
Accrued interest paid (48-month)
Monthly payment cost (48-month)
Accrued interest paid (72-month)
Monthly payment cost (72-month)

48- and 72-Month Loan Terms

How do the monthly payments compare for these two $10,000 auto loans? How does the accrued interest paid compare? What are the advantages of each loan?

Unlike homes or real estate, cars do not appreciate; instead, they *de*preciate, losing value the minute they leave the dealer's lot. According to some sources, a new car will lose as much as 65% of its value within the first five years. That means you will not recoup (get back) much of what you paid when you decide to sell. So, if you don't plan to drive the car until it stops running, you may want to consider resale value as you choose a car. (This information is available on the Web sites mentioned on the previous page.)

You can borrow the money you need to buy a car through the dealer, or you can go out on your own and get a loan from a bank or credit union. A dealer may offer certain incentives to encourage you to buy, such as a rebate (a discount on your purchase), or special loan terms (like offering 0% APR for 60 months). There are many online calculators that can help you compare incentives and financing offers.

To take on an auto loan, you will typically need to make a down payment of ten to 20% on the car. The more you put down—you can certainly pay more than 20%—the less your monthly payments will be. Because of depreciation and interest costs, saving more to make a bigger down payment means you avoid paying loans for longer than you use the car.

Auto loans generally come in 36-month, 48-month, 60-month, or 72-month terms. Because cars lose value so fast and because the longer loans tend to come with higher rates, you probably want a loan of 48 months or less. Yes, taking a longer loan will let you buy a fancier ride with the same payment, but the longer loan can be a burden. On a $25,000 auto loan, you pay $2,264 *more* in financing charges (interest) with a 72-month term (total cost: $31,559) than with a 48-month one (total cost: $29,295). You may even need or want a new car before the six years (72 months) are up. Keeping four years as a maximum is a good measure to gauge if you can afford a car's price as well; if you can't handle how much the monthly payments cost at 48 months, you might want a less expensive car.

MAKING CENT$ OF IT

You earn $45,000 a year and want to buy a $27,000 Toyota. You can make a down payment of 20% of the vehicle's price.

1. How big a loan do you need?

2. You are offered two loans: 36-month term at 6%, or 48-month term at 5%. Which do you choose and why? Take a guess at how much the payments would cost per month for both loans. Explain your answers.

Try out one of the auto loan calculators at *www.bankrate.com/calculators.aspx* to get a sense of monthly costs for different loans and terms.

Borrowing for a Home

A house is typically the most expensive purchase a person will make in his or her whole life. Since most people can't pay in cash—that would require having hundreds of thousands of dollars in the bank—they must take out a mortgage. Residential real estate often appreciates and you can get a tax deduction on mortgage interest and real estate taxes paid, not to mention you would own the place where you and your family live; so a mortgage is typically considered good debt.

A homebuyer will need somewhere between 3% and 20% of the asking price in cash as a down payment, or initial investment. (If the buyer can't put down 20%, the lender will require what's called private mortgage insurance. You pay about 0.5 to 1% of the mortgage for a policy that covers the lender if you default.) The home price, minus the down payment, is the amount you will need to borrow for a mortgage loan. Let's imagine you're buying a $200,000 house and are able to make a down payment of 20%. That would be $40,000. So you'd need a mortgage of $160,000.

With a mortgage, the house is collateral against the loan, meaning the bank can foreclose—or seize the property—if payments are not made. This is why it is very important to be sure you can afford the mortgage before you take it on; if the bank forecloses on you, you will not have a place to live. Due to the damage it will cause on your credit score, you may have to rent for many years because creditors won't be eager to take another risk on you. A common rule of thumb is that you can afford a mortgage of two and a half times one year of your salary. By that measure, if you make $60,000 a year, you should aim to take on no more than $150,000 in mortgage debt.

You can find a mortgage via a bank, savings and loan, or credit union, but you can also go to a mortgage broker, who sells products from a variety of lenders. The typical mortgage comes in terms of 15 or 30 years. Some mortgages are fixed-rate, meaning they stay at one interest rate for the life of the loan. Others are adjustable-rate, meaning the interest rate is reexamined and can be changed by the bank during the life of the loan. Mortgage rates tend to be based on personal credit risk, but also on general investment market trends. (If going rates fall below the current rate on your mortgage, you can **refinance**, or trade your loan in for one with different terms, though there are fees associated with doing this.)

Home buyers also must budget for the back-end costs of getting a mortgage, for things like attorney fees and credit checks; these are called **closing costs**, and can run 1% to 4% of the loan amount.

Renting Versus Owning a Home

Even though a mortgage is considered good debt, it does not always make sense to buy a home. Renting, though it will not build equity, may be a better choice for those who don't have savings for a down payment, those who have a lot of debt, those who don't desire to do home maintenance, as well as those who anticipate moving within three to seven years or so (with closing costs and agent fees on homes, you might lose money buying and selling so quickly).

Especially at a younger age, it's probably best to be renting, as you are likely to move a few times as your income rises, job opportunities come up, you move to a new city, and your needs change.

To rent an apartment, you will typically need to sign a **lease**, a contract between you and a landlord stating the period of time you will live in the apartment and how much you will pay per month. This document should also say when the rent is due, which utilities the landlord will pay for, whether you can have pets, what you can and can't do to the apartment (for example, paint the walls) and whether you can sublet (rent out the apartment to someone else).

The landlord will also require a **security deposit**, or sum of money up front to guarantee against any damage to the apartment, or delinquency in paying the rent. You will get this back when you move out, assuming you kept the place in good condition. Moving out before the rental term is up is called "breaking the lease," and since you are violating the terms of a contract, you could possibly be obligated to pay out the terms of the lease.

MAKING CENT$ OF IT

Danielle earns $75,000 a year, and is looking at a house that costs $220,000. Her credit qualifies for a 6% APR on a 15-year fixed-rate loan.

1. What would a 20% down payment amount to?

2. Let's say Danielle had saved that much before house hunting. Now how much would she need in a mortgage loan to cover the rest?

3. Using the rule of thumb noted earlier, is this considered affordable on her salary?

When Not to Borrow

Sometimes the costs of using credit outweigh the benefits. Some examples:

Rent-to-own. A number of chain stores offer consumers the ability to rent big-ticket items like furniture and electronics for a set fee each week or month, and build equity toward ownership. This is an installment loan in which the item itself is being loaned, and the interest is built into the price.

You can return the item at any time, and cease making payments—but you lose what you put into it. What most people who take advantage of these deals find appealing about them is that they can own the item outright if they keep paying through the entire term, usually 18 months. This is especially attractive to those with poor credit histories: The payments look affordable, and they don't have to pass a credit check.

Problem is, the payments are spread out over such a long time that buying an item through **rent-to-own** will cost you often *more than double* the retail price of the item at any other store.

Let's take a computer that retails for $1,400. At one rent-to-own retailer, the price per week is $35, and payments last 78 weeks (a year and a half). By the time you finish paying for it, you have spent $2,730—almost double its list price! You could have just saved the $35 a week instead and been able to buy the computer yourself within 40 weeks.

In-store financing. Furniture store ads often promise that you buy an item now, with zero interest APR and no payments for 12 months. That means you can get, say, a whole bedroom set without having to pay for it until the following year. It's called **in-store financing**.

Such deals can be much more costly than they appear. That "zero" rate applies only to the one-year period. Even during that time, interest is accruing, at a rate usually in the double digits, often upwards of 25%. You don't have to pay any interest within the 12 months; but at 12 months and one day, if you haven't paid off the bill completely, all that interest will be applied in a lump sum onto the rest of your bill. Generally, you're better off paying with a regular credit card for the item, unless you know you will pay off the item completely within the year period.

Payday loans. **Payday loans** are cash loans for people who, for one reason or another, need money before their next paycheck. These are short-term loans—usually two weeks—written up to the amount of the coming paycheck.

The rate for two weeks on these loans can be 15% or more! That means a $325 loan may cost $373.75 by the time the paycheck comes ($48.75 in interest over two weeks!).

The Center for Responsible Lending (CRL) calls this practice predatory, saying that almost everyone who uses this type of loan cannot afford the interest, and therefore they renew the loan. According to CRL, the average user of these loans pays $800 back on a $325 loan. Many states have put laws into play to rein in payday lenders, limiting the interest that can be charged, but the loans can still be expensive. The best way around them? Stick to your budget!

Bank overdraft protection/line of credit. These are credit products offered to checking account customers by their banks. Ordinarily, if you try to withdraw money from your account—via a check, ATM, debit purchase, or electronic payment—and you don't have the money in your account to cover the cost, the bank will charge you a non-sufficient funds fee, and the transaction usually won't be processed. If you've written a check, the business on the receiving end may also charge you a return fee. Now if you agree to **overdraft protection**, the bank will pay out what has been overdrawn, usually at a fee of $20 to $35 per transaction. You are usually required to pay it back promptly. It's basically a short-term loan of the money. Alternatively, you could link your account to a **line of credit** at the bank—which is revolving debt, like a credit card you use through your debit card or checkbook. Whatever can't be paid out of your account will be charged onto the line. You may pay an annual fee for the line, or a fee just when you overdraw, plus interest on any money charged to the line of credit. Usually, the APR is as high as a credit card's rates.

A less expensive option? Have the bank link your savings account with your checking account, so that the money comes out of the savings when you go over the checking account's balance. You may have to pay a fee if you overdraw, but it's usually around $10. Check your balances frequently, so that there's less of a chance you overdraw at all.

Pawnbrokers. Some people borrow money via **pawnshops**. They bring in a valuable item—such as jewelry, a musical instrument, a camera, or a computer—to these stores in hopes that the **pawnbroker** will make a short-term loan up to the value of the item. (These are loans typically under $1,000 dollars.) The item becomes the collateral. So if the borrower does not pay back the principal and interest within a certain period of time, he or she forfeit rights to the valuable item, and the pawnbroker will put it up for sale to *recoup* the amount loaned out. The majority of pawned items are reclaimed by the original owner, yet getting the items back is quite costly. Many states have caps on the interest charged, but it can still add up. You can expect an APR of 50 to 400% (one to 8% per week!). Again, it would be cheaper to use a credit card. Hopefully, budgeting and financial planning (from Chapter Three) will keep you on track and able to avoid forms of credit such as these.

MAKING CENT$ OF IT

Imagine these two scenarios and answer the questions.

Part 1: You decided to get that flat-screen TV you have been eyeing. At the store it costs $1,075. If you rent-to-own it, you would only have to pay $105 a month for a year and a half, and it would be yours. You don't have all the money right now to purchase it, so you consider the rent-to-own option. Calculate how much more you would pay if you rent to own vs. buy from the store. If you just saved that $105 a month, how many months would you have to wait without the TV before you could pay for it in cash?

Part 2: You need a payday loan for your next paycheck, $500. You're told that after one week, you would have to pay back $525 for the loan. What percentage is that in interest on your loan? Your next paycheck is in two weeks. How much would you owe in total after those two weeks? (Hint: interest compounds per week. Apply charges correctly.)

CHAPTER REVIEW
Master the Vocabulary

Use the personal finance terms from the start of each section to complete the following sentences.

1. _____, or a loan, is an advance of money from a lender with the agreement that the borrower will pay it back later.

2. The amount of money loaned out is known as the _____.

3. _____ is the interest rate on a loan, expressed as an annual percentage of the principal.

4. The _____ is the interest banks charge their best borrowers— typically businesses and corporations.

5. An installment loan is sometimes called _____ because there is a set term by which the amount must be paid off.

6. _____ is the display of the repayment schedule on an installment loan.

7. With revolving credit, also known as _____, you are given a credit limit and are allowed to charge up to that amount.

8. If you do not pay your credit card in full at the end of the billing period, you carry a _____ on your card.

9. Secured debt is debt that is guaranteed against some _____ that the lender can seize if the loan is not paid off.

10. If you miss one payment on a credit account, you will be considered _____; if you miss multiple payments, the lender may declare the account in _____, meaning you have not abided by the conditions of the loan.

11. Credit accounts that go unpaid may be sent to a company known as a _____, which may initiate repossession of collateral against the borrower, or worse.

12. If you cannot pay your debts, you may have to declare _____ —a last resort in which you legally declare your inability to pay in order to be freed from some debt—though doing so will impair your ability to get credit in the future.

13. Creditors may look to assess your _____, or ability to pay a loan back, before deciding to issue you credit.

14. Lenders use your _____, which documents your borrowing history, and your FICO _____, which is based on a scale of 850, to judge your creditworthiness.

15. The three _____, which prepare credit reports for lenders, are called Experian, TransUnion and Equifax.

16. The _____ on a credit card is the time between the statement date and the payment due date, during which you will not be assessed finance charges on new purchases.

17. A credit card company that uses the _____ method to calculate finance charges would add up the balances for each day during the cycle (minus any payments) and divide by the number of days.

18. The _____ is what your interest rate will go up to if you violate the terms of your credit card agreement—it can be as high as 30%.

19. Some common forms of _____ are: grants, work-study assignments and loans. To get this assistance to pay for college you must first fill out the _____ .

20. _____ and _____ are names of student loans guaranteed by the federal government.

21. _____ college loans are the types that do not accrue interest while you are in school.

22. If you rent an apartment, you may have to sign a _____, or contract with the landlord, and put down a _____, or sum of money up front to guarantee against any damage to the apartment, or delinquency in paying the rent.

23. _____ stores offer consumers the ability to rent items like furniture and electronics for a set fee each week or month, and build equity toward ownership.

24. _____ are short-term loans made in cash that are basically an advance on the next paycheck. They can have very high interest rates and have been called predatory by some consumer advocacy groups.

25. Sometimes people bring a valuable item to a _____ , in hopes of getting a short-term loan up to the item's worth.

Apply What You've Learned

1. What might some of the consequences be if you stopped making payments on a loan for several months?

2. Which of the following is not an example of an installment loan?

   A. auto loan

   B. credit card

   C. mortgage

   D. student loan

3. April is looking to borrow $5,000. These are her loan options:

Loan A	Loan B	Loan C
8% APR	8.5% APR	9% APR
36 months	24 months	48 months

   a. Which of the following installment loans will end up costing her the least?

   b. Which will have the lowest monthly payments? Try the online calculator at *www.bankrate.com/calculators.aspx*.

4. Ming borrows $1,000 at a 5% APR, with an installment loan that has a 6-month repayment period. What is the monthly periodic rate on her loan?

5. Name three advantages and three disadvantages of credit cards.

6. Javier's credit card charges interest using the average daily balance method. The following are his day-to-day charges for the previous billing cycle. If he did not pay off his card in full, what is his average daily balance for this billing cycle?

   September transactions: 15 days the balance was at $400; 12 days at $500; and 3 days at $700.

7. Assuming all the following college loans are available to you, in which order should you take them?

   A. Perkins Loan

   B. PLUS loan

   C. private loan

   D. Stafford Loan

8. Sanjay's parents are buying a new house. Their total annual income is $80,000.

   a. What is the maximum loan recommended at their income level?

   b. The house they're buying is priced at $200,000. They will be able to pay for 20% of the house's appraised cost as a down payment. How much is that?

   c. How much of a mortgage will they then need? Does that exceed the recommended level?

CHAPTER 6

Managing Risk

Chapter Objectives

Students will:

✔ Understand the importance of insurance for managing risk
✔ Learn about auto, renters, and health insurance
✔ Read about other insurance encountered later in life

Personalize It! *Think about something you've recently lost: for example, a sweater you accidentally left at the football stadium, or a video game your friend borrowed and scratched. Now consider this: what if you could have paid $1 to guarantee that you'd have been compensated with a similar item, or cash up to its value if something happened to the item? Would you do it? What if the item were worth more, like $100, $1,000, or $10,000?*

Introduction

You take risks everyday. You may get up late and chance missing the bus; you may risk hurting one friend's feelings by hanging out with another after class; you may decide to try the mystery meat in the cafeteria.

In a general sense, risk represents the probability of a bad thing happening. When we speak of risk from a financial perspective, we're referring to the chance of losing money, or something of monetary value.

One way we protect our finances from certain risks is with **insurance**. Insurance is a contract between you and a company, in which you promise to make regular, small payments in exchange for that company's promise to help you cover certain types of possible loss, monetary or other. In this chapter, you learn about how insurance works, why it's important, and what you need to know about some common kinds of insurance.

Using Insurance to Manage Risk

TERMS TO KNOW

health insurance	life insurance	underwrite
homeowners insurance	premium	exclusions
renters insurance	claim	deductible
disability insurance	policy	insurance agent
auto insurance		

Getting Started

Having the right kind of insurance—and in the right amount—can be re-assuring, especially when you need it suddenly. You know this if someone in your family broke their leg and had to go to the hospital. If you or your parents got into a fender bender. If someone broke into your house. If one of your family fell ill and was not able to work. After everyone does an appropriate amount of panicking, one of your parents probably utters: *"Thank goodness we have insurance."*

Why Insurance Makes Sense

To some extent, risks are avoidable. For example, you have probably learned already that speeding while driving increases the chances that you will cause a car accident. By not speeding you can reduce your chances of causing an accident—and also your chances of losing money to hospital bills, car repairs, and lawsuits. (Not to mention the fact that you're avoiding hurting someone else or yourself, getting arrested, or making your parents angry.)

Problem is, we can't avoid all risks. Just because you're smart enough to drive at the right speed and wear your seatbelt, it does not mean the next person is. You're still at risk of an accident caused by other factors outside your control.

Since you can't avoid everything, you try to *mitigate* some of the risk—in other words; you try to reduce the likelihood of bad things happening, or to reduce the impact if they do. In the car, that means driving safely and defensively, wearing your seatbelt. You also lessen risk by wearing a helmet when biking; by putting a smoke detector in your home; by keeping expensive jewelry in a safe; etc.

We can all afford to accept some risk. If you eat the mystery meat in the cafeteria for lunch, you know what the consequences could be. While they are not pleasant, they are also not devastating. So you go ahead and eat it, knowing there's a chance you might get to see that lunch a second time. You may accept certain financial risks in the same way: Ever gone to buy electronics and been pitched the extended warranty? Perhaps you weighed the offer then said no, figuring you could bear the cost of fixing the item should it break; if so, you accepted risk.

After accepting some risk—and doing your best to lessen others, there are some risks where a lot of money is at stake. Unless you have that money saved up, you might not have the means to accept the risk. In these cases, you might share the risk with an insurance company. Basically, by buying insurance, you are transferring some of the risk to the insurance company, and it has agreed to bear the bulk of any losses incurred from the situation it covers. Insurance is intended to be a cost-effective way of protecting against the worst-case scenario. Insurance can, for example:

- Help you pay costly medical bills if you become ill (**health insurance**)
- Cover loss of, or damage to, the place you live or the things you own (**homeowners** or **renters insurance**)
- Provide income if you're sick or hurt and not able to work (**disability insurance**)
- Pay for the costs associated with getting into a car accident, including medical bills, legal fees, and car repairs (**auto insurance**)
- Provide people who count on someone's income with financial stability if they die (**life insurance**)

While insurance sometimes helps pay for regular expenses (health insurance, for example, may cover your annual physical), its ultimate purpose is to reduce expenses in situations where costs could be devastatingly large (like surgery or long-term hospital care). The policyholder, therefore, is deciding to part with a small amount of money to protect against having to pay an enormous amount of money if and when something happens.

If your house burned down in a fire, say, it would mean that you'd lost the money you put into it, which may be in the hundreds of thousands of dollars. It would also mean that you'd have to spend money to replace it—and you would have to sacrifice future resources to do so. Insurance helps cover the costs of rebuilding. Suffering from a serious illness or a chronic health condition such as diabetes could cost you tens of thousands in medical bills. Insurance would pick up the majority of those healthcare costs. Getting into a car accident might mean damage repair and medical bills. Insurance would assist in paying for these.

How Insurers Make Money

It's important to remember that insurers, like other financial companies that have been talked about in this book, are in the business to make a profit. So how do they do that? Why would they want to take on your potential losses, anyway?

Well, first of all, the **premiums**, or payments you must make in exchange for the insurance, are related to the amount of risk you represent—which means you may pay more or less than the person sitting next to you. Insurance companies use statistics to determine the chance of certain things happening to you; and therefore the chance that you file a **claim**, a request for reimbursement for something the insurance covers. Knowing that there are certain characteristics that make people more "risky" than others—be it age, health, habits, or even where you live—the insurer will ask you about these things when you apply. The specific risks the insurer will care about depend upon the type of insurance. (Increasingly, insurers are also looking at credit scores as a tool to determine policy price. The idea is that if you show irresponsibility with credit, you may not be responsible driving, or paying premiums, and should pay more.)

An insurer prices an insurance **policy**, or contract, based on the chance it will have to pay for a claim; so if the chances are high, the premium price will be high.

All that said, you may be able to reduce your premium a bit by reducing your risk: For example, if you have antilock brakes on your car, you may get a discount on auto insurance; if you have a home security system, you may get a reduction on homeowners insurance.

If the insurance company does decide to approve a policy for you, it has agreed to **underwrite** the risk, or assume it as their own. With a relatively large base of clients, the assumption is that some of them will make many claims (beyond the cost of their premiums) and some of them will make few or no claims (not even up to the premiums). The ideal, for the insurer, is that the client base contains fewer of the former group and more of the latter. That way the risk is spread out, and the company profits.

The insurance company prices premiums moderately, because it knows people would not want to buy insurance otherwise. These premiums are made to be affordable so that the cost in premiums seem less to you than the cost of not having the insurance.

How Insurance Works

Typically, an insurance policy is a physical document. It represents a legally binding contract between you and the insurer. A policy is written very specifically. No policy covers infinite losses—there's usually an exact dollar limit on what it will cover. The amount is often up to you to choose, but the higher you go, the more the policy will cost. (A policy offering $100,000 of coverage is more expensive than a policy offering $50,000 in coverage.)

A policy usually has **exclusions**, or certain conditions that it does not cover. For example, a health insurance plan may exclude acupuncture or medical massage. That means you can't get any payment on these. You should read any policy carefully so that you know what it does and does not cover.

"It's all here in the fine print. You're not covered against huffing and puffing."

 What is this cartoonist saying about the practices of insurance companies and their policies? Define *exclusion***.**

Policies also usually have what is called a **deductible**—the amount of money the policyholder must pay before the insurance will bear some of the costs. For example, a policy with a $500 deductible will make you pay the first $500 of a claim. Plans with higher deductibles often have lower premiums, and vice versa. A high deductible policy may seem appealing since it lowers monthly payments, but it leaves you more vulnerable. It means you are running the risk, if something happens, of having to come up with that entire deductible to, say, pay your medical bills or fix your car before the insurance helps out.

When you sign up for insurance, you will get a copy of the written policy. The most important page is the declarations page, which will state:

- your name
- the name of the insurance company
- the date the policy begins and expires
- a description of what's being insured
- the premium, which may be charged monthly, semi-annually, or annually
- an explanation of coverage, including limits

Once you have a policy, you are insured. So if the thing you are insured against happens, you can submit a claim—which may include receipts or other proof—with the insurance company to receive payment. (Health insurance sometimes works differently, but we get to that later.)

Unfortunately, if you never file a claim, you don't get any money back; you are paying for the *protection* against loss, whether or not you end up needing it.

Getting Insurance

Some insurance we will discuss in this chapter may be offered to you through a job as part of a benefits package. Other types of insurance you find on your own. In such cases, you may need an **insurance agent**, someone who sells these products. You can also find insurance online, through an insurance company's Web site or an online broker site. If you're buying insurance on your own, you should get several quotes, because different companies may price certain risks differently.

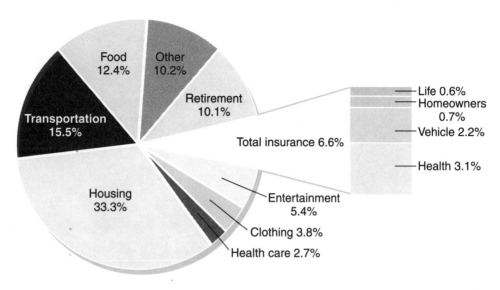

Source: Insurance Information Institute Fact Book 2009.

 Q: **Tori has vehicle and renters insurance. She spends $245 a month on both. She makes $3,000 a month net income. Her job gives her free health insurance. What percentage of her income is spent on insurance? Does this seem average?**

Unless you get insurance through work, you usually have to apply for it. That means filling out forms, to submit different documentation, or to submit to a medical exam, depending on the type of insurance.

However you find the insurance, you will want to do some research to make sure the insurer will be capable of paying your claims when you need them. A variety of investment analysis firms—including A.M. Best, Moody's, and Fitch Ratings—rate the chances that certain insurers will default on their obligations (meaning they won't be able to pay customers for legitimate claims). You should ask an agent what ratings an insurer gets and what that means; insurance brokerage Web sites should also have this information. You should also check with your state's department of insurance, which catalogs complaints against insurers.

Penny and Nick

"Ok, I guess I kind of get the point of insurance," Penny admitted as they packed up after sixth-period study hall. "But I still don't know if it's worth the money. It seems so expensive. I don't take risks. I'm young; I'm healthy; I'm a good driver. Do I *really* need it?"

"Penny, I know you're a good driver and all that, but I think insurance is like, a law or something," Nick explained. "Besides, if you ever got in an accident, you'd probably be happier if you had it."

Have Nick explain to Penny why she would be happier with insurance. Discuss how insurance works, how it would be useful, and what would happen without it.

MAKING CENT$ OF IT

Part 1: Name three insurance companies you have heard of, and what types of insurance you know they offer. If you can, search online for the ratings these companies receive through rating analysis firms like A.M. Best, Moody's, or Fitch Ratings.

Part 2: Write a paragraph: Explain the reasoning behind having insurance. Explain what it means to *underwrite* in insurance. Name three ways you can find and apply for insurance.

Basic Insurance Needs for Young Adults

TERMS TO KNOW

property insurance	no-fault laws
liability insurance	group health insurance
bodily injury liability coverage	pre-existing conditions
property damage liability coverage	co-pay
collision coverage	co-insurance
comprehensive coverage	out-of-pocket maximum

Getting Started

Right now, you may be covered on some of your parents' insurance policies. Once you move out on your own, however, you probably will need to get certain types of coverage for yourself. There are three types of insurances you may need in your late teens or early twenties: renters insurance, auto insurance, and health insurance. This section will cover what you need to know about these.

Renters Insurance

Whenever you rent an apartment, you might consider getting renters insurance. A typical renters policy has coverage for both property and liability damages. The **property insurance** portion protects your things—furniture, clothing, electronics, or other belongings—and it will cover these not just in your home, but wherever you are. It protects them from loss or damage caused by natural disasters, weather conditions, crime, or fire. The policy will provide you with money to buy replacement items. Without a policy, you will have to buy all new stuff if it is lost, stolen, or broken; and all of the money will come out of your own pocket. Renters insurance also typically provides some short-term living expenses if you are forced to stay elsewhere because of damage to the property. (Living in an apartment, you have the additional risk of being subject to issues originating in other apartments; for example, you may suffer smoke or water damage from a fire at your neighbor's place.)

Liability insurance protects you from legal responsibility. In a renters policy, it would protect you in the case you injure someone else, you damage someone else's property, or you are sued for either of these. For example, if a guest trips over your rug and breaks a bone, your renters policy would cover some of his medical needs; if your dog broke down the neighbor's fence, it would cover fixing that. It would also pay your legal costs, if he sues.

As with other types of insurance, premiums on renters insurance are primarily based on two factors: the likelihood that the insurance company will have to pay out and the amount they have to pay. To figure out the likelihood that you will file claims on your renters policy, the insurer will look at the area in which you live. Some areas of the country are more prone to natural disasters; some parts of a city are more prone to crime. The more risk you face in a certain area, the higher the premium will be. The insurer will also consider the age and construction of the building in which you live to estimate how well it could withstand certain types of risks and whether its current systems (like electric and plumbing) present any risks of their own. The price is also based on the amount of coverage you choose. The bigger your place and the more stuff you have, the more you pay. If you agree to a higher deductible, that reduces these costs, and vice versa.

Once you have a renters policy, if any of the incidents covered in the policy happen you must contact the insurer after the incident. You will likely be asked to fill out a claim form. You may need to include proof that the incident occurred, along with some evidence of value on property claims.

MAKING CENT$ OF IT

Two renters in the same building in Cleveland decide to buy renters insurance. The premiums for the policy on apartment 1A are almost double the premiums for the policy on apartment 1B. Considering the following features of each residence, why do you think the policy for apartment 1A is priced so much higher? Name three reasons.

Feature	1A	1B
Size	2 bedroom, 1 bath	1 bedroom, 1 bath
Fireplace	No	No
Window guards	No	Yes
Alarm system	No	Yes
Pets	One pit bull	Two fish in a tank
Fire, Carbon Monoxide Detectors	3, 1	2, 1

Statistically speaking, teenagers represent some of the riskiest drivers on the road (also the most likely to commit TWD, or texting while driving!). Chances are, you or someone you know will be party to an accident—hopefully minor—at some point in the next few years.

As you get older and gain more experience behind the wheel, your risks on the road decrease. The potential costs of an accident do not. As you have learned, insurance is meant to protect you in situations where the losses can be high. In this case, you may damage someone's very nice car and, at worst, need to replace it. You may hurt someone, so you may pay medical bills. You may also be sued if you did something wrong or illegal, and that could result in a court awarding the other person a certain amount of your assets or wages. For these reasons, most states require auto insurance for those who own and drive a vehicle.

We can't avoid all accidents. So, when they happen, having enough insurance to make sure you can recover from all the damages is necessary, for your health and your financial well-being.

Auto insurance policies generally come in terms of six months to a year, and are renewable. One policy may have some or all of the types of coverage listed on the following page.

- **Bodily injury liability** covers legal or medical responsibilities if another person is killed or injured and you caused the accident; no deductible.
- **Property damage liability** covers repairs needed—or replacement cost—for another person's car or other property if you caused the accident, as well as any legal costs if you are sued; no deductible.
- Personal injury protection/medical payments coverage covers medical expenses and money lost from being unable to work for you and any passengers of yours if you get hurt in an accident.
- **Collision coverage** covers damage to your car from an accident (may be required if car is leased or you have an auto loan).
- **Comprehensive coverage** covers damage to your car from anything other than an accident—a tornado or graffiti, for example.
- Uninsured and underinsured motorist property damage or bodily injury covers damage to your car or medical bills for you or your passengers if the person who hits you does not have insurance or doesn't have enough.

Your state probably requires that you have some liability coverage. Residents of Arizona, for example, must have coverage for bodily injury and property damage liability—a minimum $15,000 per person and $30,000 per accident for bodily injury, and $10,000 per accident for property damage. This might be written as 15/30/10, a common way insurers simplify the three types of liability. Your teacher will tell you what coverage is required in your state. Your property damage liability coverage pays for damage to the other person's car if you caused the accident. The other driver's liability pays if the other driver caused the accident.

In most states, the insurers for the parties involved end up paying for the medical costs incurred based upon degree of fault, meaning that if you caused the accident, the bodily injury liability part of your policy will pay, and if the other driver caused the accident, your insurance will try to get money from his insurance. Twelve states have **no-fault laws**, however, which mean your own insurance will pay for your medical costs no matter who caused the accident. These states are Florida, Hawaii, Kansas, Kentucky, Massachusetts, Michigan, Minnesota, New Jersey, New York, North Dakota, Pennsylvania and Utah. No-fault states require residents to have personal injury protection on their policy, which pays for their own medical costs. Some of these states have limits on suing for damages, as well.

The collision and comprehensive parts of a policy are often optional. Collision covers damage to your car when there is no other driver—for example, you hit a lamppost—and damage to your own car when you were at fault in an accident. Comprehensive covers break-ins or damage caused by weather or vandalism. (Unfortunately, auto insurance will never pay for normal wear and tear, such as needing a new muffler.) On collision and comprehensive, you will have to pay a deductible before the insurance will pay out. A higher deductible will lower your premium; though you need to be sure you could afford to pay the deductible should your car need fixing. Collision and comprehensive may not make sense for old cars—the policy won't pay more than the car is worth.

You can elect how much coverage you want on each part of the insurance. In fact, you may want more than your state's minimum requirement. Still, you should be aware that the greater the amount of insurance you get—and the more types of coverage—the higher the premium.

The other factors that affect insurance costs have to do with how much of a risk you represent. Some you can't change—your age for example. Teenagers and young adults pay particularly high premiums due to their lack of driving experience and higher chance of getting into an accident. If you were to maintain a good driving record, you would likely see your premiums decrease over time. How much you drive, and where you live also play a role in how much you are charged. City drivers are generally charged more as population density increases the risk of accident.

Some pricing factors *are* within your control. Among them:

The type of car you buy. The premium is based in part on how the vehicle responded in safety tests and how much it costs to replace. Also, certain cars are considered higher risk than others. Sports cars, for example, are associated with faster drivers and thus higher risk.

Your driving record. If you've had a lot of traffic violations or accidents in which you were at fault, or you've filed a lot or previous claims with the insurer, you represent a high risk. In fact, your insurance might increase premiums after you make a claim, as it sees you as a greater risk.

Your credit score. Insurers use this information to find out how good you are at paying bills on time, and to get a sense of how responsible you are.

What kind of discounts you qualify for. Most insurers offer price breaks for responsible behaviors (having been accident-free for three years, for example) or risk-prevention actions (having a car alarm). Many offer a percentage off to teens who maintain good grades.

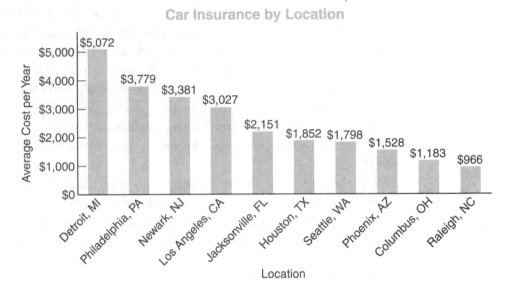

Car Insurance by Location

Source: Runzheimer International. *Note:* Assumes 100/300/50 liability limits, collision and comprehensive with $500 deductibles, and 100/300 uninsured coverage.

 Do an online search for "average car insurance costs" in your state. Make sure to look on sites that aren't trying to sell you insurance! What average did you find? Where does your state fall in this graph?

What to Do When an Accident Occurs

Pull over. In some states, you can be fined or put in jail for not stopping. Besides, physical pain and auto damage may not be immediately apparent. When you stop, pull over as far to the side as you can; you could cause further accidents by staying in the middle of the road.

Take stock. Assess the situation. Is anyone injured? Is there damage on either car? Is the accident blocking traffic? Phone 911 if there if there are any injuries, if the accident is serious, or if it is in the roadway.

Trade info. No matter who's at fault, you and the other driver should exchange names, addresses, driver's license numbers; vehicle identification numbers and license plate numbers; insurance company names and phone numbers; plus contact information for the policyholder if it's not you. (Most states require that you keep the insurance card in your car; most people put it in the glove box.)

Don't talk about the accident. Don't admit fault—you may not know all the circumstances and you don't want to implicate yourself. If you do, your insurance may have to foot the bill for the accident, and then your premiums may go up.

Document it. Write down how the accident happened. Use a cell phone or a disposable camera—carry one in your glove compartment—to take photos. If the accident involves a lot of damage, get contact info for any witnesses. Get the badge number of the highest-ranking police officer on the scene.

Report it. Ask the police for a copy of the accident report, if applicable. (You can and should file a report at the police station even if no police were needed on scene.) Call your insurer immediately afterward and give them all the information you have. You want your story told even if you were at fault—so that the other driver cannot claim it was worse than it was.

MAKING CENT$ OF IT

Sharon's auto insurance policy has the following features:

- Bodily injury and property damage liability limits are 100/300/25
- Collision has a $500 deductible
- Comprehensive has a $300 deductible

1. How much coverage does she have for bodily injury per person?
2. For bodily injury per accident?
3. How much coverage does she have per accident for property damage liability?
4. Let's say a piano falls on her car. The cost to fix the damage is $1,000. How much will her insurance pay?
5. Let's say she gets into an accident, and her car sustains $400 of damage. How much will her insurance pay?

Health Insurance

Unfortunately, none of us can predict with full certainty if and when we get sick. Even if you're healthy right now, you could, for example, fall in soccer practice and break your leg. Without health insurance, you might owe more than $10,000 for the ambulance, the hospital care and physical therapy. Health insurance is a cost-effective way to minimize and diminish potentially high health care costs, which are largely unpredictable.

Thanks to recent health reform legislation, you can stay on your parents' insurance until age 26; but you may get your own coverage once you get a job.

There are three primary ways to get health insurance: Purchase it through an employer (as you learned in Chapter Two), buy it directly from a health insurance company, or get it from the government. A recent package of health legislation will require that most Americans have health coverage by 2014.

Coverage through an employer is called **group health insurance**, and this is usually the cheapest option. Many employers pay part of the premium. Also, group insurance starts off less expensive because the risks are spread out among a number of people. With group insurance, no one who qualifies will be turned down—though certain **pre-existing conditions**, health issues that you had before the policy was purchased, may be excluded from coverage for a period of time.

Those who do not have the option of getting insurance through work will likely have to purchase individual coverage directly from an insurance company. This is typically more expensive because you don't get the advantage of a group rate and you have to pay the entire premium yourself. In most states, insurers can charge each individual a premium based upon age, state of health and risk factors. Before being approved for an individual policy, you may be subject to a health examination. Since smokers are at increased risk of lung cancer, for example, they would pay higher premiums than nonsmokers; so too would a cancer survivor in remission pay more than someone who'd never had cancer. For some people, particularly those who are in poor health or who have chronic conditions, individual insurance can be quite costly—but in coming years, the 2010 health reform legislation will provide subsidies to middle-income Americans to help make the insurance more affordable. As of now, an insurer can also completely exclude care for a pre-existing condition, or can deny a person coverage altogether; neither of these will be allowed as of 2014.

Some people have access to government-sponsored low- or no-cost healthcare programs: Medicaid, as you learned in a previous chapter, provides for Americans with limited financial resources who otherwise would not be able to afford insurance. Medicare was designed for Americans 65 and over, as well as those who suffer from certain disabilities. State Children's Health Insurance Program is for children whose parents can't afford health insurance but do not qualify for Medicaid.

No matter where you get it, health insurance typically covers a wide variety of medical costs: doctor's office visits, hospital stays, surgery and procedures, ambulance costs, blood tests and other medical tests, and prescription medicines. It typically also covers some amount of preventive care—like annual checkups and blood tests—with the understanding that prevention is cheaper than disease treatment. Vision and dental are usually not included in a health plan, but may be offered separately.

The specifics of what types of healthcare are covered, and to what extent depend on the policy. There is an array of plan types to choose from:

One kind (called fee-for-service) allows you to see any doctor you wish. Another (called an HMO) has negotiated discounts with specific doctors, hospitals and other providers, and you must use these care providers, or else you won't get any coverage. A third type of plan (called a PPO) is a hybrid of the other two, allowing you to get the highest amount of coverage if you use approved care providers, but also providing a lesser benefit if you go to doctors outside of the network. For example, you might be able to go see Dr. A, who is in the network, and pay $15 for a flu visit, or go see Dr. B, who is out-of-network, and pay $45 for the same type of visit. The more choices the policy provides, the more expensive it will be.

How costs are shared with the insurance company also depends upon the type of insurance you have. You may be charged a pre-agreed dollar figure, or **co-pay**, at the end of a visit—for example, $75 for the emergency room—and the rest of the bill is sent on to the insurer. Alternatively, the insurance may state that it will pay a certain percentage of the bill; this is called **co-insurance**. So if the percentage was 80%, and the total charge was $10,000, you would owe $2,000. Typically, the doctor will bill the insurer first then send you a bill for the remainder. In some plans, there is a deductible that must be met before insurance kicks in. Most plans state an **out-of-pocket maximum**, which is the amount you have to spend on medical bills within the year before the insurer covers all following costs.

Plans with higher premiums generally have lower deductibles, lower co-pays or co-insurance, and lower out-of-pocket maximums, and vice versa for plans with lower premiums. As with other types of insurances, the cheapest policy may not give you the protection you need or want.

Insurance Health Co. of USA

Comprehensive Medical

MEMBER NAME: JOHN DOE
MEMBER NUMBER: 123-45-678

EFFECTIVE DATE: 02-01-2009

GROUP # 876543-666-555

PRESCRIPTION GROUP#: 55522

PCP CO-PAY: $15.00
SPECIAL CO-PAY: $25.00
EMER. ROOM CO-PAY: $75.00

PRESCRIPTION CO-PAY:
$15 GENERIC
$20 NAME BRAND

MEMBER SERVICES: 1-800-987-2345
CLAIMS/INQUIRIES: 1-800-987-5432

Your health insurance card states your policy number, the basic terms of your coverage, and the insurance company's contact info. You should carry this in your wallet in case you need emergency care.

MAKING CENT$ OF IT

Ravi has a health insurance plan through his job as manager at Paco's Tacos. It has the following characteristics:

- $80 monthly premiums
- no deductible
- $15 co-pay for doctor visits
- $75 co-pay for emergency room visits
- $10 co-pay on generic prescription medicines, $25 for brand names

1. How much in premiums does he pay per year?

2. On his day off, he tries for a jump shot on the basketball court, but falls and hurts his leg. A friend helps him up, and drives him to the local hospital. The total cost of the X-rays, check-up, and crutches was $1,500. How much did Ravi pay?

3. The doctor prescribes a brand-name painkiller and a generic antibiotic. The cost of these is $400. How much did Ravi actually pay at the pharmacy?

4. Ravi follows up with his regular physician; the doctor's visit costs $150 without insurance. What did Ravi pay?

5. In totaling the actual costs of this accident and subtracting what Ravi had to pay, Ravi realizes the insurance has already saved him money. How much did he save? (Add his premiums and out-of-pocket expenses, and subtract that from the real costs of his accident.)

 *Health Insurance in the Midst of Major Change*

As of 2010, some 46 million Americans were going without health insurance—many of them because they could not afford to buy it on the private market. On March 23, 2010, President Barack Obama signed into law the Patient Protection and Affordable Care Act, which intends to make health insurance available for all people. It requires that most Americans have health insurance by 2014. To ensure this, it provides government assistance to middle-income families so they can afford insurance. It requires that companies with 50 or more workers offer group insurance, or else pay a tax fee per employee. It creates a new regulated marketplace upon which people can buy private insurance at more reasonable rates. It does not allow private insurers to deny coverage based on pre-existing conditions. Some portions of the law went into effect immediately, but the majority will be enacted by 2014.

6.3 Other Types of Insurance

beneficiary	will	living will
death benefit	estate	healthcare proxy
term life insurance	executor	worker's compensation
permanent life insurance	legal guardian	long-term care insurance

Getting Started

Over the course of your life, your financial situation will change. As it does, so will your insurance needs. This section will walk you through some of the other types of insurance you may encounter later in life.

Homeowners Insurance

If your parents own their home, they've likely put a large amount of money into it: they make a monthly mortgage payment on it, they may have spent money to remodel or otherwise upgrade it, and they certainly paid to furnish it. You can imagine, then, how devastating it would be to them—and you—if the house was damaged by a fire, was robbed, or was destroyed by a natural disaster. Your parents have likely purchased homeowners insurance to protect them against such losses.

Like renters insurance, a typical homeowners insurance policy has coverage for both property and liability. The property portion protects the house structure, and its contents from loss or damage—assuming it was caused by "acts of nature" like wind, rain, tornado, or volcanic eruption; or a fire, vandalism, criminal activity, or explosion. The difference is that homeowners insurance also covers the structure of the home and the property around it. (Renters insurance does not cover this because it is not up to you to pay for structural damage; it's up to the landlord.) Damages caused by earthquake or flood, however, are excluded; typically you have to insure these risks separately. Normal wear and tear expenses—like re-shingling the roof—are never covered.

A homeowners policy will also typically cover some expenses for other living arrangements, up to a limit, if you cannot live in your home due to any of the situations covered in the property part of the policy. The liability portion of a policy protects you from legal responsibility in much the same way a renters policy does. As with renters insurance, premiums on homeowners insurance are based on the specific risks to your home, the amount of coverage you choose, and the size of the deductible.

For insurance to work, premiums paid by consumers must exceed claims paid out, so that the company operates at a profit and can continue to sell new policies. The article below displays examples of how some companies attempt to keep costs low in areas where natural disasters can be devastating to homes.

"Homeowners still battle for higher payouts to fix Ike damages"
By Purva Patel
The Houston Chronicle

Hurricane Ike blew some shingles off William Cognata's La Porte home and loosened a lot more.

His roofer told him he needed to replace it, but his insurer offered $466 for repairs.

"Three roofers looked at it and told me to replace it. I'm no roofer, but I have some sense to know who to listen to," he said.

Area homeowners have survived the storm, waited weeks in some cases for the lights to come back on and opened their homes to insurance adjusters.

Now, as residents slammed by Ike work their way through the recovery process, some are entering a new phase: the battle for what they consider a fair settlement of their claims.

Some are complaining to regulators, hiring their own experts and, like Cognata, turning to attorneys to get higher insurance payouts.

More than 1,700 Texans so far have complained to the state about their insurance companies—everything from claims delays to unsatisfactory offers and denials.

That's a small percentage of the more than 530,000 claims filed already in the wake of Hurricane Ike, but state regulators say they're monitoring the number of reports and how they're resolved to make sure policyholders are treated fairly. The agency can require bigger payments if necessary.

"We certainly want to hear if there are any complaints about the claims process," said Jerry Hagins, a spokesman for the Texas Department of Insurance.

Cognata argues his insurance company should pay to replace the roof. The shingles can be lifted up by hand, some with creases at the top, something his roofer says can't be repaired. Getting nowhere on his own, Cognata has hired an attorney.

"You'd think they'd go ahead and do it to . . . prevent a $50,000 or $60,000 claim next year," Cognata said. "This is nothing but $5,000 or $6,000."

Chip Merlin, an attorney whose firm represents policyholders, said private companies handling claims on behalf of the flood program may be reluctant to make high offers. That's because overpayments could come out of their pockets.

After Hurricane Katrina, Merlin said, adjusters were paying out on flood claims and giving the benefit of the doubt.

"Now, for the first time, we're getting calls about national flood not paying enough," Merlin said. "Adjusters are taking a little bit longer, not paying quite as freely, and we think that's because the independent contractors will be responsible for any overpayment."

But the flood insurance program had held companies responsible for overpayments even before Katrina, said Butch Kinerney, a spokesman for the Federal Emergency Management Agency.

When the Texas Windstorm Insurance Association declined to send an engineer out to his home, Tom O'Brien hired an engineer and an attorney to help get more than the $43,000 offered by the association so far. "It's been hard to deal with this for the last two months," he said.

O'Brien, who has been remodeling and selling houses for the past six years, estimated it would cost at least $100,000 to repair a hole in the roof above his bedroom, bricks blown out of two different walls, cracks in his walls, and structural damage that occurred as his roof shifted.

A claims consultant said O'Brien's house in Dickinson would be too costly to repair and should be rebuilt from scratch.

Jim Oliver, director of the windstorm association, would say only that the adjuster's report didn't indicate an engineer was required.

He said the association would ask O'Brien to submit an estimate from a contractor and work with the adjuster to determine if more needs to be paid.

A larger payout would be welcome, but O'Brien shouldn't have to jump through so many hoops, said Javier Delgado, an attorney he hired on a contingency basis.

"No homeowner should have to hire their own experts. That's the duty of the insurance company," he said. "They're supposed to act in good faith and hire the experts if an expert is needed."

1. Describe exactly what the homeowners are fighting against.

2. Why are they taking legal action? Do they have the right to take this action?

3. Why do you think an insurance company would not want to pay a client what is needed to fix their home?

4. Do you think states have a responsibility to insure homeowners who knowingly build in higher risk areas? Why or why not?

MAKING CENT$ OF IT

Seamus O'Leary's parents have just renewed their homeowners insurance policy. It has the following specifications:

Annual Premiums cost $600

Policy Specifications	Coverage Limit	Deductible
Dwelling Protection	$200,000	$500
Personal Property	$100,000	$500
Loss-of-Use Living Expenses	Up to 12 months	$0
Family Liability Protection	$100,000 per incident	$0
Guest Medical Protection	$1,000 per person	$0

1. How much do they spend per year to keep the policy active?

2. The neighbor's kid accidentally threw a baseball through the window. Replacing the window cost $800. If this is the first claim the O'Learys have filed this year, how much would insurance pay?

3. Later in the year, a tornado damaged a portion of the roof. The damage cost $5,000 to repair. How much would insurance pay of this?

4. If their house was damaged by a flood, and repair cost them $20,000, how much would they get from insurance?

Life Insurance

Most families depend on earned income to make ends meet. So what would happen if a person who brings in a needed paycheck suddenly died? It could compound an emotionally difficult time by adding in financial stress. The point of life insurance is to eliminate this potential stress. A life insurance policy is meant to replace a certain amount of income upon one's death.

Typically, the people who need life insurance are those who have people depending on their income. These may be parents of young children, a single person who supports an elderly relative, or a couple who rely on each other's salary for quality of life.

The spouse and children of workers who pass away may also be eligible for Social Security Survivors Benefit, a kind of government-paid life insurance that is funded through people's payroll taxes. Many people get additional coverage, however, to offset the potential losses to the family. Life insurance is often offered as a benefit from an employer for free or little cost; it can also be purchased from an insurance agent. When you buy a policy, you get to name the **beneficiary**, or person who will inherit the money.

Three factors play into the cost of a life insurance policy: the type of policy, the risk someone represents, and the **death benefit**, or total amount that insurance agrees to pay.

First off, there are two main types of life insurance policies: **Term life insurance** covers a certain period of time—say, 15 years; so if the policyholder dies in that period, his or her beneficiary gets the benefits. **Permanent life insurance** doesn't expire as term does; it pays out as promised as long as premium payments are made. Also, policyholders are promised some kind of cash value, meaning they could cash out the policy at any time and get money back, with an investment return. Permanent life policies tend to be more expensive than term policies, because they cover a longer period of time and provide this investment option.

Second, the cost of a policy is dependent on the applicant's current health and relative risk of mortality—usually, applicants must submit to a medical exam. This means that it's cheaper to buy a policy at a younger age than when older.

Finally, the size of the benefit is a factor in determining price. The greater the benefit, the more expensive the premiums will be. The right benefit depends on future expenses for the years ahead. A family might also add an additional sum to cover big costs in the coming years (like a kid's college tuition) or the mortgage, as a way to ensure funds for these expenses if income is lost. Typically, experts recommend factoring in funeral expenses, too.

What a Will Accomplishes

Just as life insurance allows people to make plans contingent upon their death, so too does a **will**. A will is a legal document that states a person's plans for his or her **estate**—that is, all the assets he or she has accumulated, including a house, stocks, bonds, savings and any valuables like jewelry—after death. Without a will, the court chooses who will inherit the person's estate. Typically, the court will distribute the money to family members (a spouse and children get first priority), but this process takes time and the money may not end up in the hands the deceased would have preferred. Having a will reduces the risk of this taking place.

With a will, you name your own heirs, which can include people or even charities. Plus, you name an **executor**, or person who will responsible for making sure the money is distributed per your wishes. A will also allows parents to name a **legal guardian**, who will be charged with taking care of their minor children should anything happen. Within a will, you also can name a person to have certain responsibilities if you become sick or incapacitated to the point of being unable to make decisions: A **living will**, for example, states your medical wishes. A **health-care proxy** can make medical decisions on your behalf.

Disability Insurance

Just as a family might struggle financially if one of its breadwinners were to die, it also might be in a tough spot if one of the earners became sick or injured and could not work. Such a possibility is far more common than you might imagine: according to the Insurance Information Institute, 43% of all 40 year olds will have a disability lasting more than 90 days (out of work for three months or more) by age 65. Disability insurance protects against the financial damage that something like this would do. Policy-holders pay regular, nominal premiums; if an accident or sickness prevents them from working, the insurance company will replace a certain amount of income for that time.

If disabled, workers may be eligible for Social Security Disability Insurance (SSDI), a government program that comes out of Social Security taxes. If approved, payments begin six months after illness or injury occurs. If hurt on the job, an employee might also be eligible for **worker's compensation**, a kind of insurance that employers pay to cover wages and medical costs for workers who are injured at work.

Because these programs often do not replace enough income, some people also buy private disability insurance. There are two types: short-term and long-term. Short-term provides replacement of a certain portion of salary—usually no more than 70%—for up to two years. Long-term picks up where short-term coverage leaves off, and can replace up to the same or less income, often up through retirement.

Many people get some private disability insurance through their employers. Or someone can also purchase it or get additional coverage with an agent.

Long-Term Care Insurance

Perhaps you've had a grandparent who needed to go to an assisted living facility, an adult day care or a nursing home. If so, you may have heard your parents talk about how expensive these were. A year in an assisted living facility averages more than $36,000, while nursing home care runs more than $62,000 a year, according to a recent MetLife survey. Medicare covers only certain kinds of short-term nursing care, so some people purchase **long-term care insurance** to cover the rest.

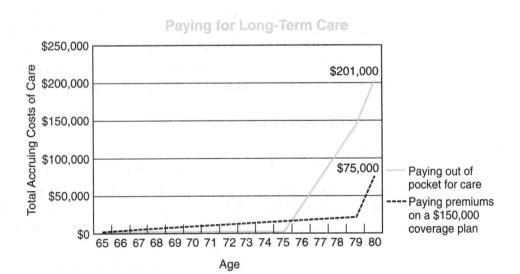

Paying for Long-Term Care

The previous graph shows long-term insurance total premium costs (with a max payout of $150,000) bought at age 65, vs. out-of-pocket payment for four years of assisted living and one year in a nursing home ($36,000/year and $57,000/year, respectively) starting from age 75. How much over the maximum payout ($150,000) from insurance was paid out-of-pocket the last year? What was the total cost saved because of insurance?

Typically, those who buy this insurance are people in their 50s or 60s who feel that paying out-of-pocket for long term care would compromise their finances. They may also be looking for ways to avoid becoming a burden to their children. As with other insurances, pricing is based on risk. So the older you are and the poorer your health, the more expensive a policy will be. (A medical exam is almost always required.) This insurance is often sold by employers at discounted rates; it can also be purchased from an agent or broker.

Other Types of Insurance

The aforementioned are among the most common types of insurance you will encounter. Of course, there are numerous others:

Type of Insurance	Who It's For	What It Does
Private mortgage insurance	People who are buying a home but can't afford to make a 20% down payment	Protects the lender from losing money if the borrower defaults
Pet insurance	People with domesticated animals	Helps pay veterinary bills
Extended warranty	People who are buying items like electronics or cars	Covers costs of servicing if they break within a certain period of time
Cell phone insurance	People with cell phone contracts	Provides a replacement phone if one is lost or damaged
Travel insurance	Those about to take a trip	Reimburses costs if trip must be cancelled or changed for certain reasons

Type of Insurance	Who It's For	What It Does
Wedding insurance	The soon-to-be married	Helps couple recoup costs if something comes in the way of the big day
Motor home insurance	Anyone who drives an RV	Provides property damage and liability coverage
Malpractice insurance	Doctors	Protects them from liability in case they are sued for an act that caused injury or death
Rental car insurance	People renting cars	Covers any damage or liability incurred while driving the vehicle

MAKING CENT$ OF IT

Choosing the right death benefit isn't an exact science. There are plenty of online calculators that can give you an estimate. Use the calculator at *www.lifehappens.org/life-insurance/life-calculator*, or find a different calculator by using a search engine to search for "life insurance calculator." For this exercise you can also just add up costs and losses as though the sole earner of the family plans for life insurance that could not already be covered by savings.

Come up with an estimated insurance benefit for a family's sole earner who:

- would have $15,000 in funeral expenses
- has two kids, ages 5 and 10, in public school
- has $250,000 outstanding on a mortgage, but no other debt
- has $10,000 in non-retirement savings and $300,000 in retirement savings
- brings in $60,000 a year that would need to be replaced for 20 years
- has no other life insurance

What might be a good policy amount for them to get? Explain your answer.

CHAPTER REVIEW

Master the Vocabulary

Use the personal finance terms from the start of each section to complete the following sentences.

1. _____ is a tool that helps protect you from the financial risk of loss.

2. The amount that you pay periodically in order to secure insurance coverage benefits is called a _____.

3. You may have to submit a _____, or request for reimbursement, in order to get money from your insurance company when something happens.

4. You may have to spend a certain amount of your own money—called a _____—before coverage kicks in.

5. A person who sells insurance is called an insurance _____.

6. _____ helps cover medical bills.

7. _____ reimburses homeowners for property damage or liability costs.

8. _____ helps pay for bills incurred in a car accident.

9. _____ helps older people pay for stays in nursing homes and assisted living facilities.

10. Renters insurance has two separate parts: _____ and _____ coverage; the first protects the structure of the apartment and your things; the second protects you from legal responsibility.

11. In states with _____ laws, your insurance will always pay for your medical bills after an auto accident, even if the other driver was responsible.

12. The kind of health insurance you get through an employer is called _____.

13. A flat fee you are charged at the doctor's office that represents your portion of the bill is called a _____; if you are instead charged a percentage of the total bill it is called _____.

14. With certain health insurance plans, after you spend up to the _____ maximum on your health insurance policy on medical costs, the insurance will pick up the rest.

15. The _____ is the amount of money the beneficiary of a life insurance policy stands to inherit.

16. _____ life insurance offers a benefit only if the policyholder passes away during a set period of years; _____ life insurance will provide the benefit if the policyholder dies any time after the policy has been written.

17. _____ replaces income if a person is unable to work due to sickness or injury.

18. The document that specifies your wishes for your assets after you die is called a _____ .

19. The person you have named to make sure your inheritance wishes are granted is called the _____ .

20. A will can also name a _____ , who will be charged with taking care of minor children if both parents are unable to.

21. A _____ is a document that states what your medical desires are if you are incapacitated. A _____ can make medical decisions on your behalf in such cases.

Apply What You've Learned

1. Give two reasons why insurance can be a valuable investment.

2. Match the type of auto insurance to the risk it covers.

   1. _____Bodily injury liability

   2. _____Property damage liability

   3. _____Personal injury protection

   4. _____Collision

   5. _____Comprehensive

   6. _____Uninsured motorist property damage or bodily injury

   7. _____Underinsured motorist property damage or bodily injury

   A. Covers medical expenses and money lost from being unable to work for you and any of your passengers

   B. Covers damage to your car or medical bills for you or your passengers if the person who hits you does not have insurance

   C. Covers damage to your car from an accident

   D. Covers damage done to your car or medical bills for you or your passengers if the costs exceed the other person's policy limits

   E. Covers repairs needed—or replacement cost—for another person's car, as well as any legal costs if you are sued

   F. Covers legal or medical responsibilities if the other driver or his passengers are killed or injured

   G. Covers damage to your car from anything other than an accident

3. Jamal is in a health insurance plan through his job. In the following table are the costs to Jamal for certain services, along with the deductibles:

Expense	In-Network	Out-of-Network
Yearly deductible	$0	$200
Doctor visits	$25 co-pay	20%
Emergency room	$50 co-pay	$50
Hospitalization	$0	20%

a. Jamal has a check-up appointment with Dr. Smith who charges $150 for such an appointment. If Dr. Smith is in-network, what will he have to pay?

b. If Dr. Smith is out-of-network, and Jamal has met his deductible, what will he pay?

c. If Jamal has not yet met his deductible, what will he have to pay?

d. Jamal has to have his tonsils taken out, and he must spend a night in the hospital. The cost is $4,000. How much of that will his insurance pay if the hospital is in-network?

e. How much if it is out-of-network?

4. You have the following homeowners insurance coverage:
Annual Premiums cost $750

Policy Specifications	Coverage Limit	Deductible
Dwelling Protection	$325,000	$1,000
Personal Property	$100,000	$1,000
Loss-of-Use Living Expenses	Up to 12 months	$0
Family Liability Protection	$100,000 per incident	$0
Guest Medical Protection	$1,000 per person	$0

a. The house burns down. You haven't yet filed any claims for the year. How much money will the insurance company pay out?

b. Your friend was in the house cat-sitting for you when the fire started from one of the electrical outlets. She got out in time, thankfully, but suffered smoke inhalation and had to go to the hospital. Up to how much will the insurance reimburse her?

c. You lost $80,000 in property that wasn't part of the house itself (furniture, electronics, etc.). How much will the insurance pay for what's lost if you had not used the deductible yet that year?

d. How long will the insurance pay the costs of you living elsewhere?

5. Come up with a benefit estimate on a life insurance policy that would be needed for a family's sole earner who:

- would have $15,000 in funeral expenses

- has one child, age 16, in public school

- has no outstanding mortgage and no other debt

- has $40,000 in non-retirement savings and $600,000 in retirement savings

- brings in $80,000 a year that would need to be replaced for 15 years

- has no other life insurance

Explain your reasoning.

6. Which of the following are typically covered by a homeowners insurance policy?

a. _____ repairs for wind damage

b. _____ painting to cover graffiti

c. _____ belongings stolen in a break-in

d. _____ repairs for water damage from flood

e. _____ a computer of yours that is stolen in a public library

f. _____ medical bills for someone who is bitten by your dog

g. _____ the washer/dryer that broke down suddenly

GLOSSARY

adjusted gross income: Earned income (wages or salary) and unearned income (interest income) added together.

advance-fee fraud: A scam artist promises something of value: a loan, a job, or access to some kind of discount, on condition that a fee is paid beforehand. The client pays the fee, but then does not get what was promised; the scam artist disappears with the client's money.

amortization: The reduction of a debt over time. An amortization table is used by lenders to show how payments are applied (part to pay interest and part to pay principal) over the loan term, and how that leads to paying off the loan.

annual percentage rate (APR): The percentage cost of credit on a yearly basis. The interest rate on a loan is expressed as an annual percentage.

annual percentage yield (APY): The percentage interest payments on a bank account on a yearly basis. The Truth in Savings Act of 1991 required that banks calculate and demonstrate to consumers a standardized APY for an account, so that various accounts are directly comparable.

appreciate/ appreciation: To gain in value/the gain in value.

apprenticeship: A formal training period, during which an individual is taught a trade or skill by someone more experienced.

asset allocation: Distributing investments among different asset classes. Stocks, bonds, options, mutual funds, CDs, T-bills, etc. are examples of different classes of assets.

assets: All the items of value that a person owns: whether properties, cash, securities, or other investments.

ATM (automated teller machine): A bank device that allows customers to make withdrawals and deposits at a machine instead of through a teller at the bank.

ATM card: A plastic card from the bank needed to use an ATM.

audit: A tax audit is when the government scrutinizes a tax return to check its validity, choosing someone either at random or purposely. The IRS audits a certain number of returns each year, requiring those taxpayers to provide proof for what they have claimed on their returns.

authorized user: A person issued a credit or debit card with their name on it, where that person is not the one in charge of paying the bill. They are authorized by the account holder to use the account.

auto insurance: Insurance a driver buys to protect against paying for the costs associated with getting into a car accident, including medical bills, legal fees and car repairs. Car owners are required by law to purchase such insurance.

average daily balance: A calculation that the credit card company uses to bill finance charges. With this method, the card company averages the balance on the card from each day of the month. Finance charges are based on this average balance.

balance: On a credit card account, the outstanding debt left on that card past the first billing period, when interest will start to accrue. In a bank account, the amount of money in that account at any point in time.

balance transfer: Taking the balance from a credit card and moving it to a different card account. Usually done to reduce interest charges, often by taking advantage of a special offer.

bank statement: A monthly report from the bank sent to the account holder, showing transaction history and bank account balances for the month.

bankruptcy: A last resort for a debtor. The person declares in court the inability to pay his or her debts, in order to be freed from debt. First, by law, the individual would have to go through a credit counseling program and submit to a repayment plan.

basis: In calculating capital gains, it is the price of an investment security minus commissions or fees.

bear market: When the stock market is trending downward (losing value) over a period of time.

beneficiary: The individual named on a life insurance policy, or a will, who will receive the insurance benefits or the deceased's estate.

benefits: Economic rewards offered to employees of a company that are additional to salary. They are an added form of compensation, because they have monetary value.

bodily injury liability coverage: Part of auto insurance that covers legal or medical responsibilities if the other driver or passengers are killed or injured.

bonds: Certificates issued by a corporation or government agency in exchange for a loan, usually long-term.

brokers: Investment brokers are people who are licensed to act as go-betweens for buyers and sellers of investments.

budget: A spending plan that helps balance present and future income/revenue and spending flows.

budget deficit: When expenses and savings exceed income.

budget surplus: When expenses and savings are below income.

bull market: When the stock market is trending upward (gaining value) over a period of time.

business plan: A detailed plan indicating the nature of a potential new business, its market, source of funding, and the risks, expectations, and marketing approach involved in starting the business.

capacity: What a lender determines is a borrower's ability to take on a loan. The lender may want to see proof of income, assets, and other debt (for example, pay stubs and account statements) to assess whether they have the capacity to make loan payments.

capital: Money invested for use in creation of more income, investment opportunities, or production. Can also mean working assets, like machines, tools, and buildings used in the production of goods and services.

capital appreciation: An increase in the value of a security/investment. Also, an investment strategy emphasizing money growth.

capital gains: Positive returns on an investment that involve selling the asset for a higher price than was paid for it.

capital losses: Negative returns on an investment that involve selling the asset for less than was paid for it.

capital preservation: An investment strategy that emphasizes maintaining capital already accrued, through buying secure, less risky investments or assets.

career: One's area of work over a long time; a professional path in which there is room for growth.

cash advance: Money withdrawn directly from an ATM as a loan against a credit card account.

check register: A booklet used to keep a detailed list of transactions, both debit and credit, in one's checking account.

checking account: Deposits in a bank allowing the depositor to make withdrawals by issuing checks or debit card charges against the account. The most liquid type of retail bank account. Many pay no interest, but are secure places to have money on hand instead of carrying cash.

circular flow: The economic circulation of goods, services, and payments among households, businesses, and government.

claim: A request for reimbursement from a policyholder to the insurance company, for a loss covered by their insurance.

closed-end credit: A one-time advance of a sum of money that the borrower agrees to pay back over a predetermined length of time (called a term). Examples of this type of loan include mortgages, car loans, and student loans.

closing costs: Costs that home buyers must budget for when getting a mortgage; for one-time expenses like attorney fees and credit check fees incurred when finalizing the purchase of the house.

co-insurance: When health insurance requires the policyholder to pay a percentage of medical bills and drug costs as part of the policy.

collateral: Money or items of value used to back up a loan, to be seized if the borrower defaults.

collection agency: A company that tracks down delinquent debt in exchange for a commission from the credit card company or bank.

collision coverage: Part of auto insurance that covers costs of damage to one's car from an accident.

commission: Money earned as a percentage of a sale of an item.

compound interest: A way interest can accrue on borrowed money. Interest is earned on the principal and on interest previously earned. Compounding can happen annually or monthly. The equation for compound interest is:

$$\text{Future value} = \text{principal} \times (1 + \text{interest rate})^{\text{number of compounding periods}}$$

comprehensive coverage: Part of auto insurance that covers costs of damage to the car from anything other than an accident—a tornado or vandalism, for example.

co-pay: A predetermined dollar amount that one must pay at the end of each doctor or hospital visit, as determined by a health insurance policy. The rest of the bill is sent on to the insurer.

cost of living: The cost of food, rent, transportation, and all other necessities to live in a certain city or area.

coupon: The promised interest rate to be paid on a bond to the bond holder periodically.

cover letter: A letter that accompanies a résumé when applying for a job. In the letter, an applicant introduces himself or herself to the hiring manager, and makes a case for why he or she is the best candidate for the position offered.

credit: An advance of money to an individual, with the understanding that they will pay all or part of it back within a specified time limit. Credit cards are a form of credit; so are home mortgages, student loans, and auto loans.

credit limit: Instead of a set loan amount, a maximum amount of money one is allowed to borrow from the company or bank at any one time (usually refers to credit cards or lines of credit).

credit reporting agencies (or bureaus): Companies that prepare credit reports on individuals that lenders and other service agents (such as insurance companies) can use to assess an individual's ability to handle credit. The three major agencies are TransUnion, Experian, and Equifax.

credit report: A document that chronicles an individual's borrowing over the past several years. A report shows every loan or credit line taken out over a certain period by the individual, as well as payment history on those loans.

credit score: The information in a person's credit reports is turned into a numerical assessment of creditworthiness, known as a FICO credit score, which is provided to interested lenders. Lenders use these scores to determine who should get loans and at what rates.

credit union: A nonprofit owned by its members, who typically have a common interest. Offers members services similar to those offered by a retail bank.

death benefit: Total amount that a life insurance policy agrees to pay the beneficiary upon death of the policyholder.

debit card: A plastic card directly linked to a checking account, which can be used at ATMs and store cash registers. The purchase amount is withdrawn automatically from the account.

deductible: The amount of money the insured policyholder must pay before the insurance will bear the remaining costs.

deduction: Something that directly reduces taxable income; the dollar amount of the deduction is subtracted from gross income, leaving a smaller amount of income to be taxed.

default: When the borrower has not abided by the loan terms, by not paying or not being able to pay. Also in bonds, when a bond issuer is unable to pay back the original principal because they have no money to pay.

deficit: Occurs when spending exceeds income or revenue.

deflation: An extended period of decline in prices.

delinquent: When an individual misses a scheduled loan payment, the loan is considered delinquent. At that point, the lender will probably start charging late fees.

depreciate/depreciation: To decrease in value/a decrease in value.

disability insurance: Replaces a portion of the policyholder's income in the event that he or she becomes sick or disabled and cannot work.

discretionary income: Income left over after allocating income toward necessary expenses, or needs; money left to spend on wants.

disposable income: The amount of income received after taxes and other deductions, available for living expenses or savings. Also known as *take-home pay.*

diversification: Including in a portfolio different kinds of investments with varying volatility, return potential, and market exposures in order to reduce overall risk.

dividends: A share of a company's profits issued to stockholders.

dollar-cost averaging: This investment strategy involves investing in an asset over time, rather than all at once. An investor allots equal amounts of money in a certain investment on a regular schedule; so that as the price rises and falls over time, the cost to the investor is averaged.

down payment: The initial amount of money one is required to pay when buying a good or service on an installment loan. For a house, a percentage of the total cost that the mortgage issuer requires to be paid before granting a loan for the remainder.

earned income: The money a worker is paid as compensation for labor.

emergency fund: Money set aside specifically for paying unexpected expenses.

entrepreneur: An individual who starts a business, organizes and develops it, and assumes the risks and rewards of ownership.

equities: Stocks or shares of a company.

equity: Value of real estate or other property owned; the part that has been paid for is the owner's equity. (What is still owed on the mortgage loan is not equity to the homeowner.)

estate: Accumulated assets, including a house, stocks, bonds, savings, and any valuables like jewelry that someone owns. Upon death, can be distributed in whole or part to beneficiaries in a will.

estate tax: A tax imposed on inherited money or property.

exclusions: Specified conditions or circumstances that an insurance policy does not cover.

executor: Person who is named responsible for making sure the provisions of a will by the deceased are complied with.

exemptions: Circumstances that reduce taxable income (establishing a certain portion of income as not to be taxed). For example, in a bigger household (where a greater number of dependents rely on one income), more income is exempt from taxes.

Fair Isaac Corporation (FICO): The company that turns the information in people's credit reports into a numerical assessment of creditworthiness called a FICO credit score.

fake-check scams: A common Internet scam, where the sender wants to send the targeted person a large check, with the requirement that they send back a portion of the money through legal means. The sender's check ends up a fake, and bounces, while the money the victim sent has gone to the scam artist.

Federal Deposit Insurance Corporation (FDIC): A government agency that guarantees deposits to individuals if a bank goes bankrupt. The FDIC was founded during the Great Depression to restore trust in banking institutions.

Federal Insurance and Contributions Act (FICA): The government agency that oversees payroll taxes that fund government services, such as Social Security and Medicare.

Federal Trade Commission (FTC): An office of the government responsible for consumer protection. They deal with cases like identity theft, credit card mistreatment, and fraudulent sales schemes.

fee schedule: A complete list of fee charges on bank accounts. Banks are mandated to create and provide these schedules to customers by the Truth in Savings Act.

finance charge: The cost of credit (in dollars) that is charged by the lender; both interest owed on a loan or a credit card, and also any fees on the loan.

financial aid: Ways of paying college tuition that come as help from outside sources such as governments or banks. Financial aid can include grants, scholarships, work-study, and loans.

financial planner/advisor: This professional helps individuals create comprehensive, individualized action plans to reach their financial goals.

financial planning: Applying personal finance principles to manage money in ways that will help to achieve financial security and other money-related goals.

529 college savings plan: An account meant for college savings, named after the section of tax law that allows it preferential taxation rates. There are two types of 529s: savings plans and prepaid plans. Within these, students or their parents choose mutual funds from a selection offered, to invest college savings.

fixed expenses: Expenses that do not change from month to month, like rent, a car payment, or a gym membership.

forbearance: A relaxed payment schedule on a loan that the borrower asks for during a time of financial hardship. During the forbearance period, interest may still accrue and be added onto the loan as a lump sum when the period is up.

foreclosure: Repossession of a house by the mortgage company that owns it, when the homeowner can no longer make mortgage payments (they default on their loan).

Form 1040EZ: A tax return form. The main federal tax return is known as a Form 1040. Those who are single or married filing together, and earning less than $100,000 a year, can fill out a simple version called the 1040EZ.

Form 1099: A required income statement, totaling the income for the year on which taxes are owed. A Form 1099 reports income on which tax was not withheld.

Form I-9: A government form used to verify that the hired employee is a U.S. citizen or otherwise authorized to work in the United States.

Form W-2: This form, provided by the employer, reports an employee's taxable income for the year. It also shows the federal and state income tax and payroll tax already withheld.

Form W-4: A tax document an employee fills out, that signals to employers the income tax an employee is estimated to owe over the year.

formal education: Education that takes place in a classroom. High school, college, and graduate school are all formal education. So is trade school, a place to get training in a specific technical field.

401(k)/403(b): Retirement investment accounts, where employees contribute a portion of their pre-tax incomes into a selection of investments chosen by the employer for retirement savings. 401(k) plans are for private company employees, and 403(b) plans for public and nonprofit employees.

fraud: Intentional deceit for the purpose of gain.

Free Application for Federal Student Aid (FAFSA): Getting financial aid begins with filing the FAFSA. This government form directs the calculation of a student's eligibility for grants, work-study, and government loans.

government transfer payments: Government programs that provide money, valuable services (such as health care), or vouchers for food to citizens with particular needs. Among the beneficiaries of such programs are low-income individuals and families, retired persons, very ill or disabled people, and veterans.

grace period: The time between the credit card bill's statement date and the due date, in which one can pay off purchases made during the period before any finance charges accrue.

grants: Money from the government, corporations, or a university, given to those with extra financial need for tuition costs. Like scholarships, grants do not require repayment as loans do.

gross pay: The income amount a worker earns before deductions or taxes are taken out of the paycheck.

group health insurance: Health insurance coverage through an employer is called group health insurance (since there is a large number of people insured), and this is usually the cheapest way to get health care. It is less expensive because the risks are spread out among a large group.

growth investing: Investment choices made with the emphasis on increasing total capital worth. Growth investors seek out capital appreciation, an increase in the value of the security in which they invested.

health insurance: A way of managing the financial risks of getting sick or injured. In exchange for a monthly fee (called a *premium*), the insurance will pay for hospital, medical, and drug costs.

healthcare proxy: The individual that a patient has named in charge of making medical decisions on his or her behalf, in the event that the patient cannot make his or her own decisions.

homeowners insurance: Protection to cover costs of various types of risks to the owner's house or apartment and its contents.

identity theft: The unlawful use of an individual's personal information by another individual.

income investing: Investing with the emphasis on maintaining a constant level of income. Some people use investments to increase their current cash flow rather than wait for future capital appreciation. They buy certain investments that pay out money on a regular basis.

income tax: Tax levied on income, both earned and unearned. Almost everyone who has income must pay income taxes.

indexes/indices: A selection of stocks that are tracked, and used to represent the overall market trend. Among the more frequently cited indexes are the Dow Jones Industrial Average, which tracks 30 of the largest public companies in the United States; and the S&P 500, which tracks 500 of the largest U.S.-traded companies.

inflation: A sustained rise in the prices of goods and services over an extended period.

informal education: Training that happens outside of a traditional school. It may occur while on the job, or through an apprenticeship or internship.

initial public offering (IPO): The first time a company sells stock on the stock market, making it a public company.

installment loan: A one-time advance of a sum of money that the borrower agrees to return through regular payments over a predetermined length of time (called the *term*). Examples include mortgages, car loans, and student loans.

in-store financing: Loans made by retail companies when they let an individual take an item home and pay for it over time. These loans often come with high APRs and hidden fees.

insurance: A contract between an individual and a company in which the individual makes regular, small payments in exchange for the company's promise to cover certain types of possible monetary losses.

insurance agent: One who earns a living selling insurance policies.

interest: The cost for the use of borrowed money. Paid to the lender by the borrower of the money.

interest rate: The charge for the use of borrowed money, expressed as a percentage of the amount borrowed.

Internal Revenue Service (IRS): The federal agency that collects tax money.

internship: A position in which young workers take a low-level position in their field of interest in order to try it out and gain experience.

invest: To buy different types of financial products that have the potential to provide growth in value; but the chance of taking a higher reward brings with it a risk of losing money.

investment club: A group of people who share a common interest in investing and come together to educate one another on investments and investment practices.

IRA (individual retirement account): A kind of retirement account that anyone who has income can set up through a bank, brokerage, or investment company.

job: Originally meant to refer to work done in the short term for pay. Has become a general term used for any employment, even a career position, although they are two different things.

job interview: When an employer calls in a job applicant to answer questions in person, about why the applicant wants the available position, and what makes the applicant qualified.

joint account: A bank account where two individuals share responsibility and access to the account.

lay off: When a company must let some of its employees go, for financial reasons. This is different from being discharged (fired), which is dismissal of an individual for cause.

lease: A contract between a tenant and a landlord, stating the period of time the tenant will live in the apartment, monthly rent amount, and the responsibilities of the landlord and the tenant in maintaining the property.

legal guardian: The person named to take care of minor children should anything happen to the parents. The person legally charged, by the state, to oversee a minor child.

lenders: Those that advance money to others, with the expectation of being repaid with interest. Banks are the most common lenders for individuals.

liabilities: Any debts outstanding, such as a credit card balance, or student loans. Financial obligations owed to others are liabilities.

liability insurance: Part of homeowners or renters insurance. Covers legal responsibility should anything occur to visitors on the property.

life insurance: An insurance policy that protects against income loss to a family, by promising a specified sum of money should one of its income earners die.

line of credit: A form of revolving debt, like a credit account, linked to a checking or savings account. It often comes with yearly maintenance fees and a high APR.

liquidity: The ease by which an asset or investment can be converted into cash.

living will: States one's medical wishes in circumstances where one becomes unable to speak for oneself.

long-term capital gains: Unearned income created on the sale of an asset that has been owned for more than a year.

long-term care insurance: Insurance that covers the costs of long-term nursing care or hospitalization in the event of its necessity. Medicare covers only certain kinds of short-term nursing care, so some people purchase long-term care insurance to cover the rest.

marginal tax rates: The tax percentage rate that applies to the last dollar one earns. Also called a *tax bracket,* the highest bracket (rate of taxation) one falls into at one's income level.

maturity: The date at which a bond can be redeemed.

minimum payment: The lowest amount of money one can pay on a credit card bill or other line of credit to avoid delinquency and late fees. Usually a minimum payment equals 2% to 5% of the balance owed, or a set amount like $25.

minimum wage: By law, the lowest hourly rate an employer may pay a worker.

money market deposit account: Similar to savings accounts, these accounts combine some of the features of savings and checking, typically with higher interest rates.

mortgage: A loan used to buy a home.

mutual fund: A kind of investment made up of a group of securities (stocks or bonds). The fund is created and managed by a business, with the intention of increasing profits and returns for the fund's shareholders.

needs: Goods or services that one cannot do without—such as food, housing, etc.

Net Asset Value (NAV): The price per share of a mutual fund.

net pay: The amount remaining of a paycheck after all of the payroll deductions and income tax are taken out. Also known as *take-home pay*, or *disposable income.*

net worth statement: A listing of all of a person's or family's assets and liabilities: assets – liabilities = net worth.

no-fault laws: State laws that require an insurer to pay for the policyholder's medical costs in a car accident, no matter who caused the accident. States with no-fault laws are Florida, Hawaii, Kansas, Kentucky, Massachusetts, Michigan, Minnesota, New Jersey, New York, North Dakota, Pennsylvania and Utah.

nominal interest rate: The interest rate quoted on a loan or bank account; it does not account for inflation.

nonsufficient funds fee: The fee charged to a checking account if the user spends past the balance in the account. Often this fee is in excess of $30.

open-end credit: An account that offers a credit limit instead of a set loan amount. The borrower can spend any amount up to that limit at any one time. Credit cards are a form of open-end credit, also called revolving credit.

opportunity cost: That which must be given up in order to get something else; a trade-off.

out-of-pocket maximum: The amount specified in a health insurance policy that must be spent by the policyholder before the insurer covers all following costs; also called the total yearly deductible.

overdraft (overdrawing): Charging one's bank account for more than the balance in the account. Depending on the account, the transaction will be denied, or the transaction will be paid but a nonsufficient funds fee will be charged to the account.

overdraft protection: The bank agrees it will pay when charges are overdrawn on the account; but a nonsufficient funds fee will usually be charged.

par value: The face value, or cost, of a bond when it is issued.

pawnbroker: Someone who runs a pawnshop.

pawnshops: Places to *pawn*, or bring in, a valuable item—such as jewelry, a musical instrument, a camera, or a computer—in hopes that the pawnbroker will make a short-term loan up to the value of the item, in trade for holding that item as collateral and charging interest. (These are loans typically under $1,000 dollars.)

payday loans: Cash loans for people who need money before their next paycheck. These are short-term loans—usually two weeks—written up to the amount of the coming paycheck.

payroll taxes: Taxes deducted directly from a worker's paycheck, applied to specific government programs such as Social Security.

penalty APR: The rate charged on a credit card if an individual violates the terms of their credit card agreement. Often it is paying the bill late, or going over the credit limit, that triggers this rate.

pension: A retirement plan an employer offers an employee, conditional on an extended term of employment. It requires no investment of the employee's salary, but is direct pay from the employer.

Perkins Loan: The least expensive government student loan offered to students with extra financial need.

permanent life insurance: A life insurance policy that remains in force as long as premium payments are made, with no set term end date. In addition, this policy accrues cash value, meaning the policyholder could cash out the policy at any time.

personal finance: Relates specifically to how people—as individuals or part of a household—manage their money.

philanthropy: Giving to charities or other causes, either with a donation of money or time as a volunteer.

PIN (personal identification number): Four or more digits used as a password for an individual. This code is needed when using the ATM, for instance.

PLUS loan: The Parent Loan for Under-graduate Students, a special loan for college students where their parents must cosign the loan.

policy: A contract between an individual and an insurance company, outlining payment should the policyholder incur specified losses.

Ponzi scheme: A scheme set up to look like an interest-earning investment, where actually there is no investment, but the new deposits are cycled to older clients to look like returns. Eventually the arrangement is discovered or collapses from a lack of new investors, and all the money is taken by the scam artist.

portfolio: All of a person's investment holdings.

pre-existing conditions: Health issues that existed before a health insurance policy was put into effect.

premium: The amount of money an insured person must pay regularly to maintain an insurance policy.

prime rate: The interest rate banks charge their best customers, usually corporations rather than individuals; this is often used as a reference point for personal loan rates.

principal: The original value of a loan or deposit/investment, to which interest or returns may be added.

private student loans: These are issued by banks to help pay college costs. They are not regulated by the government. There are no limits on how much one can borrow, but these loans also typically come with high interest rates.

profit: Money earned from the operation of a business after expenses have been paid.

progressive tax system: One that imposes a higher tax rate as an individual's income increases.

promissory note: A contract with a lender (of a student loan, for example), stating that the borrower will repay the loan amount.

property damage liability coverage: Part of auto insurance. Covers repairs needed—or replacement costs—for the other person's car or other property if the policyholder caused the accident; also covers any legal costs if the policyholder is sued.

property insurance: Part of homeowners/renters insurance. Financial protection for an insured person's property, furniture, clothing, electronics, or other belongings. It protects against loss or damage caused by natural disasters, weather conditions, crime, or fire.

prospectus: An explanatory document containing details about a mutual fund investment, and the fund manager's intentions with the investment.

public companies: Companies that issue stock to the public are known as public companies, in contrast to companies that are privately owned.

pyramid scheme: An illegal investment scheme in which new investors make up the bottom of the pyramid, with their investment money going to those on the level above. The only gains are the dollars that come from new recruits. Because there is no real investment or growth, the pyramid inevitably collapses.

real estate: Commercial or residential property, including land and buildings, that is privately owned.

real interest rate: The interest rate calculated to account for inflation.

recession: A period of economic decline.

recurring expenses: Expenses that are incurred and must be paid regularly.

refinance: To trade in a loan for one with different terms, usually something done with mortgages. There are often fees associated with doing this.

renters insurance: Protection to cover costs of various risks to someone who rents a house or apartment; particularly covers belongings, and liability of injury to guests or neighbors.

rent-to-own: An installment loan in which the item itself is being loaned and the interest is built into the price of eventual purchase.

repossession: Taking back a good or property due to the failure of the purchaser (or borrower) to make required payments.

résumé: A personal career document, outlining professional job history and experience, which highlights abilities and education.

retail bank: A financial institution that takes deposits and makes loans to individuals and small businesses.

return: The gain or loss on invested capital, usually represented as a percentage.

revolving credit: Credit that offers a credit limit, instead of a set loan amount, where the borrower can spend up to that limit at any one time. Also called *open-end credit*.

rewards cards: Many credit card companies offer rewards programs through which the cardholder can earn airline miles, points, or money back on each dollar spent on the card.

Roth IRA: A retirement account that does not offer a tax deduction up front (like a traditional IRA), but instead allows withdrawals tax-free after age 59½. The reason people invest in Roth IRAs is that they think they might be in a higher tax bracket at retirement than they are in now.

Rule of 72: This rule states that dividing 72 by the interest rate or rate of return, gets an estimate of the years required to double the initial investment. For 4% returns: $72 \div 4 = 18$ years to double the investment.

safe deposit box: Rented boxes within a bank's vault, meant to keep important documents and small valuables safe.

salary: A yearly income figure earned by an employee, with the expectation of working a set number of hours per week.

sales load: A commission paid to the salesperson of a mutual fund.

savings: The portion of personal or business income that is not spent or invested.

savings account: A very liquid account, like a checking account, but usually with fewer withdrawals allowed per month. It pays interest on the money kept in it.

scarcity: The economic condition of having insufficient resources (like money) to cover all that one might like. Also, the condition resulting from the fact that there is not enough of everything to go around to everyone.

scholarships: Money for education given to a student based on criteria such as academic ability or athletic skill.

secured loan: A loan in which the borrower pledges something of value in case the loan is not repaid.

Securities and Exchange Commission (SEC): A government agency that provides regulation and law enforcement actions on behalf of investors. The SEC was founded in 1934, during the Depression and not long after the great stock market crash of 1929.

security/securities: Financial instruments or investments that represent some value; stocks and bonds.

security deposit: A sum of money given to the landlord upon leasing an apartment, to guarantee against any damage to the apartment or delinquency in paying the rent.

shares: Stocks or equities; called *shares* because they represent part ownership of the corporation that issued them.

short-term capital gains: Unearned income on an asset that has appreciated in value and that has been owned for less than a year.

signature card: A card signed by the owner of a bank account, enabling the bank to compare the signatures on future transactions to verify identity.

simple interest: Interest that is not compounded, but only paid on the principal balance each given period. Simple interest earned = principal × interest rate × periods.

Social Security: A government benefit program that is paid for by taxes; provides income to retirees after a certain age.

Stafford Loan: A government loan for students, fixed at a low interest rate. Any student is eligible for unsubsidized Stafford Loans. This is the best available loan for many students.

stock exchanges: Places or markets where securities are bought and sold.

stocks: Shares or equities, which represent ownership stakes in a company.

subprime: Risky credit borrowers with under "prime" credit scores, typically those with credit scores 620 and below. These borrowers are considered at high risk of defaulting on their loans, and often will either be denied credit or assessed at the highest interest rates.

subsidized student loans: Student loans that do not accrue interest until after graduation.

surplus: Occurs when spending is less than income or revenue.

tax credit: Government incentives that reduce taxes owed dollar-for-dollar. A $1,000 tax credit means $1,000 less in taxes for the year. Recently, credits have been offered for buying a home or buying a hybrid car.

tax liability: Amount owed on yearly total taxable income.

tax liens: Claims by a state or federal government on something a person owns, in order to secure money for unpaid taxes.

tax return: Any one of several standard forms for reporting to the IRS all the income an individual has made (both earned and unearned), and taxes already paid. It is a way for the government to assess whether the appropriate amount of taxes have been paid given income.

tax-deferred: Describes certain investments or retirement accounts where taxes are not owed on the money until it is withdrawn for use.

taxes: Households and businesses give a certain amount of their income to the government in the form of taxes. The government—federal, state, or local—then spends this revenue on items it deems necessary for society, putting money back into the economy.

term life insurance: Life insurance that covers a certain period—say, five to 15 years. If the policyholder dies in that period, his or her beneficiary gets the benefits.

ticker symbols: Stocks are identified by ticker symbols, three- or four-letter codes that identify the company on the stock market.

time value of money: A certain amount of money saved today is worth more than the same amount saved in the future. The reason is that money saved now has time to grow with interest.

tips: Money (income) given by a customer for good and friendly service to a service-sector employee (like a waiter).

traditional IRA: A tax-deferred retirement account, set up by an individual at a bank.

tuition: The costs of attending school or college.

U.S. Savings Bonds: A type of bond issued by the U.S. Treasury, originally designed as a way for the government to raise money to pay for World War I.

underwrite: To assume risk as one's own. Insurance companies underwrite risk when they sell policies.

unearned income: This type of income is passive—not produced by working. Types of unearned income include interest income, capital gains, and dividends.

unemployment rate: The percentage of the workforce not employed but looking for work.

union: A collective of laborers in one sector, which bargains for benefits, good working conditions, and wage increases. Examples of unions include the Airline Pilots Association, the United Auto Workers (UAW), Major League Baseball Players Association, the American Federation of Teachers (AFT), and the Screen Actors Guild.

unsubsidized student loans: Student loans that accrue interest from the moment they are taken out.

variable expenses: Expenses that may increase or decrease from month to month.

volatility: The extent of an investment's price fluctuation.

wage: An hourly fee for work performed.

wants: Things that are desired, but that are not necessities.

will: A legal document that states a person's plans for his or her estate—that is, all the assets he or she has accumulated—after his or her death.

withholding: The amount of taxes paid per paycheck, determined by how many exemptions one can claim, and total salary or wages.

worker's compensation: Benefits paid by employers to workers who are injured in accidents on the job.

work-study: A job given to a student by or through a university or college, that pays wages through government resources. This is another form of financial aid.

INTERNET RESOURCES

Chapter One

Mind Your Finances, by the In Charge Education Foundation

http://www.mindyourfinances.com
A Web site of personal finance education material and interactive learning tools. Includes online calculators that estimate interest costs of loans, compound interest growth, college savings, and even calculate net worth, balancing a checkbook, or retirement savings.
http://www.mindyourfinances.com/calculators
http://www.mindyourfinances.com/calculators/savings-goals

The Financial Planning Association

http://www.fpanet.org
An organization of financial planning professionals, plus free personal finance information, and educational material.

The National Association of Personal Financial Advisors

http://www.napfa.org
An organization of financial planning professionals, with free advice and personal services.

CNNMoney.com, by CNN, *Fortune*, and *Money* magazines

http://money.cnn.com
A Web site for current investment news, stock trends, and investment advice. Includes a personal finance section with financial planning information and news stories. Also has a list of personal finance wealth calculators; for retirement, investing, savings, etc.
http://money.cnn.com/pf/
http://money.cnn.com/magazines/moneymag/money101/index.html
http://money.cnn.com/tools

Cnet, of CBS Interactive

http://www.cnet.com
Consumer reviews, news, and feedback on new technology and high-end products and merchandise.

Edmunds.com

http://www.edmunds.com
Information on new and used car market prices, consumer reviews, and information on purchasing from car dealers across the United States.

Kelley Blue Book Official Guide
http://www.kbb.com
Certified car reviewer, with information on new and used cars, "blue book" market values, and tips on buying.

MyMoney.gov, from the Financial Literacy and Education Commission
http://www.mymoney.gov
A government Web site dedicated to personal finance matters. It has pooled personal financial advice found at over 20 government agency Web sites, and listed them together at one convenient location.

Chapter Two

Department of Labor Wage and Hour Division
http://www.dol.gov/whd/minwage/america.htm
Facts and details on minimum wage requirements, both federal and by state.

Bureau of Labor Statistics
http://www.bls.gov
The government Web site for news, numbers, and recent information on American employment and economic statistics. Includes the Occupational Outlook Handbook, with facts and figures on job possibilities, salaries, and current employment trends for hundreds of occupations. Also includes a CPI inflation calculator, to compare dollar worth for any years after 1913.
http://www.bls.gov/oco/
http://www.bls.gov.oco/cg
http://www.bls.gov/data/inflation_calculator.htm

Salary.com
http://www.salary.com
A Web site dedicated to current job information and salary demands for different occupations, taken from national averages. Contains information for both employers and employees on career benefits and human resources.

Monster.com
http://www.monster.com
A job market Web site, that links employers and those looking for work in a large number of occupational fields.

Wegmans Grocery Stores

http://www.wegmans.com

The Web site to the national grocery chain Wegmans. Used in Chapter Two to locate employer information for practice in a job interview setting.

Internal Revenue Service

http://www.irs.gov

Government information on tax paying, for individuals and businesses. The Web site contains all standard IRS federal tax return forms available to download.

http://www.irs.gov/formspubs/index.html

http://www.irs.gov/app/picklist/list/formsInstructions.html

Chapter Three

The U.S. Better Business Bureau

http://www.bbb.org/us

An organization dedicated to better business practices, supporting trusted and transparently run businesses for decades. A place for consumers to file complaints, check a business's validity, and find trusted reviews of businesses and services.

The American Institute of Philanthropy

http://www.charitywatch.org

A trusted place to find charity reviews, and learn about the practices of registered charities across the country. Contains a charity rating guide and a "Watchdog Report."

Charity Navigator

http://www.charitynavigator.org

An independent charity evaluation Web site, works to honestly examine the financial actions and business practices of America's registered charities.

Internal Revenue Service

http://www.irs.gov

See description under Chapter Two resources.

ConsumerReports.org

http://www.consumerreports.org

A nonprofit, independent, expert Web site dedicated to objective product reviews. Potential customers can see other customer reviews of products, including electronics, cars, or sporting equipment.

The National Credit Union Administration

http://www.ncua.gov

A place for customers and organizations to get information on credit unions, for credit unions to register, and to find information on credit union functions, actions, and legal requirements.

The Credit Union National Association

http://www.cuna.org

An organization of credit unions, with information for the unions and their customers on legal regulations, business practices, and a list of other credit unions in their area.

Federal Deposit Insurance Corporation

http://www.fdic.gov

The Web site for the government organization created to protect bank customers, and provide deposit insurance, customer protection, and regulate retail banking services.

Federal Trade Commission

http://www.ftc.gov

The government organization created for the protection of America's consumers. The Web site offers education and information on credit loans, ID theft, business scams, and has a section where consumers can file complaints.

Mint.com

http://www.mint.com

Free online software that can help individuals manage, budget, and track their money flows. Voted the best personal money management site by *Money* magazine, the *New York Times*, and the *Wall Street Journal*.

Chapter Four

Yahoo! Finance

http://finance.yahoo.com/

A current business and finance news Web site. Contains pages on personal finance and investment strategies, including up-to-the-minute stock quotes.
http://finance.yahoo.com/personal-finance
http://finance.yahoo.com/marketupdate?u

The *Wall Street Journal* Web site

http://www.wsj.com

The Web site for the *Wall Street Journal*, for business news and financial reporting. Includes an up-to-the-minute stock quotes page.
http://online.wsj.com/mdc/public/page/marketsdata.html?mod=WSJ_hpp_marketdata

CNNMoney.com, by CNN, *Fortune*, and *Money* magazines
http://money.cnn.com
As described in Chapter One resources. Also see the stock market page, which includes up-to-the-minute quotes.
http://money.cnn.com/data/us_markets/index.html

Vanguard, an investment company
http://www.vanguard.com
A company with products for investing for: college, retirement, small businesses, health care costs, etc. Has a large number of mutual funds to invest in, with prospectuses to review.
https://personal.vanguard.com/us/home?fromPage=portal
https://personal.vanguard.com/us/funds/vanguard

Savingforcollege.com, a Bankrate Company
http://www.savingforcollege.com
Information on college savings plans, choices, and investment strategies. Includes information on the 529 Plans; which are state-run investment plans with tax breaks for saving for college costs.
http://www.savingforcollege.com/intro_to_529s/what-is-a-529-plan.php

FinAid.org
http://www.finaid.org
A Web site for guiding students through the financial aid application process; with information on scholarships, grants, and loans available.

The Free Application for Federal Student Aid
http://www.fafsa.ed.gov/
The direct link for information and for filing the government FAFSA.

Know How 2GO
http://knowhow2go.org/
A Web site dedicated to information, support, and real student advice on getting to college from high school. For students interested but needing encouragement, Know How 2GO came up with a student-friendly "college checklist," and has real college students write blog posts about their experiences.
http://knowhow2go.org/main_4steps.php
http://www.knowhow2go.org/ambassadors/

The Stock Market Game, from SIFMA Foundation for Investor Education

http://stockmarketgame.org

A free online teaching tool that gives students the freedom to investigate, purchase, and track companies on the stock market, with their own portfolio and their own investment "money." It is the only educational stock market simulation game supported by the New York Stock Exchange.

Chapter Five

Bankrate.com

http://www.bankrate.com

An objective Web site that catalogs bank information, interest rates, and personal finance tools, including calculators for all types of personal finance accounting.

http://www.bankrate.com/calculators.aspx

AnnualCreditReport.com

http://www.annualcreditreport.com

The Web site to receive free yearly credit reports from TransUnion, Equifax, and Experian.

Federal Trade Commission

http://www.ftc.gov

See description in Chapter Three resources. Here, with special information for consumers and credit users.

http://www.ftc.gov/bcp/consumer.shtm

http://www.ftc.gov/bcp/

CardRatings.com

http://www.cardratings.com

Educational material, credit card company information, and tips on credit card use. Rates a variety of credit cards available by their customer service, quality, and fees.

CardTrak.com

http://www.cardtrak.com

A Web site for educational material, credit card company information, and tips on credit card use. Rates a variety of credit cards available.

Advantage Credit Counseling Service

http://www.advantageccs.org/

A free online nonprofit consumer credit counseling service provider, which offers budget advice, and credit/debt counseling services. It also has money management advice for teens and young adults.

http://www.advantageccs.org/debt_management_plan_teens.html

Chapter Six

A.M. Best
http://www.ambest.com
A credit rating organization that rates investments and companies on the market.

Moody's
http://www.moodys.com
A credit rating organization that rates investments and companies on the market.

Fitch Ratings
http://www.fitchratings.com/index_fitchratings.cfm
A credit rating organization that rates investments and companies on the market.

The Life and Health Insurance Foundation for Education
http://lifehappens.org
A nonprofit organization dedicated to teaching about different insurance needs, how to buy and properly understand insurance policy benefits. Includes a life insurance calculator.
http://lifehappens.org/life-insurance/life-calculator

INDEX